T0368147

FIRE AND FORGIVENESS

THE CINDY AMES STORY

ANDREA NEPTUNE

authorHOUSE®

AuthorHouse™
1663 Liberty Drive
Bloomington, IN 47403
www.authorhouse.com
Phone: 833-262-8899

Published by AuthorHouse   11/19/2024

ISBN: 979-8-8230-3578-1 (sc)
ISBN: 979-8-8230-3579-8 (hc)
ISBN: 979-8-8230-3577-4 (e)

Library of Congress Control Number: 2024921767

Print information available on the last page.

Any people depicted in stock imagery provided by Getty Images are models, and such images are being used for illustrative purposes only. Certain stock imagery © *Getty Images.*

This book is printed on acid-free paper.

DEDICATIONS

<u>Andrea</u>
To Auntie Cindy; my mother, Jeannie;
my sons, Nolan and Trevin;
and my husband, Gary—
thank you for believing in me.
I love you!

<u>Cindy</u>
I dedicate this book to *all* the hard-working people who helped me through my tragedy:

- To the doctors, nurses, and therapists who daily had to push me, encourage me, and cause me pain so that I could survive.
- To my family, who stopped their lives as they knew it and concentrated their efforts on me and my boys' needs.
- To my boys, Michael and Jeremiah, who not only were the beacon of light keeping me going but also helped me immensely on my road to recovery after the hospital.
- To my husband, Don, who has encouraged me and supported me for the last twenty-plus years.
- Finally, and most importantly, to God, my Savior, who guided me through the most trying and painful time of my life and sent me back to live more. Thank you, Jesus.

DISCLAIMERS

This account is to the best of Cindy Ames Harding's recall ability; these memories reflect her perception and perspective. Some names have been changed to protect the not-so-innocent. Other names remain unchanged to celebrate those individuals who helped Cindy on her journey.

WARNING

Please note that this book contains graphic depictions of burn treatment and recovery. Content includes perilous situations, blood, and bodily functions, and may not be suitable for all readers.

PROLOGUE: PARADISE

November 8, 2018

Early-morning phone calls rarely bring good news, especially to a night owl.

The sound of her cell phone buzzing caused Cindy to stir in bed. Don shifted under the blankets. Pulled from a deep sleep, Cindy opened her eyes and looked at the clock: 7:35 a.m. *Something must be wrong. Who would be calling me this early?* Cindy sat up and looked at her cell phone. Seeing it was her son Michael, she quickly answered.

"Hi, Michael. Is everything okay?"

"Hi, Mom. I wanted to let you know there's a big fire heading your way. You need to get out of there," Michael urged, anxiety in his voice.

Adrenaline shot through Cindy's body at hearing the word *fire,* and a sense of dread filled her veins. Her mind momentarily flashed back to the smell of burning flesh—memories she was always trying to suppress. "What do you mean, a fire? How close is it?"

"It's in Concow, and the winds are blowing bad. You need to evacuate right now."

For those living in Paradise, evacuating for a fire was common practice. Cindy could recall a handful of times they had evacuated to the local church, only to be sent home a few hours later. *Lightning doesn't strike twice*, she thought, looking at the burn scars on her arm. Her body relaxed. "Michael, it's probably just a false alarm, but I'm getting up."

"Mom, please pack up and get out of the house now. The fire is heading toward Paradise."

Cindy sighed. She'd much rather go back to bed, but she could hear the fear in his voice. "Okay, Michael. I'm waking Don up now."

Don roused. "I'm gonna need a cup of coffee first."

Cindy picked out some clothes to wear and got dressed for the day, pondering what she would need to pack in her overnight bag. She then sat at the table with a cup of coffee and began making phone calls to neighbors to make sure they had heard the news. Her ninety-four-year-old neighbor George responded with indignation: "I'm not going anywhere. I'll hop in the pool if a fire comes."

Cindy sighed and called George's daughter, Barbara, who lived in Southern California, and explained that George refused to evacuate. "I've tried, Barbara, but I can't argue with him anymore, and I need to get going. I'm going over to get his dog, whether your dad comes with us or not, so he might as well just come with us. Can you call and talk some sense into him?"

She then called Sherry across the street, who was already talking to Carol, another neighbor. Then Cindy's friend Tracy, who lived in nearby Magalia, called to make sure Cindy had heard. "Cindy, I want to make sure you know there's a fire, and it's heading your way. And I just want you and Don to know that I love you! Now get out of there!" Cindy conveyed her gratitude and, before hanging up, learned Tracy was also packing. The phone kept Cindy at the table for another half hour.

Michael called back. "Mom, are you still there? Are you out of there yet?"

"I'm having a cup of coffee and making some phone calls to the neighbors, and I'm figuring out what I need to pack."

"Mom! You don't have time for a cup of coffee. Just get yourself out of there!"

Cindy heard the urgency in his voice and set her coffee down, placing one last phone call to Sherry.

"Hi, Cindy, we're loading stuff in the car now. Carol has a police tracker, and they're saying it's really bad. Some of the neighbors have already left."

Cindy looked at the clock: 8:32 a.m. She grabbed her phone and started taking pictures of each room in the house for documentation; then she grabbed a box and started going from room to room, filling it with things she wanted to bring with her. She picked up the large bag of holiday baking supplies she had just bought, but then changed her mind and put it back. She felt indecisive and distracted.

In her frantic state, she walked past her favorite pictures hanging on the wall—of her son Jeremiah, her son Michael and his family, her parents, and a family photo of her siblings when they were kids. She picked up her favorite little rock, stamped "The purpose of life is a life of purpose," and placed it in the box.

Glancing in the sunroom, she saw the two bags of paperwork and pictures for the book she was writing and, putting the box down, picked them up to put them in her car at once.

As soon as Cindy stepped outside, her heart raced. She could smell the heavy smoke, and there was ash the size of quarters floating in the air. Her car was covered in ash and filament. The fire was closer than she'd expected. This was not a drill. She looked at her watch: it was 8:58 a.m., an hour and a half since Michael had called her.

"Don, we need to leave now," Cindy urged when she raced inside. She was no longer packing but grabbing.

The phone rang, and it was Barbara, George's daughter. "Okay, Dad says he'll go with you. I told him to find all of his wallets he keeps hidden in the house as he's getting ready."

Cindy thought about what treasures and heirlooms she wanted to bring. She had tubs already put together with some of her valuables from when they had been evacuated before. From her glass cabinet, she added the priceless heirlooms from her grandfather who was Cherokee Indian, including his parents' handmade wedding basket, a handmade rug that was over a hundred years old, a tomahawk, and his peace pipe. Once outside, she placed the tubs in the trunk.

Don was outside packing up the camper, loading up items directly from the garage. He figured if they needed to be gone for a while, they could stay in the camper. The plan was for Don to drive the Chevy truck and the overhead camper and for Cindy to drive the Ford Edge after she picked up George.

Looking down the street and seeing the deserted driveways and the ash still falling from the sky, Cindy began to panic. They were out of time. Feeling suddenly frightened, she ran back into the house, although her frazzled mind made it difficult to focus. She started reevaluating what was in the last tub, taking things out and putting them back in. She then remembered that she had her cousin's Indian stuff up in the attic. Jeff had asked her to store them for "safekeeping."

In the hallway, she pulled down the stairs to the attic hatch and went up to hand Jeff's stuff to Don, surveying what else was up there. She saw some empty tubs and thought about grabbing and filling them too, but then thought, *No, we'll be back. This will all be here when we come back, and we'll just have to unpack it all.*

Cindy then went into her bedroom and did a quick scan: *What do I need to bring? What might I need for a day or two?* She reached into her closet, gripped a six-inch handful of clothes on their hangers, and placed them in the remaining tub. Then she grabbed a couple pairs of shoes, some underwear, and makeup. She went into her jewelry box and grabbed a handful of her nicer jewelry, forgetting that the night before, she had taken off her wedding ring and diamond earrings and placed them on the nearby dresser.

She snatched a box of mementos and put it in the tub—including her mom's driver's license, a series of two-dollar bills, and silver coins. Cindy raced the tub out to the car and, again seeing the floating ash and smoky sky, agreed to herself on one last trip.

She went into the office to get their birth certificates, but, in her frenzy, forgot to secure the insurance papers. She grabbed her laptop and a few things on the desk. In the hallway, she carefully grabbed her son Jeremiah's urn and his picture, and by the door, she took a photo of her and Don off the wall. Outside, she placed these on the floor behind the passenger seat. While she had room for more, she had no more time to pack it.

"Don, I'm ready to leave. Let's get going!"

Don walked over to her car, and they hugged. "Follow right behind me. Stay on my tail," he urged, looking her in the eye. "Stay with me."

Cindy nodded and got in the car. Gizmo, their cockapoo shih tzu, sat on the seat next to her. By now, it was a quarter to ten. Don pulled out of the driveway and let Cindy go by on her way to George's around the corner. George was in his driveway standing with his cane and his white terrier, Grizzly.

"Hi, George," she said. "We need to hurry and grab some of your stuff."

Cindy ran into his house and grabbed his varying wallets off the counter, his medications, some clothes, and toiletries, and put them in a suitcase. George hobbled back outside while Cindy put the suitcase in the car. They looked up at the foreboding sky, the air full of thick soot and ash. To the right, the clouds were charcoal black without a speck of blue.

Don was waiting for them in the truck, and Cindy pulled behind him in the car, following the camper on the way out. Sherry and Carol, their neighbors, soon followed behind them on the way to Skyway, where traffic was bumper to bumper. Cars cut in between Cindy and Don, separating them and forcing them into different lanes.

They soon came upon traffic controllers who were in place to guide cars and avoid chaos. Some cars were directed to go down the left and right lanes of Skyway, converting the opposing traffic lane to help cars exit the town. Others were directed to go down Neal Road, which seemed to be closer to the fire. The traffic controller sent Don and Cindy to separate lanes, and eventually, a lane divider separated them.

George urged, "Don't let Don get out of your sight. Stay close!" Looking down the road, Cindy could only see a block ahead. Beyond that, it was a blur of black smoke.

Bumper to bumper, Cindy fought traffic to stay close to Don and eventually was able to change lanes to get behind him again. With the big overhead camper looming in front of her, she felt Don was drafting her to safety.

The traffic was moving slowly but steadily, about thirty miles an hour. Driving on the inbound lane, Cindy knew there were cliffs on the left side. When the road turned a corner, Cindy exclaimed, "George, the fire is right there, on the shoulder of the road! Oh my God, they want us to drive right through the fire!"

George responded calmly, "Just follow your honey. Just stay on his tail."

Due to the density of the smoke, Cindy could not see more than a car's length in front of Don, except the orange of the fire flickering like a devil's tongue through the black. Looming on the right, Cindy saw a cluster of condominiums in flames, and the fence along the road was also burning.

Cindy could hear the static electricity as lines snapped from the heat. She could see electric poles that were down and trees that were on fire—trees that could fall on them at any moment. Flames rose on both the left side and right side of the road, and Cindy realized, *Oh my God, I'm actually IN the fire.*

Staring at the camper ahead was the only thing keeping Cindy together. It became her beacon in the flames. Uncontrollably, she began having a panic attack. Her chest started rising and falling as her breathing quickened. She gripped the steering wheel as if hanging on for dear life. Her eyes started to well up with tears.

Stop the car. You need to get out. You need to run. Cindy glanced at the wall of fire closing in on the road out of Paradise. *This can't be happening. I can't go through this again. I can't live through another fire like Truckee. I just can't …*

CHAPTER 1

TRUCKEE

May 10, 1982

Cindy drove along Donner Pass Road with her windows cracked, her long strawberry blonde hair fluttering in the breeze. She admired how calm Donner Lake could be in the morning and noted the empty docks. *School is almost out,* Cindy thought. *Those are going to be crowded with teenagers soon.*

Cindy loved living in Truckee, a small mountain town where everybody knew everybody, nobody locked their doors, and you identified your phone number only by the last four digits since everyone had the same area code and prefix.

Looking forward to the upcoming weekend, Cindy sang along to "Ebony and Ivory" playing on the radio. As she inhaled the scent of pine trees, her inhalation turned into a yawn. She was exhausted after four back-to-back shifts in the ER at the Tahoe Forest Hospital, although last night she had gotten a reprieve and worked in the OB unit, helping deliver two babies. Even though it had been a rewarding night, she couldn't wait to get home and crawl into bed.

Cindy drove her Subaru up the winding, snow-covered road toward her house at the top of Denton Avenue and pulled onto the steep driveway. Even though it was early May, snow covered the higher roads and mountaintops after the latest storm, and there were some deep snow patches on the sides of the road. Cindy sat in her car in the driveway for a moment, enjoying its luxurious feel. She loved her brand-new 1982 burgundy Subaru, which she had just purchased. For years, she had been driving an old Maverick, a car that had been known to explode when rear-ended. A month earlier, Cindy had had a vivid nightmare in which she was in a serious car accident in the Maverick, and believing in omens, she'd decided the very next day it was time to go car shopping.

Before climbing the stairs to enter the house, Cindy paused and took in the view overlooking Donner Lake, which always brought her a sense of peace. She would need to feel calm before facing Ken, her estranged husband for almost a year now. Over the holidays, they had given it another try, but that only lasted a couple of weeks. Even though their situation was messy, it helped that he was still willing to stay overnight at the house with the kids while she worked the night shift. *I hope he doesn't want to talk about the divorce. I'm too exhausted right now,* she thought.

"Good morning!" Cindy greeted, surveying the living room. Ken stood in the kitchen, hovering over the oven, with their four-year-old son, Jeremiah, standing nearby in his underwear. Jim, Ken's friend and coworker, sat at the dining room table reading the *Sierra Sun*, the local newspaper.

"Did Michael make it to school okay?" Cindy asked. She hadn't passed the school bus on her way home, but it was almost nine a.m., and he should've already been picked up on his way to second grade.

Ken nodded, opening the oven door to peek inside.

"What's in the oven?" Cindy asked.

"Frozen burritos," Ken replied with a chuckle. "Breakfast of champions!"

"Why don't you let me make you and Jim a decent breakfast before you go? It's the least I can do to thank you for watching the boys these last few nights."

Cindy got busy in the kitchen making scrambled eggs, hash browns, and toast while the men refilled their coffee cups and talked at the table. As Cindy popped the bread in the toaster, she glanced up at the smoke alarm to see that the battery was still out. The darn toaster always smoked and set off the alarm, so they had dismantled it.

She then poured the scrambled eggs into a pan on the gas stove and let them cook. She enjoyed cooking for the men. Even though she knew there wasn't any chance of reconciliation, she felt grateful that Ken was still willing to help and remained involved with their boys.

"How are you doing with money?" Cindy asked Ken as he got ready to leave. She knew that construction was slow and that he was picking up little jobs and selling wood. They hadn't settled any of the financial details regarding their separation yet, but he did drive to Truckee from his parents' house in Coleville to help with the kids while she worked. Ken was even willing to drive back the next day so she could head to San Francisco for the weekend.

"Do you need some gas money?"

Ken nodded, saying, "That would be great."

Cindy went to her purse on the table and opened her wallet, shuffling through the fifty dollars in bills and handing him a twenty.

"That'll fill up the tank. Thanks!" Ken tucked the money into his flannel pocket and headed downstairs and out the door.

Cindy watched him leave and flashed back to him leaving after she had kicked him out for good. There were several feet of snow on the ground then, and he had almost slipped before getting into Jim's truck. He had always been a belligerent and angry drunk, and she didn't miss his outbursts.

Only two days earlier, Cindy had called her sister, Gail, and confided that she was committed to getting a divorce. For the first time, she admitted to someone the truth about their marriage and confessed that she had been enduring emotional abuse. There had been times during Ken's alcoholic rages that Cindy felt scared for her life. She was embarrassed and ashamed and had hidden the abuse from the outside world. Ken could get violent, but fortunately, he was never physical with her. Emotional scars were easier to hide than bruises would've been.

Gail had been shocked. "Cindy, I had no idea. Does Mom even know?" she asked.

"No. I haven't told anybody," replied Cindy. "I've been embarrassed and humiliated, and I didn't want anyone to know. But I'm leaving him. I need to protect the boys. I don't want them growing up around that."

Cindy's entire family had been oblivious, living so far away in Los Angeles. Truckee, in the Sierra Nevada mountain range near Lake Tahoe, was only an eight-hour drive from LA, but they still only saw each other a couple of times a year, which had made it easy for Cindy to keep her marital issues secret. Knowing now that Gail supported her gave Cindy the emotional strength she needed to move forward and work toward a divorce, splitting her life from Ken in the most cordial way possible. Fortunately, getting kicked out of the house and staying with his parents seemed to have sobered Ken up.

Cindy's mind turned toward the weekend. She was excited to be getting away. Cindy was going away with Steve, her longtime friend from the ER; they had acknowledged an attraction months earlier but had felt it was too soon after her marital separation, so they'd decided to wait it out. Now, it had been nearly a year since her initial separation from Ken, and Cindy was ready to move on.

She was going with Steve to San Francisco to get a tour of the city, check out Sausalito, and meet some of his friends, giving them a chance to explore the chemistry between them. She felt excited about getting out of town, since she had been picking up extra shifts lately and was looking forward to a break, but she was mostly happy to finally spend some time with Steve away from prying eyes.

She personally thought she could use some happiness in her private life. She felt like a teenager, giddy with anticipation. Nothing could ruin this weekend!

Cindy picked up Jeremiah and took a quick look around the living room before heading upstairs. It was time for the four-year-old's nap, and the pillow was crying out her name.

At the top of the stairs, Cindy surveyed the unfinished third floor, which was more like a large open loft meagerly furnished with a dresser, nightstands, and a large waterbed. While the rooms did not yet have walls and the floor was still bare plywood, the floorplan for several rooms was easy to navigate visually. Ken had insisted on doing all the construction work himself and refused to take out a home loan. The four-year project so far had been a slow labor of love. Unfortunately, he had not yet finished the house before they separated.

Cindy tucked Jeremiah into bed, kissing his forehead good night. "Sweet dreams, Miah."

Jeremiah quickly fell asleep while she got ready for bed. Slipping off her white tennis shoes and blue scrubs, Cindy climbed onto the other side of the bed, slipping her naked body between the warm sheets, eager for sleep.

At twenty-nine, Cindy felt good about her body. She was strong and had endurance for hiking and long shifts in the ER. And she had given birth to two healthy babies. She still carried some of the pregnancy weight, but she had lost thirty pounds since she and Ken had split, and she felt confident about losing thirty more. She was taking advantage of the equipment in the physical therapy department for toning and strength training, a free employee benefit, and she walked the steep one-mile road down to Donner Lake and then another mile up the steep incline back to her house at the top of the hill every day.

She was young and strong, and while her five-foot-ten frame gave her a larger presence than most women, she carried her stature with confidence. Plus, her long hair, blue eyes, and playful smile gave her confidence too. She felt good about where she was in her life.

After putting her long hair into a bun, Cindy rested her weary head on the pillow as the warm waterbed melted into her bare skin, pulling her under into a dreamy abyss.

CHAPTER 2:
FIRE!

The sound of the dog barking woke Cindy from a deep slumber, the kind of sleep you fall into before your head hits the pillow. Four back-to-back night shifts in the ER and OB had taken their toll. Cindy groggily lifted her head from the pillow and glanced at the clock: 1:06 p.m. *Why is Candy barking like that?*

Crackle! Pop! Cindy turned her head toward the open stairway down to the second floor. Feeling hot, she pushed off the blanket. Pop! Pop! The sound of lightbulbs bursting made her sit up quickly. She stared momentarily at the flickering lights and the smoke spiraling up the hazy stairwell before she realized she wasn't waking from a bad nightmare. *Fire,* she thought to herself, seconds before adrenaline raged through her body. *Oh my God, the house is on fire!*

Cindy looked over at Jeremiah, who was sound asleep, before pushing herself out of the waterbed. Candy, their collie chained outside on a lead, continued to bark incessantly. The sounds of popping and breaking coming from downstairs grew more frequent. She looked around the unfinished third level, with its plywood floor and open-framed walls, and through the smoky haze saw no other exit, no way downstairs beyond the flickering stairwell and growing inferno below.

"Miah," Cindy urged. "Miah! Get up, honey!"

Cindy went around the bed and saw the flames crawling up the stairs. Within minutes, the smoke became so thick that she could only grab what she hoped was a robe from the nearby chair to cover her naked body.

Jeremiah jumped out of bed and headed toward the closest window, just as Cindy had practiced with him in case of emergency only a couple of weeks before. *Please God*, she prayed. *Please don't let him panic and run to the stairwell. I can't see him in this smoke!* Cindy looked down at her hands and could barely make them out. She looked toward the dim light coming from the window and saw his silhouette contrasting against the sunshine outside.

Feeling the stifling heat and seeing the dancing flames leaping up the stairs, Cindy suddenly feared the floor could collapse. *Oh my God, how are we going to get out?*

"Jeremiah, honey, we have to get out of the house. The house is on fire," she explained as calmly as she could. She grabbed the thick quilt off the bed as she went toward Jeremiah by the window. She could tell he was looking at her but could not see his expression clearly through the smoke.

Cindy's mind raced. *How can we get out?* She had wanted to buy a ladder to attach to the window in case of an emergency but hadn't yet. She had nothing to break through the walls. She looked across the large room to the window on the other side and wondered what was out there, but she was afraid to cross the floor because it might fall through.

In her panic, she saw limited options, but she knew they could not go down the stairs and knew that if they didn't get out soon, they were both going to die. The heat alone and smoke inhalation were almost suffocating.

Cindy looked out the window down to the ground three stories below where a large granite slab awaited. *I'm going to have to drop Miah out the window*, she thought, mentally steeling herself, *and the fall alone might kill him*. She had seen grown men in the ER who hadn't survived falls like this. She looked around once more and saw no other way. Already, she felt her face throbbing from the heat.

"Jeremiah, we've gotta jump out the window, honey. That's the only way we can get out," she explained quickly.

"Okay, Mommy, okay," he said, fear and acceptance entwined in his trusting little voice. He coughed and gasped from the heavy smoke filling the room.

"Stand back, Miah. I'm going to open the window."

Jeremiah stepped back into Cindy away from the window as she reached over his head with both hands and slid the window to the side, tossing the quilt and her robe out the window down to the ground below.

In less than thirty seconds, the flames, greeting the fresh oxygen with vigor, rushed up the stairs, rolled across the ceiling, and raced out the window in a flash, the heat scorching Cindy's naked back and body. The flameover happened so quickly that Cindy involuntarily closed her eyes and opened them again, and it was over.

Jeremiah, shielded from the flames by Cindy's body, cried out in fear.

Knowing they were running out of time, Cindy looked down at the crumpled quilt, hoping somehow it would soften their fall. Below, a large, flat granite slab and dirt awaited them on the mountainside.

Cindy could feel the raw heat intensifying on her back as she quickly picked up Jeremiah and put his little body through the window. Holding both his hands, she dangled him in the open air. Fear gripped her heart as she struggled with the finality of her options. She knew she had to let go, but as a mother, she did not know how. This was the unthinkable. She knew she could be dropping him to his death, or a broken neck or back and a life of paralysis. She held on.

Knowing that he could die, she wanted him to be having pleasant thoughts. She looked over through the pine trees toward Donner Lake, always a source of beauty and happy family memories. "Jeremiah, look at the lake," she urged. "Look how pretty the lake is ..."

"Mommy!" Jeremiah cried out as he looked down, feeling the pain in his wrists and wanting the suspense to end. "Mommy, let go!"

Cindy let go—praying as she did.

Jeremiah landed face down, bracing his fall with both arms and a leg, the other leg flailing upward. He turned around and sat up.

Cindy let out a sigh of relief, thanking God he was alive.

Oh God, he lived, she thought. *Now I have to jump!* There was no looking back, the unbearable heat and hellish flames now too close to face. Jumping out the third-story window was her only choice if she wanted to live, her only salvation before the entire room was engulfed in flames by flashover.

Satan's fury roared behind her. Cindy put her feet through the window and twisted on her stomach until she was hanging from the windowsill by her hands, her naked body convulsing as the fire engulfed the third story and her fear of heights preventing her from letting go onto the rocky abyss below. She could hear the raging whirl of flames coming from the bedroom and could feel the burning on her fingers—and she knew she had no other option.

"Mommy, hurry! Come on!" Jeremiah screamed, seeing the fiery inferno that was their house.

I have to push myself away from the house, she thought. *I can't land on Miah, or I'll crush him* ... And then, with a push, she let go.

CHAPTER 3:
THE ER

As Cindy pushed herself into a sitting position, she felt pain rip through her right hip. *I'm hurt*, she thought. Still, she pushed the pain to the back of her mind and surveyed their situation. She knew they had to get away from the fiery house in case it collapsed or exploded. As she glanced over at the propane tank not too far from the house, she quickly reached over, grabbed the robe on the ground, and slipped it over her head.

"Mommy, the kittens. The kittens!" Jeremiah cried out, concerned for the safety of their two newest family members.

"Okay, stay here, and I'll go get them," Cindy assured him, taking a step toward the basement door. Suddenly, debilitating pain shot through Cindy's hip, and she knew the injury was serious. *I can't open the door. The fire is right there, and I'll get burned!*

"I'm sure they already got out, honey. Animals know how to do that," Cindy assured him, looking at the house in flames and realizing they had probably already perished.

Cindy reached for Jeremiah's hand to pull him up when he cried out, "It hurts, Mommy. It hurts!"

She looked at his hand and immediately noticed that it was deformed, which meant he had broken his wrist during the landing. As Cindy helped Jeremiah off the ground, he cried out, "Mommy, my leg hurts too."

She picked him up in her arms and hobbled over behind her Subaru, where she thought they would be safe from flying debris. Thinking they would be okay if she could drive them away from the house and to the hospital, Cindy tried to open the driver's side door, hoping to find the keys inside, but it wouldn't open.

As they used the car as a shield, Cindy realized that someone must have seen the fire by now and called the fire department. A loud crashing noise came from the house, and Cindy realized the first floor had probably just fallen through. She started to feel dizzy.

Suddenly, Cindy heard yelling and saw two young men running down the road, surveying Cindy and Jeremiah and the burning house. "Oh my God, are you okay? Was anyone else in the house?"

"No, no, it's just us," Cindy said, seeing the relief on their faces.

"We saw the fire from up on the freeway," one of the men explained, insinuating that they had pulled over and hopped the guard rail down to her house. "I'll go find a phone and call the ambulance."

Cindy suddenly became aware that Candy was still barking. "First, can you please go untie our dog? I don't want her to get injured."

One of the men nodded and went to untie her. Candy ran to the side door and began pacing, worried that her family was still inside the house. Cindy was too weak to call for her but felt reassured she was free to escape the fire. *She'll be safe until Ken comes and gets her,* she thought.

Wanting to get to the hospital as soon as possible, where she knew her doctor friends and nurses would take care of them, she said, "We really need a ride to the hospital. My son is hurt. Can you drive us there?" Cindy nodded over toward her Jeep at the bottom of the driveway, where she knew the keys were inside.

The two men looked at Cindy in surprise. "Don't you want to wait for the ambulance?"

"No, no, I just really want to get to the hospital. Most of these houses are empty vacation homes. It'll take too long to find a phone and call them. We could be at the hospital before the ambulance even gets here ..."

Suddenly, there was a loud crashing sound from the house, as if the second or third floor had collapsed, and the four turned their heads in time to see fire shooting out of the side windows. Fear ripped through Cindy, and she wanted to get away from the house as soon as possible.

The men decided to split up. "You go look for a phone and call 911, and I'll drive her to the hospital!"

The taller man picked up Jeremiah and set him on the hood of the Jeep. He then returned and helped Cindy limp down to the car and put her on the front seat, placing Jeremiah's naked little body on her lap. He was wearing only his white underwear from his nap.

Cindy looked down at Jeremiah's little face, and the horror of their situation set in. His face was white with shock, contrasting the red burns on his cheeks and forehead, and his blonde hair was singed and ragged. Both his wrists look deformed too. Cindy prayed there were no internal injuries. With fear in his blue eyes, he looked back at his mother, seeing the more dramatic consequences of the fire on her face. *I probably look horrible,* Cindy realized. *I probably look just as bad as him.*

The man started the Jeep and began driving the rugged, curvy road down the hillside toward Donner Lake. As they approached the bottom, Cindy heard the sirens.

Cindy urged, "Don't stop. Just go. By the time you stop and get me into the ambulance, we could be at the hospital. I'm a nurse. I work in the ER. Just get me to the hospital."

Just as the Jeep hit the pavement of Donner Pass Road, two firetrucks and an ambulance passed them, turning right onto her road.

"Go. Just go. I don't care if you stop at the stop signs," Cindy urged.

The man drove the nine miles through the town of Truckee as fast as he could and pulled up to the ER at the Tahoe Forest Hospital with a halt.

He then ran through the sliding emergency room doors yelling, "I have a mom and a little boy who jumped out of a third-story window because their house was on fire!"

Medical staff ran out to the Jeep, having already heard there was a fire on Donner Lake. Cindy felt a sense of relief, knowing they were in good hands.

One nurse took Jeremiah off Cindy's lap, and another went to help Cindy out of the car. "No, no, I can stand up," Cindy stubbornly assured them. But as soon as she stood up, she felt her body collapsing, the gravity of the situation catching up with her.

"Here's a wheelchair!" a nurse exclaimed, thrusting it forward as Cindy turned and sat in the chair. The nurse pushed her into the ER and into the newly established burn room, which Cindy had helped set up only months before. She was its first burn occupant.

Jeremiah was placed in a bed next to her so they could share the room. He lay on the bed crying as the nurses assessed his vital signs.

"It's Cindy! It's Cindy Ames and her son Jeremiah!" Word spread like wildfire throughout the medical staff. A nurse's worst nightmare is seeing one of their own come through the ER doors.

Having just adjourned a staff meeting, the nurses swarmed into the room to aid Cindy in any way they could. The familiar faces were comforting.

"Where's Jan?" Cindy asked, knowing that Jan was one of the best ER nurses. "I want Jan to help me."

"I want Papa Black to look at Jeremiah's bones," Cindy directed, giving orders like she was on the clock. Papa Black was the nickname Dr. Black had gotten over the years. He was a gruff doctor, but they all knew he was just a big teddy bear and was more like their dad—thus, Papa Black.

"Okay, Cindy, just relax," Jan assured her. "We're going to give you pain meds now." The burn room was chaos as a flurry of nurses attended to the urgent needs of both patients.

Cindy replied, "Okay, but not too much. I want to talk to the doctor when he gets here." Suffering from traumatic shock, Cindy did not see herself as they did. She felt the pain in her hip, but because the fire had obliterated her nerves, she did not understand the severity of her burns.

Cindy heard the heavy footsteps of cowboy boots coming down the ER hall at a rapid pace. *Thank God, it's Dr. Boone!* Cindy thought, recognizing his footfall. Dr. Howard Boone was a local surgeon and one of Cindy's friends. She felt a sense of relief, as she knew she was in good hands.

Dr. Boone, a hippie doctor whom everyone admired for his skills, came in to assess Cindy, checking her vitals and listening to her chest. He then sat her up and pulled aside her hospital gown to listen to her breathing through her back with his stethoscope. As he pulled away the stethoscope, a large layer of Cindy's skin pulled off and stuck to his gloved hand. Stunned, Dr. Boone paused. The nurses saw it too, their eyes wide in comprehension. As Dr. Boone pulled off his glove, Cindy saw debris fly into the air but didn't comprehend what she was seeing. He quickly hid his hand behind his back.

"Okay, we're done here," he assured her.

"Are you sure?" Cindy asked.

"Yes, but Cindy, we're going to have to transfer you to a burn unit. You have burns on your back, and we're not equipped to treat them," said Dr. Boone, still minimizing the gravity of the situation. The nurses continued to console Cindy and offer encouragement.

Immediately, the staff started making calls to burn units in California to see who could take her. She needed to be flown and transported as soon as possible. They called one in San Francisco and another in the Bay Area, but these could only take one patient, not both.

"Nope," Cindy insisted. "Jeremiah and I must go together. We need to stay together."

Sherri, the ER nurse supervisor, had worked at a burn unit in Southern California, Brotman Medical Center, and made a phone call.

"Hey, I know you don't have any beds," she implored, "but I have one of my nurses and her son who need to stay together. Is there any way you could move some patients around and make room for them? Please, can you do something?"

The staff consulted and were able to make a room available. "Perfect. Thank you! I also want her to see Dr. Hoefflin," Sherri requested, knowing he was one of the finest doctors there.

Cindy looked over at Jeremiah and saw the nurses applying saline soaks to his arms, face, and body. Then they turned to Cindy and started with her. *Oh God, oh God, it's so cold, and it hurts so bad!* Cindy wanted to scream but couldn't. She had to be strong in front of Jeremiah, who was being so good.

Cindy looked at the clock and realized it was almost three in the afternoon. "Oh my gosh, my son Michael! He should be getting home from school. I don't want him to get home and see the house on fire!"

The nurses looked at the clock and realized that Michael would already be on his way home on the bus from Truckee Elementary. The nurses assured her they would contact the fire department and let them know to keep an eye out for Michael and that they would take care of him—the way that folks in a small town do.

Jan, her favorite nurse, attempted to place an IV in Cindy's arms but couldn't seem to get one started, so now a team was trying her foot. Cindy could tell that things weren't good, as they were all being serious and working fast. She knew this body language, having worked with them in the ER for a few years now. Cindy felt the blood drain from her face as her stomach tied up in knots. She suddenly realized she might be in grave condition.

Cindy turned to Jeremiah as a distraction for them both. "Honey, Daddy will be here soon. Everything's going to be okay."

Nancy, a fellow nurse and a good friend, turned to Cindy. "Jeremiah has breaks in both his arms. Is there a particular doctor you want for him?"

"Yes. Papa Black. No one else. I know he'll come and take care of us."

Cindy closed her eyes and took a deep breath, saying a quick prayer and asking God for His healing and guidance.

CHAPTER 4:
THE FLIGHT

After Michael was brought to the hospital, the staff wouldn't let him see Cindy or Jeremiah, partly because seeing them both burned might be too upsetting for his tender heart but also to keep germs and contamination out of the sterile burn room.

Cindy asked Nancy to call Linda, another friend and coworker, to pick up Michael and take him to her house. A second phone call went out to Ken, who had already heard about the fire and was getting ready to go back to Truckee from his parents' house in Coleville. He had a two-hour drive but would first go to the hospital to see Jeremiah and then go pick up Michael at Linda's. Cindy felt relieved knowing Ken was there to be with Jeremiah in the hospital. Knowing her boys were taken care of allowed her to focus on what was going on around her.

Before flying out that night, Cindy wanted to talk to Michael on the phone, needing to hear his little voice and reassure him they were okay. When she was handed the phone, Linda told her Michael was already asleep.

"That's okay, please wake him up. I really want to talk to him before we leave." *And there's a chance this may be the last time I ever talk to him*, she realized.

Michael got on the phone. "Mom?"

"Hi, honey, we're okay. Linda is going to take care of you, and your dad will be there soon. I'm okay, and Miah is okay. I just want you to know that you're a good boy, and I love you very much, Michael." Cindy's voice started to crack as her blue eyes welled up with tears. If this was going to be the last time he heard her voice, she wanted him to remember how deeply she loved him.

"The doctors are sending us down to LA where they're going to take care of us," she continued. "You'll come down later and stay with Grandma and visit us." After Cindy hung up, she lay in bed and took a breath. Since she knew Michael was safe and secure, she was now mentally ready for the flight.

Cindy had been in the Truckee Hospital for twelve hours. Her hospital room and the outside hallway were filled with staff members, both on and off duty, all there to support one of their own. Plus, Truckee was a small town, and everyone had heard what happened to sweet Cindy and Jeremiah, and had flooded to the hospital in support.

They gathered in the hallway to say goodbye as they prepared her for the flight. Jeremiah was scared and put up a little fight about going on the airplane until a staff member offered to give him a 7-Up for the trip, and he quickly agreed.

Around midnight, there was a break in the windy weather, so the airplane was able to land at the Truckee Airport instead of Reno, which had been the backup plan.

Between Cindy's asthma and smoke inhalation, her breathing was becoming laborious. The staff debated on intubating her for the trip but decided to wait as long as she could breathe on her own. Intubating her meant that she couldn't talk to Jeremiah or express her needs to the accompanying flight nurse, so they kept it as a last resort.

As the staff discussed their options, Cindy thought back on the countless times she had assisted with an intubation, a procedure used if patients could not breathe effectively on their own. They would first open the patient's mouth and, using a curved blade, sweep the tongue out of the way. Keeping the blade there, they would stick the tube down the patient's throat into the trachea.

Once in place, the tube was attached to a ventilation machine so air could be pushed into the lungs. It was an uncomfortable procedure for the patient, but it provided immediate and urgent relief. In all the times Cindy had helped save a patient's life with an intubation, she'd never thought she'd be on the receiving end.

The ambulance arrived at the airport, and the staff quickly loaded the two gurneys into the tiny plane, having to tip Cindy sideways to get them both inside. Cindy's gurney was side by side with Jeremiah's and both were hooked up to IVs. Two pilots and a flight nurse were already on board, eager to get Cindy to the Center.

About midway through the bumpy flight, Cindy started having difficulty breathing. Her lungs felt scorched. "I can't. Breathe. Very good," Cindy said with fear in her voice. "I can't breathe."

"I have everything ready if I need to intubate you," the nurse assured her. "If I need to do it, I'm ready, and I won't let you get too bad because I don't want it too swollen." The nurse spoke to Cindy in nurse-talk, knowing that Cindy understood that her throat would swell if she struggled to breathe for too long, making it a more difficult and painful procedure to get the tube down her throat. The procedure would already be difficult to do while on a bumpy plane ride.

"Show me. Show me you have it ready," Cindy demanded. Whether it was her ten years of nursing experience or her need to control her fear that drove her, Cindy needed to see that it was, in fact, ready.

She felt assured when the nurse held out the equipment. She then turned toward Jeremiah, feeling the need to explain what was happening to help ease his fears. "Honey, if Mommy has a hard time breathing, it's okay. The nurse is going to put a tube down my throat to help me. If I stop breathing, don't get too scared; just let the nurse do what she needs to do."

"Okay, Mommy," Jeremiah replied in his little voice.

Cindy focused on her shallow breathing, fear constricting her blood vessels as the world shrunk with each labored breath. *Inhale. Exhale.* Time slowed down as she became acutely aware of her breathing. She felt the air pass slowly over her dry lips.

Inhale. Exhale.

"How much longer until we get there?" the nurse asked the pilots. "I can't wait much longer to intubate her."

"We've got five minutes," the pilot responded.

"No, they're asking us to hold off landing for ten minutes," the copilot informed.

The nurse urged, "Tell them we don't have ten minutes. Tell them my patient needs to land *now.*"

The pilot relayed the message and was reprioritized to land immediately before Cindy's breathing got worse. An ambulance was waiting at the Santa Monica Airport terminal when the airplane pulled in. Once Cindy and Jeremiah were loaded in the ambulance, it was a short ride to Brotman Medical Center.

As the gurneys were wheeled into the hospital, Cindy spotted her parents, who lived nearby in West Covina, waiting for her arrival. It wasn't until Cindy saw her mom and dad that she felt the weight break free of trying to keep it together for her kids. Knowing that her parents were there and would take care of everything, Cindy let down her guard and fell apart. She had been trying to stay strong for her boys, but under her own mother's wing, she finally let go.

Cindy sobbed as she looked at her parents' faces, stricken with fear upon seeing Cindy for the first time. Her long blonde hair, which she had worn with pride down her back or in a long braid, was now a singed ball on top of her head. Her puffy face was almost unrecognizable, her skin swollen and red with angry, open wounds. Both her eyes were almost swollen shut. Her hands and arms were wrapped completely in bandages.

The medical staff rushed to help Cindy first and began to wheel her away. "Please, stay for Jeremiah," Cindy asked her parents between labored breaths. "Please, make sure he is okay," she implored, relinquishing her parental responsibility onto them.

"It's okay, Cindy. We're here," they reassured her. And Cindy was wheeled away.

CHAPTER 5:
ASSESSMENT
Day 1: Intensive Care Burn Unit

From this moment on for the next several months, Cindy was no longer an active force in her life but merely a passive body in a hospital bed, as life revolved around her. As soon as Cindy was whisked away into the emergency room, the medical staff swarmed to give her a formal assessment. Immediately, a doctor told her, "Cindy, you can't breathe. We need to intubate you." She nodded, as she already knew she needed help.

"Yes, do it," she whispered.

"We'll still tell you everything we're going to do as we're doing it. We're going to give you medication, but we know that you can still hear us even though you won't be able to talk to us after we intubate you." Cindy nodded that she understood and quickly succumbed to the medication, falling asleep.

The medical team at Brotman Medical Center quickly assessed Cindy and prioritized her immediate needs. Dr. Hoefflin, a plastic surgeon who had a reputation for being the best, and Dr. Tamir, an orthopedic surgeon, were assigned to her. Dr. Waxburg, an ophthalmologic surgeon, was scheduled to cleanse her eyes and debride her eyelids immediately. She was also scheduled for a double procedure in the operating room in two days, with Dr. Hoefflin performing the first skin graft procedure and Dr. Tamir putting a Kirshner/Steinman pin in her leg to help pull the fractured hip back into place with traction.

When Cindy woke up in the Intensive Care Burn Unit, she immediately felt throbbing pain and thought for a moment that she had been in a car accident. Then she remembered the fire. She knew that she was on a ventilator and was relieved that breathing was no longer a struggle. What she didn't realize was that she would remain on the ventilator for several days.

"We need to take you to surgery right away to debride and clean your eyes out, Cindy," Dr. Waxburg said, speaking gently with his face close to hers. "Your eyes and eyelids have been burned, and we need to do some repair so you don't lose any of your vision."

Cindy nodded, still feeling groggy from the medication. She knew she should feel scared but believed she was in good hands. As her life lay in the balance, she knew she had the best team of doctors and that they were in control.

"We're going to let your parents come say goodbye to you before we take you to the OR." Cindy nodded as she felt herself starting to fade and fall into the abyss, the pre-operation sedative taking effect.

The surgery went well, and Cindy was taken back to the burn ICU. After they cleaned out her eyes, they put a salve in her eyes to protect them and help them heal. For a few days afterward, her eyes remained bandaged, and she could not see the medical staff as they attended to her and spoke to her. These first few days at the Center were a blur to Cindy, as she faded in and out of consciousness, in and out of assessments.

"Cindy, most of your body has been damaged by the fire. You have third-degree burns on 70 percent of your body," Dr. Hoefflin explained in a soft, gentle voice.

She nodded, hearing the doctor but not grasping the gravity of his words.

"We need to do skin grafts to protect the most severely burned areas."

Cindy nodded.

"We're consulting with your parents and your husband to determine your medical care plan and course of action ..."

Cindy's parents, Reota and Larry, were making the best decisions for their daughter that they could, prioritizing her quality of life.

"Cindy, you have fourth-degree burns on your fingers, and you have exposed bone. We have discussed amputating them, but we know that as a nurse, you will need the use of your hands, so we are going to try skin grafts."

Cindy nodded again.

One after another, the medical staff treated the triage of dire health issues that Cindy faced, prioritizing each procedure through protocol. For Cindy, time was a blur, and she felt herself bobbing in and out of consciousness as hours and days and then weeks flowed together.

Over the next couple of weeks, the doctors continued to talk to Cindy and inform her about each surgery, even though the conversations were distorted in her mind as they spoke to her between bouts of consciousness.

"Cindy, your right hip and pelvis are shattered, but our main priority right now is helping your skin heal. We're going to first harvest skin grafts off the front of your legs and place the skin on your arms ..."

What Cindy didn't know, and what the doctors later explained to her parents and to Ken, was that they had calculated her chance of survival, and it was grim. They acknowledged that due to the great patient care she had received in Truckee, her chances were better. However, using a medical diagnosis formula, the doctors had calculated her chance of survival by subtracting the percentage of body burns and the patient's age from 100 percent and then deducting an additional 10 percent for any other major issues. Cindy's age of 30 (rounded) and 70 percent burns took her to 0 percent. Then they deducted 10 percent each for her being overweight, having smoke inhalation, and not getting to the burn unit for over twelve hours.

Therefore, Cindy's chance of survival was calculated to be –30 percent.

CHAPTER 6:
THE OFFICIAL MEDICAL REPORT (VERBATIM)
May 13, 1982

Dr. Hoefflin's Operative Report:

Patient was admitted for inhalation and burns over half of her body.

She is of significant risk due to the weight, size, the inhalation injury, the fractured pelvis, and the size of her burns.

The patient has large surface burns on face, both upper extremities including the hands, upper chest wall, the entire back, buttock, bilateral flanks, and both leg areas. There are extreme burn wounds on left hand.

The diagnosis, anticipated procedures, risk, limitation alternatives, postoperative course has been discussed in detail with the patient and family, and they understand and wish to proceed.

Procedure Report:

Multiple strips of donor skin were taken from the left calf area, the dorsal aspect of the thigh, abdominal areas, chest and right thigh areas.

Utilizing the Watson knife, a large surface area of obviously necrotic 3rd degree and deep secondary degree skin was removed from the left posterior thigh, lateral flank and hip areas.

The sheath skin was then utilized to cover the dorsal aspect of the left hand in a very meticulous fashion. The remainder of the skin grafts were taken and applied to both hand areas, both upper arms, and then applied to the left posterior leg area, left flank and hip areas.

Once completed, Dr. Tamir placed a Kirshner/Steinman pin through the right tibia for the traction of the fractured pelvis.

CHAPTER 7:
TRUCKEE SHERIFFS

A few days after the fire, Truckee sheriff Phil Harrison and fire investigator Don Delaney traveled south to Brotman Medical Center to check on Cindy's status. They were hoping she was conscious and could answer some questions. They had spoken with the firefighters on the scene, and no obvious cause of the fire had been identified yet, making this an open case. They knew Cindy was in critical condition and might not survive the fire, so they needed to question her as soon as possible.

Sheriff Harrison and Investigator Delaney first spoke to her doctor to determine Cindy's status and found out she was in and out of consciousness. Cindy's family was also there in the waiting room—including Cindy's husband, Ken Ames, who was a person of interest.

Then they both went to the waiting room to introduce themselves and ask the family to stay for questioning. Since time was of the essence, they went to Cindy's room next to see if she was able to answer any questions. Fortunately, she tilted her head slightly when they entered the room, acknowledging their presence.

Cindy lay in bed with her arms and hands bandaged and gauze wrapped around her chin and face. Her eyes were bandaged as well. It was difficult to assess her injuries, but it was obvious she was in critical condition.

"Hi, Cindy. It's Sheriff Phil Harrison," he said gently, not sure if she would remember him in this state.

Cindy nodded her head slightly. She had worked with Phil when he had come into the ER on many occasions and recognized his voice. Cops were always coming in and out of the hospital.

"I've traveled here from Truckee to talk to you about the fire. I need to know if you remember *anything* about what might have caused the fire. Any details could help."

Fire, Cindy thought groggily. *What started the fire? Candy barking. Smoke. Miah. Dropped him from the window ...* She tried to recall details. *Ken. I heard something downstairs. Ken came back.*

"Ken," Cindy whispered.

"What's that, Cindy?" Phil asked, wanting to confirm what he had heard.

"Ken came back. Noise ... downstairs. Ask Ken," Cindy murmured, hoping Ken could shed some light on what had happened.

"Okay, Cindy, that's great. We'll talk to Ken. Anything else?" Phil asked.

Cindy nodded her head no. She just wanted to sleep.

The men left her room and went back to the waiting room, hoping Ken hadn't left. He was still there.

"Hi, Ken. We need to ask you a few questions," Phil stated, getting out his notepad. "Can you tell us anything you know about the morning of the fire?"

"Sure," Ken answered. "I had stayed the night with the boys while Cindy was at work. Michael caught the school bus at 8:20 a.m. like normal. Cindy got home around 8:45 a.m. My friend Jim was with me, as we were going to do a job that morning. Cindy made us breakfast, and we left at about 9:30 a.m. Cindy and Jeremiah were home alone. It wasn't until about three o'clock that I got the call from the hospital about the fire. I was already at my parents' house in Coleville, but I left right away to head back to Truckee."

"Okay, thank you," Phil responded. "To clarify, your marriage to Cindy is estranged?"

"Yes," said Ken meekly. "We got back together over the winter, but it didn't work out."

"Did you return to the house after you left at 9:30 a.m.? Cindy said you came back to the house."

"Came back? No. I didn't go back to the house," said Ken, confused. "Wait, am I a suspect? I didn't start the fire, if that's what you're thinking."

"We're just following up on all lines of inquiry, Ken."

"Well, I didn't do it. I mean, I could have done it. I learned all about making explosives in the military and could have rigged it up, but I didn't do it. I wasn't there."

Cindy's family stared at Ken incredulously.

Ken looked over at Reota, Cindy's mom, and saw the look on her face. "What? I didn't do it. I wouldn't have done it. I wasn't even there!"

Phil looked at Ken and wrote in his notepad. He and Don spoke to the other family members before leaving. Meanwhile, Cindy's brother, Larry, stared at Ken from across the waiting room, clenching his teeth.

CHAPTER 8:
JEREMIAH

One day, in a lucid moment, Cindy asked Gail a serious question. She knew that she could trust Gail because she never lied; anyone could see the truth on her face. Several days before, Cindy recalled seeing Jeremiah next door just beyond the curtain before they wheeled him to surgery, and then he never came back.

"Gail, tell me the truth. The nurses keep telling me Miah was moved from next door to a different wing in the hospital, but please tell me the truth. Is he dead? He died, didn't he? Just tell me if he's dead. I need to know!" Her voice cracked.

Cindy knew that Jeremiah had third-degree burns on both his right arm and right cheek—on 10 percent of his body. He had also broken both of his wrists when trying to brace himself from the fall, and he had broken two bones in his lower left leg, his tib fib.

"No, Cindy, he's fine," Gail insisted. "He's okay."

Cindy nodded her head, her lip trembling and tears welling in her blue eyes. Even though she trusted Gail, she thought for sure everyone was lying to her, trying to protect her.

To reassure Cindy, Dr. Tamir, who was treating both of them, stopped by her room to discuss Jeremiah's status and broke down the medical issues in detail.

"To start, Jeremiah broke both arms and wrists, so he is scheduled for surgery on both of his wrists next. Instead of pins, we will put wires in both wrists to help them heal, and later, we will have to remove the wires.

He also has second-degree burns on his right arm, and his left arm has third-degree burns and required skin grafts, which we did a couple days ago. During the fall, he also broke the tibia and fibula in his left leg." Dr. Tamir paused. "Because of his three limb casts, he can't walk and has to be in a wheelchair, but this is only temporary."

Cindy nodded her head in understanding as tears rolled down her cheeks. Her poor little boy. This was a lot for a four-year-old to deal with.

While Jeremiah wasn't burned as badly as Cindy, his burned arm was also broken, which made it tricky for a cast. Dr. Tamir explained that Jeremiah would have an "open cast" because his burns underneath needed to breathe, so they couldn't put on a regular closed cast.

"We can leave his wrists and not do surgery, but I don't know how well he'll be able to use them," Dr. Tamir continued. "Or we can do surgery, but I don't know how well his burns will heal because we will have to keep the casts partially open so the surgical wounds can heal …"

Dr. Tamir tried to give Cindy all the available possibilities so she could make an educated decision, and normally she would have appreciated being treated with respect like that. But as Cindy lay in bed listening, the situation became so complex, and there were so many variables, she couldn't make a decision. The morphine certainly didn't help.

Even though she appreciated being informed and being told what the options were when she was lucid, she ultimately left it up to her family to make the best choices. She knew her family—her mom, dad, sisters, and brother—would deliberate when they were all at the house and decide the best course of action. When Ken was in town, he was included in the discussion too. Cindy trusted them all and knew they would run their choices past her.

After any procedure was performed, the doctors always stopped by and visited Cindy to keep her updated.

"I just want you to know what we did today," Dr. Tamir said. "It's so hard to help him heal. So far, we've been lucky with him."

Sometimes, Cindy would just look at her family's faces to read their response. Usually, they looked at her and nodded their heads reassuringly.

Other times, she would look at the doctor and just say, "Fix it." It was all Cindy could do to put her faith and trust in her family to make the right decisions, in the medical team to do their best, and in God to watch over Jeremiah.

CHAPTER 9:
MICHAEL AND MIAH

Unbeknownst to Cindy, the staff and the family discussed whether to let the boys see their mom in her condition. Early on, Cindy had expressed that she didn't want them to see her like this, to remember her in this state, but her family also knew she needed to see their smiling faces and hear their little voices to give her a reason to live.

Ken, who had been staying at Cindy's parents' house—in the trailer in the backyard—first brought Michael to see her. Michael had been asking about her for days, and it was clear his eight-year-old mind was apprehensive about her absence. He entered the room wide-eyed, leaning back against his father's body.

"Hi, honey," Cindy said softly. "Come here. It's okay … I'm fine. The doctors are gonna do their work, honey, and they're going to help me get better so I can come home." Cindy was aware of how her burned skin and singed hair and tubes might look to him. She knew that she probably looked a little scary, maybe not even at all like the mother he remembered.

Michael turned his body and buried his head in his dad's chest. But it was enough. Cindy had seen him and reassured him, and that was all she could do right now.

To ease her fears, the medical staff next brought Jeremiah to her, escorting him in a wheelchair down to her room. Relief flooded her chest, easing her unfounded fear, and she burst into tears, happy beyond words to see him. *Oh, he is alive. He is doing good! Praise God!*

As Gail picked up Jeremiah, Cindy saw the casts on his arms and leg. *Oh, my little boy*, she thought. Tears ran down her face. *Oh, my poor children. They have lost their home and everything they own. And I am so badly burned and must look terrifying to them. Thank God for my family!*

Cindy took a breath and spoke to Jeremiah. "Miah, you get to leave the hospital soon, and you're going to go home with Auntie Gail, and she is going to take care of you."

Gail, who was a teacher, had quit her summer job to help take care of Michael and Jeremiah, who needed round-the-clock assistance.

"You can share a room with me at Grandpa and Grandma's," Gail said, looking directly at Jeremiah in her arms. Jeremiah nodded.

Cindy added, "Michael will be there too, sharing a room with Auntie JoJo."

"Okay, Mommy," Jeremiah responded quietly.

Cindy felt a flood of relief. In her heart, she had honestly thought he had died and they were hiding it from her because they didn't want her to know. This had been one of her deepest fears. Now she knew he was really okay.

Cindy knew that between her two sisters, her brother, and her parents, the boys would be safe. Ken needed to return to work in Coleville, and Cindy didn't want them so far away, with Ken and his parents. Cindy's parents had offered to keep the boys close by, and Ken had agreed with the understanding that he would take them for periodic weekends.

Cindy's dad had taken some time off work to stay at the hospital with Cindy and to help with the boys. When their church found out about Cindy and what she was going through, they held a blood drive, donating blood marked directly for her. Another church where Larry had worked one weekend found out about Cindy, and they also held a blood drive. Before Cindy left the hospital, she ended up using every donated pint, and she was eternally thankful to each and every donor who helped save her life.

CHAPTER 10:
TRAUMA AND TREATMENT

The largest organ of the human body is the skin, and over 70 percent of Cindy's had been burned by the heat of the fire. Of those burns, only 5 percent were first-degree, which simply meant the skin was red and painful. Another 20 percent were second-degree burns, which meant the skin was blistered and swollen. The remaining 75 percent of her burns were third-degree.

Third-degree burns are essentially charred skin, making the skin look white, dark red, or even black, much like the charred skin on a piece of barbecued chicken. Skin with third-degree burns cannot regenerate itself like the first two layers. While the skin damage is quite severe, third-degree burns are initially not as painful as expected—because the burns also damage the nerves—until the burns start to heal and the nerves recover.

Cindy's skin with third-degree burns was no longer viable, so it needed to be replaced with synthetic or grafted skin. This was essential so that the body tissue underneath did not get infected—and also to avoid *sepsis*, an infection that happens when bacteria gets into the bloodstream, or *tetanus*, a disease caused when a certain type of bacteria gets into the body through an open wound.

The doctor's first choice was to harvest as much unaffected skin as possible from Cindy's body before exploring alternatives. When Cindy had leaned against the windowsill as she opened the window during the fire, her pelvic and pubic area were unaffected, so this was the first place they conducted a skin graft.

Cindy's left hand was burned to the bones, nearly fourth-degree burns—the most severe injury affecting all layers of the skin, tendons, and bones—and so the doctors had put all their attention there first. One nurse inquired about amputating several fingers or possibly her hand, but Cindy's surgeon, Dr. Hoefflin, a compassionate soul, argued, "Cindy is a nurse, and if she lives, she's going to want to go back to work, and she'll need her hands."

Instead, Dr. Hoefflin meticulously reconstructed Cindy's hand and used the shaved skin from her delicate pubic area to cover her fingers, a location that became a source of friendly jokes later.

The next best area to graft from was the front of Cindy's legs, which were only lightly burned. The doctors first gave her second-degree burns time to heal and then grafted the skin to cover the third-degree burns, first on her arm and then on her back.

To do grafts, the doctors used a cheese slicer–like instrument to remove the top layers of healthy skin. The skin graft was usually a three-inch-wide strip. This strip was placed onto a plastic carrier and cranked through a metal Tanner mesher to stretch it out. Unlike the burned areas, donor sites still had their nerves intact. Once the grafts were removed, the donor area was an open wound and was quite painful, despite the dressing placed on top of it.

After scrubbing and sterilizing a third-degree burn, the dead tissue was excised, or cut out, down to the healthy tissue. The newly harvested skin was placed on top of the healthy base and stapled in place all around the edges. Then the medical staff applied a dressing on top to protect the skin graft and hoped that her body would accept the graft as new skin.

The graft started developing blood vessels and connecting to the skin around it within thirty-six hours. If blood vessels didn't begin to form shortly after the surgery, it was a sign her body was rejecting the graft. While they didn't always take or grow, most of Cindy's skin grafts were successful. The burns on her back and shoulders had the most difficult time healing and required multiple grafts.

The donor sites healed within one to two weeks, but the graft sites took a bit longer. The hundreds of staples used to adhere the grafts were removed from Cindy's body over the course of her recovery. Every time she was put under, the doctor would reuse any donor areas that had healed for more skin grafts. Called an *autograft*, the procedure of grafting tissue from one point to another on Cindy's body was essentially a type of organ transplant. She was her own savior donor.

As fate would have it, Cindy's skin had rapid recovery. Human skin typically regenerates within five to seven days, but Cindy's skin regenerated every three to four days. As Dr. Hoefflin told her parents, "Her rapid regeneration is truly a blessing. It's helping to keep her alive, as we are able to go back into the donor site and take another graft quickly."

The doctors wanted to cover as much of her skin as possible to keep the open burn site from being exposed to infection. Infection is what usually kills a burn patient.

After grafting skin onto Cindy's hands, the doctor performed skin grafts on her arms. Cindy's breasts had burned, especially on the sides where the fire had rushed past her. Cindy also had grafts on her lower legs. Her feet, her pubis, and the top of her thighs were the areas least affected by the fire. In contrast, her back and buttocks were affected the most.

The doctors repeated this process over and over, bringing Cindy back into surgery to harvest skin from the same regenerated areas, with her upper thighs being the most common donor site. Over time, her body became a mosaic of skin grafts.

Since Cindy couldn't eat, nutrients were provided two ways. One was intravenously (IV) with total parenteral nutrition (TPN). Lipids, or broken-down fats; sugars; proteins like amino acids; and electrolytes with vitamins were custom-mixed based on a daily analysis of her blood and delivered in her IV. The other method was via a thin NG tube inserted through her nose and down her esophagus to her stomach. This stayed in place 24/7, and liquid nutrition was dripped in constantly. The tube was also used to administer medications. A burn patient needs an excessive amount of nutrition and calories, sometimes three or four times more than normal, to help heal the injury.

Due to the liquid diet, along with the antibiotics, Cindy had horrible diarrhea. While she had a catheter to assist with bladder control, she frequently had diarrhea episodes in bed, sometimes volatile. On a regular basis, the staff would roll her over to give her a bed bath, cleaning her buttocks and legs from diarrhea and changing her sheets. She often found herself on her side with her open back and butt exposed, which was humiliating.

The stomach acids, digestive enzymes, and bile present in diarrhea damaged her skin tissue, causing a burning sensation in her rectum, and her buttocks became so raw it was painful. Recovering from the burns was not just about her skin. It was about every aspect of her body responding to both the trauma and treatment.

Sometimes, Cindy felt embarrassed that the staff had to clean her up, and she apologized profusely: "I'm sorry. I'm so sorry." But Cindy had no control over her body or its functions. Moving her body and limbs around for the sponge bath was painful, but the pain helped mask her humiliation, and she let pride go out the window. Pride was a luxury she could not afford. She was in survival mode, and she knew she could not focus on something as frivolous as feelings.

The nurses tried to assure her that it was not unusual to have these issues. Often, they would talk to her and try to distract her from what was going on by asking her about her boys. She appreciated their conversation and their efforts.

While Cindy knew she didn't have room for pride, she still occasionally found herself feeling ashamed and embarrassed as a natural human reaction to being immersed in diarrhea and other excretions ... to being naked during the Betadine baths ... to being given a sponge bath in all of her private areas while remaining helpless ... to having every hole poked and prodded. She couldn't even use her own hands because they were bandaged up. She had to ask for help if she had a simple itch that needed to be scratched. Her life was not her own, and her body was out of her control.

Cindy's days were filled with diarrhea outbreaks, skin grafts, surgeries, and physical therapy. They started physical therapy almost immediately on her hand, making each finger bend through resistance. They also bent her ankles at ninety-degree angles and made her toes point up straight using splints to keep her from getting *foot drop*, a condition that makes it difficult to lift the front part of your foot. Then they exercised her legs; this had to be done carefully because of her skin grafts, and it was a tormenting exercise.

Cindy had also fractured her hip and pelvis, which contributed to her suffering. Sometimes, when the staff moved her in certain ways, Cindy's screams filled the room. There wasn't an inch on her body that didn't feel tortured and in anguish. The fire and its effects had impacted every fiber of her being.

Every part of her was in physical pain. Mentally, as a nurse, she could understand what was happening, but being a patient was a far different experience than serving as a nurse. And her emotional state was stripped down to the bare minimum. All she had left was her will to live, and even that was teetering on the edge.

CHAPTER 11:
THE BOYS

Cindy's parents, or Ken when he was visiting, would bring the boys by on a regular basis to visit Cindy in the hospital, which was good for Cindy's spirit. She refused visits only when she was in a lot of pain, and her pain levels varied depending on her surgery schedule. Her mom would let her know a day ahead when they planned on bringing the boys by. If she was in agony, which was occasionally, she would put them off. She didn't want them to see her that way, writhing in pain or doped up on morphine.

Cindy was also concerned about how she looked to the boys. She knew that she must look terrifying and was worried about the effect it might have on them. She didn't want to give them nightmares. Her five-foot-ten-inch frame was bandaged from head to toe in the hospital bed, although she was mostly covered in blankets. Her bedhead hair was in a melted bun, and her face was blotchy, swollen, and angry-looking. The only thing that had not changed about her were her blue eyes, which, as always, looked upon them with love.

Michael entered the room and touched his mom's hand, which was wrapped in bandages. Although she didn't have much mobility, Cindy moved her eyes to Michael's face and looked him in the eye. Sometimes she felt too ill to talk. The only way she could communicate with the boys was to wink at them, and then they would wink back. In her mind, every time she winked, it was her way of saying, "I love you."

Michael held his mother's hand and looked around the room, taking in the surroundings and the heart monitor. He seemed to hold his emotions inside so that he wouldn't cry in front of her, although Cindy imagined he probably cried after he left. It saddened her heart knowing he was being brave for her. She knew Michael had a hard time expressing his feelings and hoped he was talking to someone at home.

Since Jeremiah was in a wheelchair, he had to be carried into the room with his three casts. Gail picked Jeremiah up out of his wheelchair in the hall and sat him in a chair by Cindy on the side of the bed.

Cindy could not hold back her tears as they ran down her cheeks. Seeing her boys set off a strong surge of emotion and willpower that flowed through her body. She loved her boys so much and hated to watch them suffer because of seeing her in such bad shape. She struggled with the decision to allow them to see her, but she knew that they wanted to come, and she, too, wanted to be there for them. Also, if they didn't come, they might start imagining the worst, like she was dying or was already dead. She wanted to assure them that she was okay and that she loved them.

She cried as she thought about all their precious souls had been through. With Jeremiah's burns, skin grafts, broken bones, and casts, he couldn't go to the bathroom by himself, let alone run across a playground. The boys had each lost some of their childhood innocence, and it broke her heart.

Cindy had learned that Michael saw the house on fire from the school bus and had run from the bus stop uphill the entire mile to their house. When Michael saw the house in flames and that the top two floors had already fallen, he thought she was inside. He started screaming as he ran toward the house until a firefighter caught him and stopped him from getting closer. With tears running down his face, he kept telling the firefighters that his mom was inside, assuming Jeremiah was with their dad.

"That's my house on fire!" Michael frantically shouted to the firefighter. "My mom is inside!"

Trying to keep Michael at a distance as his little body twisted to get out of his hold, the firefighter said, "Son, you need to stay back. It's not safe to get closer."

Teary-eyed and panicking, Michael had said, "You don't understand! My mom is in the house! I saw the top floors fall down! My mom is in there! You need to save her!"

Another firefighter said, "We're doing our best, son, but it's a dangerous situation. We're doing everything we can. It's not safe for you here. Let's stay here away from the fire." The firefighter stayed by Michael's side and tried to console him.

There were sirens blaring in the background as more emergency personnel arrived. All the while, Michael thought he was watching his mom burn to death, his eyes blurry with tears as he watched the flames consume his home. Meanwhile, a dispatch came through the firefighter's radio.

Dispatch relayed, "Firefighters, we have confirmation. The dwellers of the burning house are already at the hospital, and they're okay. Their names are Jeremiah and Cindy Ames."

Immediately, another firefighter approached Michael and told him, "Son, we just heard from dispatch. Your mom and brother are at the hospital, and they are all right."

Overwhelmed with relief, Michael said, "Thank you, thank you," as he broke down sobbing.

Cindy couldn't imagine what was going through Michael's head when he thought they were inside the house and the trauma it must have caused him. While Jeremiah's injuries were external, Michael's injuries were internal.

Reota asked the boys to tell their mom how they were doing.

"I'm good, Mom," said Michael. "I get to stay with Auntie JoJo in her room, and Miah stays with Auntie Gail."

Cindy thought what a blessing it was that Joy had moved back into their parents' home the year before to save money for her upcoming wedding. Now, she was a huge help to her and the boys.

"And Miah, what about you?" Joy prompted.

"I'm good. Grandma makes us yummy crepes!"

Cindy smiled. Along with chuck roast with carrots and potatoes, her mom's crepes were Cindy's favorite too.

As the boys said their farewells, Cindy gave them both a wink, and they each winked back.

CHAPTER 12:
THE MONKEYS

From the outside, Cindy often looked like a quiet patient in bed when she was sleeping, but internally, she was living a revolving nightmare.

While the medical staff had her on a regular rotation of skin graft surgeries, they kept her morphine dosage high to help ease the pain. For no rhyme or reason, as Cindy faded in and out of consciousness, in and out of morphine stupors, in and out of excruciating pain, she associated staff members with her pain and manifested nightmares involving them as part of her morphine mania.

In one nightmare, Cindy dreamed that a swarm of monkeys was trying to tie her down against her will. Dr. Porter, the anesthesiologist assigned to Cindy, was helping the monkeys pin Cindy to the bed as she fought against them for her freedom. The monkeys grabbed her arms and forced them down into straps as they ran around her bed. As she fought in vain, she looked up at the basement-like windows at the top of the room walls, and she thought that if she could just get up to the windows, she could shout for help and let people know they were holding her down there against her wishes. She thought that if someone could find her mom and explain what was happening, her mom would find her and save her.

A few days later, as Cindy's morphine decreased, she remembered how scared she had been of the monkeys and of being held against her will. She then suddenly realized the monkeys were actually the recovery nurses who had to tie her down because she was trying to pull her NG tubes and IVs out. She lay there feeling a sense of surrealness, not knowing what was real and what had been a fantasy. She had felt so frantic in her nightmare, and with or without monkeys, she knew that the fear she felt was real.

Another time, Cindy felt like she was in a dungeon, and they were burying her alive. She was suffocating, and they were burying her in the ground so she couldn't breathe. She could feel her body sinking. She tried to move her hands to claw her way out, but her hands were tied, and she was helpless. In her mind, Cindy yelled out, *Why are the nurses ignoring me? Don't they know I'm still alive? Help me. Help! I don't want to die. I'm sinking deeper. Help me, please! Don't let me suffocate. Just untie my hands, please. I don't want to die ...*

Later, Cindy woke up and found that she had floated to Hawaii. It was hot and humid, and she was having trouble breathing. She was in a room up on the top floor, so none of her family could find her to help her. She thought that if her family could just climb up the stairs to where she was and bring Dr. Boone, her surgeon and friend from Truckee, he would make sure she was all right.

In another dream, Cindy and Jeremiah were running for their lives up a hill to get away from people who were chasing them. Cindy had been shot and was in a lot of pain, but all she could focus on was to keep running. They had reached a steep embankment next to the freeway, and she was having difficulty climbing to the top. She yelled to Jeremiah, "Go! Go! Don't let them hurt you. Go!" Cindy was crawling up the steep hillside as her feet kept slipping on the dirt. Jeremiah wanted to climb back down to help her, but she told him no. She could feel the presence of their pursuers gaining on them, and she was terrified for their lives. She never found safety before waking up; her sleep was in a suspended state of fear.

Another time, Cindy woke up to find herself floating on a boat that was drifting. There wasn't a motor, so she was stranded on the boat, feeling alone and scared. She believed nobody knew where she was and that nobody could find her. She drifted into the dark abyss alone, with only her fear for company.

Cindy was then floating on a tube in water, going round and round like a Disneyland ride, lost in a mindless loop that she couldn't disembark from.

Cindy called out, "I am so tired. Can you get me out of here? I'm so tired. Mom? Where are you? Can you get me out of here? Mom, come find me! Come get me out of here, pleeeaase!"

"My mom has to find me," she whined. "If she doesn't find me, I don't know what I'm going to do!"

Later, when Cindy's mom came in for her regular visit, she took a seat in the room chair and waited for Cindy to wake up.

When Cindy opened her eyes, she murmured, "Mom. Mom, you found me. I knew you'd find me!"

Reota looked at Cindy and then shifted her eyes to the nurse in the room as if for an explanation. "Yes, honey, I have found you. I'm here. I've been here all afternoon."

"No. No, you just found me. I've been floating."

"Okay, honey," she said, nodding her head sympathetically. "I'm glad I found you. I'm here."

As Cindy's mind tried to make sense of the nightmare her body was in, as she drifted in and out of consciousness, as morphine dripped through her system to help her cope with the pain, she experienced dreamlike fantasies as well as nightmares. While each episode was based on a nugget of truth, the fear and pain in her mind transformed them into life-threatening experiences—experiences where she struggled alone in terror. Her hallucinogenic nightmares were something she would never forget.

CHAPTER 13:
RAPUNZEL

When a patient is in the burn ICU, the staff likes to ask a family member to bring in a picture of the patient to keep by the bedside. The photo helps to humanize the patient to the medical staff, even if the patient is not conscious or recognizable. As such, Cindy's mother brought a picture from the house and placed it by Cindy's bedside.

In Cindy's picture, she was wearing her scrubs with her long strawberry blonde hair in one thick braid pulled to the front. She had been growing out her long hair for much of her adult life, and it reached down her back. Naturally wavy, it was often kept in a long braid.

When Cindy straightened her hair, it reached down to her waist. When she went swimming in the lake, it dried into curly ringlets. She enjoyed playing with it in new styles. Along with her blue eyes, she felt it was her best feature, and it was a source of pride for her.

What Cindy did not realize was that as the fire rushed past her backside toward the window during the flameover, it immediately melted all her beautiful hair, which had been in a bun, into a molten mess at the back of her head. One afternoon, she saw the nurses talking to her mom in the corridor. Cindy was often in and out of consciousness, but since she was alert, the staff recognized a good time to have a lucid conversation with Reota and Cindy about a concern.

Reota came into the room and spoke to Cindy gently and with compassion. "Cindy, there is something the nurses would like to do. We know how much you love your hair, but honey, it is singed into a ball at the back of your head, and there is no saving it. I know you've been asking them to comb your hair, but they can't. With your permission, the nurses would like to cut off your damaged hair."

Cindy felt dismayed. "Can't Gail or somebody take their time to comb it?"

"No, honey, they can't. It has melted together into a ball, and it's harboring germs that can cause an infection. We need to get it off before your scalp gets infected."

Cindy sighed. What was her hair to her now? Beauty was a thing of the past. In her dismay, she nodded her head. "Do what you have to do."

Later that day, her favorite nurse, Elaine, came into the room, touting her pregnant belly and sharing stories of the baby's latest kick. Elaine was tall and blonde, with a sweet disposition, and Cindy had connected with her right away.

Elaine took a pair of scissors and patiently cut away at the melted mass on Cindy's head. She tried not to grimace as the occasional whiff of acrid, burned hair caught her nose.

Cindy lay there calmly as Elaine slowly clipped off her hair, one careful snip at a time. She felt like Rapunzel having her long, beautiful hair cut away.

When she finished, Elaine held a mirror out for Cindy to see, but Cindy did not want to look at herself and averted her eyes. She wanted to remember the person she saw on the morning of May 10. She knew her hair was short, and her face was oozing in some places and scabby in others. Her eyes felt puffy and swollen. She could not bear to face that reality. She just wanted to go back to sleep. *Will I ever look like myself again?* she wondered. It would be weeks before she could look at herself in the mirror.

Cindy's face was part second-degree and part third-degree burns, but the doctors didn't want to put grafts on her face if they didn't have to. Grafts would have a thicker texture, and the seams would be obvious, creating scars. Scars on her hands, arms, back, and legs were inevitable, but the plastic surgeon did his best to preserve her face.

The nurses came in and put a special salve cream on her face on a daily basis, which helped to stimulate skin growth and nerve recovery. Cindy loved the way the cool cream felt on her face and looked forward to the treatments. Elaine was often the one who applied the cream, massaging it into her skin and making Cindy feel like she was getting a facial. In all the countless procedures she had done to her, this was the only one she enjoyed.

She closed her eyes, and her mind drifted to a peaceful afternoon at Donner Lake, relaxing with her boys. In her mind's eye, she could see the mountains looming on the other side of the dark blue lake, the twin peaks covered with pine trees, and the train tracks midway up the mountain running parallel with the waterline. For a moment, she could almost hear the squeal of the train tracks.

CHAPTER 14:
NANCY

Nancy and Cindy had been friends since they were babies, having been next-door neighbors in West Covina their entire childhood, and they had always shared a special connection. Their dads worked together, and their families spent a lot of time together, so they were destined to be best friends from the start.

In elementary school, they played together almost every day, running around the neighborhood like tomboys, climbing the large oak tree in Nancy's yard, higher and higher each year as their bravery grew. In the summer, they picked the plums off the trees and ate them until their bellies swelled. In the fall, their job was to pick up the rotten plums on the ground, the overripe scent filling the air. Every year, their families spent the Fourth of July together with the rest of the neighborhood, the girls dancing with sparklers in the streets.

In middle school, they were pranksters together, playing various jokes on their dads—who, for unknown reasons, playfully called each other "Hogan"—and playing doorbell ditch with the neighbors. Once, they fed a neighborhood girl cat food, mixing it with garlic and spices and then having her take a bite to guess what it was.

Occasionally, they covered rocks and trash with a blanket in the middle of the road and watched as drivers stopped to inspect what it was. On other days, they rode their bikes to the mall and walked around JCPenney. They especially liked to look at the cute baby-boy clothes and say how much they wanted to have baby boys when they got older, which they both eventually did. They were young, wild, and free, as only young friends without a care in the world can be.

While they both attended Covina High as teenagers, Nancy was a year older than Cindy, so they didn't have many classes together. Also, they had separate friends in their own grade levels—Cindy hung out with her hippy friends and Nancy with the drill team. However, they still walked to school together every day along with their friend Cheryl, who was the third Musketeer, and they always spent time together after school.

When Nancy was a senior, she was given her grandfather's '56 Pontiac, and she began driving them to school. On the weekends, they headed to the beach or the movies, or they shopped at their favorite local store, Zodys.

Every summer, they spent at least one day a week at the beach, usually taking Beach Boulevard to Huntington Beach or sometimes heading to Laguna or Del Mar, often with Cheryl and other friends. They always had a comfortable acceptance of each other and even an intimacy, applying suntan lotion on each other or peeling each other's backs. It was almost as if they were sisters. There was an unconditional love in their deep friendship.

When Nancy first heard about Cindy and the fire, she knew she had to travel to see her in the hospital as soon as possible. Nancy lived in the Bay Area with her family, so it took her over six hours to drive to West Covina. She visited Cindy in June after Cindy had made it through the first critical weeks and was allowed nonfamily visitors.

When Nancy got to the hospital, Cindy was in the basement of the hospital in the burn ICU. Nancy felt like she was traveling down into a dark dungeon, and she felt the darkness of the windowless floor sink into her spirit.

On her way down, Nancy prayed: *Dear God, please let me connect with Cindy. Let her feel my presence and know that I love her. Let her feel my love and not any of the fear I have about her burns and how she looks.*

Cindy had been in and out of consciousness, and the doctors warned Nancy that Cindy most likely would not be conscious. When Nancy entered the room, she paused to take a deep breath and to take it all in.

Nothing really surprised her. She felt like God had prepared her for this moment.

With a glance, Nancy could see at once that Cindy's long, beautiful hair was gone. Her swollen and puffy face was an angry red color. Her lips were bright purple from drinking grape juice. Cindy's body was bandaged and covered, concealing the necrosis of dead, burned tissue, but Nancy knew it was there.

Nancy took a step into the quiet room and walked over to Cindy's bed. Cindy had always had a beautiful face, and underneath the swelling, Nancy could still recognize her friend and see her beauty. Nancy was grateful that the burns had not damaged her face so much as to make her unrecognizable.

Nancy stood next to the bed and gently placed her hand on Cindy's arm, hoping Cindy could feel her presence. Uncontrollably, warm tears fell down her cheeks at the sense of helplessness she felt, unable to help her friend or alleviate her pain. She spoke aloud, in a soothing, soft voice, but loud enough for Cindy to hear: "Cindy, it's Nancy. You're going to get through this. It's going to be okay in the end; just keep fighting. I'm praying for you. I love you, and I'm here for you."

Nancy could not say that she knew how Cindy felt because she didn't, but she tried to encourage Cindy as best she could. She thought about little Jeremiah and how Cindy had saved his life by dropping him from the window, three stories from the ground. Jeremiah was the same age as her own daughter, Danielle, and she couldn't imagine being faced with such horrors. Tears continued to roll down her cheeks.

Nancy had such a love for Cindy that she had been praying about her friend's pain, praying for relief and healing. Nancy thought about the unconditional love of their friendship and how, as they had gotten older, she had come to realize that what was important in life wasn't things but relationships. It was all about encouraging each other and accepting one another unequivocally. She knew with a solid conviction that her relationship with Cindy was special and rare, and she could not imagine a day without her friend.

Despite the scorched hair, the bandages, and the unconsciousness, Nancy looked at Cindy and knew with conviction that she was going to live. Cindy had always been a fighter. She would get through this. Cindy always had an amazing sense of humor about life and was incredibly resilient, and Nancy knew that those traits would help her endure.

Still, it hurt to see Cindy in pain. It was hurtful to know that something so tragic had happened to her, to such a beautiful and giving person. Nancy also knew Cindy would not want to be seen as a victim and that she wouldn't be victimized by this tragedy.

Cindy lay in bed in a comatose state, but she knew her friend was there and could feel Nancy's love. She felt her friend praying for her and let the well wishes flow over her and through her. Weeks later, when Cindy was fully conscious and aware, she remembered with clarity that Nancy had been there. Knowing how much her friend loved her filled her with warmth and fueled her drive to recover.

For years afterward, whenever Nancy was depressed or upset about something in her life, she would think about all that Cindy had endured and ask herself, "You're going to complain about *this*?" Cindy became a pillar of strength for Nancy. If Cindy could survive the fire, Nancy could overcome anything God put in her path.

CHAPTER 15:
DON'T MESS WITH
MY HEART

The year before the fire, Cindy had been having pain in her lower right abdomen, so she sought medical care from Dr. Boone, a surgeon in Truckee. After several tests, she was diagnosed with reoccurring chronic appendicitis and also a cyst on her nerve, both of which were addressed during surgery. During the surgery, Dr. Boone noticed that Cindy was having irregular heartbeats. Later, Dr. Lombard diagnosed her with a heart condition called *bigeminy*, where every other beat is an irregular heartbeat.

In LA, as Cindy lay in bed in the burn ICU, she overheard doctors talking about her heart condition. Dr. Nakano, a cardiologist, had been called in to monitor her heart and bouts of *atrial fibrillation*, or fast heart rate, and her *ectopic beats*, or irregular rhythm. She could hear them talking about what procedures they should follow, and she started to panic that they did not know her history and that she was already being monitored for a heart condition.

Cindy tried to get their attention, whispering, "Don't mess … with my heart."

Engrossed in their conversation, neither heard her, so she whispered again, "No, no," shaking her head in her mind.

Finally, Dr. Goldberg, a tall blonde man with thick eyebrows and blue eyes, noticed her trying to get their attention. He walked over and gently put his hand on Cindy's arm as he spoke. "Do you want to say something, Cindy?"

Cindy nodded, whispering, "Don't ... don't mess with my heart ... Dr. Lombard."

"Oh, yes!" They both nodded. "Rest assured, we know you have a cardiologist, Dr. Lombard. It is in your chart. We'll be sure to talk to him," Dr. Goldberg reassured her.

Cindy felt relieved. She wanted them to talk to Dr. Lombard, who knew that the bigeminy was normal under regular conditions when she wasn't stressed. She didn't want them to do any procedures on her that they didn't need to do. She was under enough stress as it was.

CHAPTER 16:
SUSPECT

Ken frequently came down to see Cindy and to spend time with the boys, staying in the trailer on the side of her parents' house. Ken's friend, Jim, often came with him, offering moral support. Whether or not Ken was in town, Michael stayed in the house in his Auntie JoJo's room so she could get him up, feed him, and get him ready for the day.

Ken would visit Cindy in the hospital almost daily when he was visiting. His visits after the first few weeks, however, created angst for Cindy's family and were a stress for Cindy. He was a frequent visitor to her hospital room, and the family didn't know if it was out of love, out of obligation, as a cover-up, or out of a dire need to control Cindy and their relationship.

Ken often sought a private audience with Cindy in the early morning, asking Cindy to come back to him and their marriage or asking if he was wasting his time staying in LA and visiting her in the hospital. Ken pleaded with her, assuring her of his commitment. "No matter what you're like after this, I'll stay married to you anyway. I'll take care of you. I love you. Just come back to me."

Cindy sighed and shook her head. "Ken, I can't make any decisions right now. I need all my energy to get well. I'm just trying to get by day by day, hour by hour. I can't think about this right now."

She couldn't even breathe on her own half the time, but he wanted her to make major life decisions as she lay in a hospital bed. She just didn't have the emotional capacity to deal with him. She couldn't take the pressure. She knew in her heart that she did not love him like she should and that she couldn't go back to him, even if she could never walk or feed herself, but she was worried about telling him how she truly felt. Her greatest fear was that he'd take off with the boys and disappear while she was vulnerable in the hospital. *Oh God, please don't let him do that to me. I would die. I need my kids. I love them so much.*

Ken visited her each morning, only to have Cindy become upset and stressed. She would wake up groggy and disoriented, wake up feeling afraid, and wake up to find him sitting in her room. This distress caused her irregular heart rate to set off the heart monitor. The staff had noticed a correlation. Whenever Cindy opened her eyes and saw Ken in the room, her heart rate increased, and her abnormal heart rhythm caused the heart monitor to beep a warning that something was wrong. Immediately, the staff kicked any visitors out of the room in order to get her heart rate leveled.

The staff discussed this connection between Ken's visits and Cindy's irregular heartbeat with her parents. Reota and Larry knew this was an issue, and they knew there was more to this situation than the staff knew about.

The next day, Cindy's mom and sister Gail had a private meeting with Dr. Goldberg, the general doctor in charge of Cindy's overall care. Cindy had come to appreciate that he spoke to her like she was a nurse, not just a patient, giving her the detailed medical explanations she wanted.

Dr. Goldberg sat in his office with Reota and Gail, who felt that the hospital staff needed to know a few things about Cindy's husband.

Gail began, "First, we thought you should know that Cindy and Ken have been separated for some time now, and Cindy had asked him for a divorce before the fire."

Dr. Goldberg said, "I'm aware of that."

"He's been staying at my parents' house in the camper in the backyard, but our brother doesn't want him here. He is convinced Ken is the one who set the house on fire."

Dr. Goldberg's eyes widened. This, he had not known.

"Look, Cindy is afraid of Ken," Gail continued. "He threatened to take her life when they were together, and he'd say things like, 'If you leave me, I'll kill myself.' He's a mean drunk. She couldn't wait to get away from him. She's really afraid of him. This is why her heart monitor keeps going off when he visits."

Dr. Goldberg understood the immediacy of the situation and said, "As I can see, there are serious legal complications to the situation now."

Gail continued, "Ken has also talked about getting the house insurance money, which really upset my mom and dad. He should be focusing on his wife getting better, not on how much money he's gonna get. We haven't told Cindy because we don't want to upset her, and she needs to focus on her health. But our brother can't stand to be around him. He's convinced Ken was making good on his threats and set the house on fire to get back at her for leaving him. The sheriffs have him under suspicion too."

Dr. Goldberg nodded. "Clearly, we need to protect Cindy and do what's best for her well-being. Do you want to ask Ken to stop visiting, or would you like us to do it?"

Everyone agreed it would sound better if it came from the medical staff.

The next morning when Ken came for a visit, the nurse asked Ken to wait in the hallway. When Dr. Goldberg came over, he pulled Ken aside and spoke with him. "Hello, Mr. Ames. We have noticed that your visits seem to agitate Cindy. We'd like to ask you not to come back until Cindy is more stable. Right now, we need her to focus on her recovery."

When Gail and Reota told Cindy that Ken would not be coming by anymore, she felt a huge sense of relief, like a weight had been taken off her chest. She didn't know in what condition she was going to leave the hospital, but she knew she would be going home, one way or another, an emancipated woman.

CHAPTER 17:
STAGE TWO

There were three stages to Cindy's recovery. The first stage was in the burn ICU in a state of "conscious unconsciousness," where she slipped in and out of consciousness and was fighting for her life—essentially the first four weeks or so. The second stage was when she was fully conscious and in incredible pain, and every day, she fought for her will to live. The third stage was conscious healing, but this stage was still weeks away. The second stage was by far the worst, and today, Cindy was struggling.

Cindy lay in bed, chills running up and down her body, praying to God and offering up her deepest thoughts and fears: *Oh, God, when will this end? Will it ever be over? I'm so tired. I'm fighting to get better. Why? Why did this happen to me? Will I ever be myself again? What will I be like when this is over? Will I ever be able to hug my boys again? Will I ever be able to hold a man again? Will a man ever want to hold me? To make love to me? Am I going to be so scarred and ugly that people will stare or be offended to look at me? I can't even move my legs or arms by myself. How can I expect my life to be normal again? Why am I even living?*

Cindy took a deep breath as tears rolled down the sides of her face— tears she could not wipe away. *I will be normal. I have to, Lord. I have to think positively. I need to be a mother to my boys. I will be a whole woman again. I just have to. Give me strength, oh Lord. Please. I pray to you.*

Day after day, as Cindy lay in the hospital bed, she prayed and fought for her will to live. Each day was a battle, not only physically but emotionally and spiritually as well.

CHAPTER 18:
BETADINE BATHS

As Cindy's nerves healed themselves, she felt immense pain and anguish. As such, Betadine baths became the part of the day she hated the most. When it was time for her Betadine bath, the nurses turned her on her side, put her in a bath lift, rolled the lift to the tub room, and then lowered her into the Betadine bath. Cindy's body screamed in agony.

The baths were one of the worst parts of her day as the nurses painfully scrubbed off the dead layers of skin to reveal raw skin beneath. Debridement was horrifying. She dreaded bath time, but as a nurse, she understood she had no choice. And the staff had no choice.

She had very little control over life at all at this point. So she turned her life over to the staff and over to God. Each day, she prayed that God would help her get through it.

Today, it was nurses Robbie and Karen giving her the Betadine bath. Robbie was a burn technician with a dark complexion and dark hair, fitting the description of *tall, dark, and handsome*. He had a big stature, which made Cindy feel safe when he lifted and moved her. Karen, on the other hand, was a petite blonde who was particularly good with nursing skills. They made a good team. Cindy found out later that they were dating.

In preparation for the bath, they first stripped Cindy of all her bandages. Sometimes, the bandages stuck to her skin and couldn't be removed, so they had to soak them off in the tub. While in the tub, the nurses used soft scrub brushes to disinfect her wounds and remove all the blackened, decaying skin, including skin grafts that didn't take. The iodine burned, and it literally felt like they were scrubbing off her skin—which they were. The process was reminiscent of the Old West days when they used to tar someone as a form of torture and punishment. Removing the tar involved ripping it off along with several layers of burned skin.

"You're doing just fine," Robbie said soothingly. "We're gonna get you through this. We've got you."

The nurses had to give Cindy a bath twice a day in the Betadine solution, and each bath took almost three hours. Through all of this, Cindy did not have time to be modest or have a sense of humility. Her body was an open vessel from which the medical staff would work. Exposing her breasts, her pubic area, and her buttocks was a daily occurrence. And while Cindy understood the need for immodesty and humility, as she had seen her own share of private body parts exposed while working in the hospital, unconsciously, she still harbored a sense of humiliation and embarrassment.

The torturous baths put Cindy in excruciating agony. Afterward, her back throbbed the most, but her body ached all over. Either the skin was an exposed burned area needing grafts, the area was a new graft freshly stapled onto her, or it was a donor site where new skin had just been harvested.

Each time they took a graft and placed it on an area on her body, they stapled the edges of the entire patch of skin onto her during surgery when she was unconscious, but then about five days later, the titanium staples were removed while she was awake, which was painful. *Pinch, pull, pinch, pull*—each titanium staple was pulled from her skin with medical staple removers, one by one. Sometimes, staples traveled deep into the tissue and, in the end, were never removed. Sometimes it was the pain from the staples that put her over the edge; they felt like needles stabbing her over and over.

Cindy also had pain in her hips and back from her fractures, and she experienced pain in her regenerating nerves.

Even with weeks of ongoing grafts, there was not enough healthy skin to cover Cindy's burns. As the skin is the largest organ in the human body, healing was imperative. The doctors' primary concern was promoting healthy skin regeneration and covering her with healthy grafts.

The human body's ability to heal and regenerate its skin is miraculous. The average human has twenty-one square feet of skin, and since 70 percent of Cindy's body had third-degree burns, they needed to look at outside sources for additional skin tissue. The doctors used cadaver skin and pig skin as temporary coverings for wound surfaces, called *heterografts*, before using a permanent placement with her own skin, the *autograft*.

After surgery, the cadaver or pig skin was put over various clean wounds on her body and then covered with a dressing. The temporary covering was removed when her own skin had regenerated for permanent autografting. The cadaver skin and pig skin helped save her life.

All in all, there was almost no area of skin on her body that was unharmed by a burn or graft. The excruciating pain as they scrubbed her during the Betadine baths, twice a day, day after day, only increased with each session as her nerves began to heal. She moaned in pain and sometimes cried out, pleading for them to stop. The nurses would grit their teeth as they labored over what they knew needed to be done to save Cindy's life. For Cindy, however, each bath felt like she was being burned all over again.

CHAPTER 19:
THE PACT

While working in the Tahoe Forest Hospital ER, Cindy had two friends with whom she worked closely—Steve and Alice. Steve was the doctor she had been planning to travel to San Francisco with before the fire. Alice was a free-spirited nurse Cindy had instantly bonded with when they first met. They became so close that Alice asked Cindy to be godmother to her daughter Mia. The three of them always talked about the condition of patients who came in—including, on occasion, patients who were brain-dead and who were hooked up to machines without any quality of life.

The three of them had made a quality-of-life pact: If any of them was ever really bad, one of them would obtain a big dose of a certain medication and put it in their IV. They promised each other repeatedly that they would not let each other suffer, and they trusted each other enough to let the others make that determination.

After the fire, Alice flew down to LA to visit Cindy in the hospital. This was during Cindy's "purple stage." Her mouth was purple, her gums were purple, and even her tongue was purple.

Alice gasped when she entered the room. It was hard to see her friend in full-body bandages, hooked to monitors, missing her long hair, with blotching red skin and purple lips. Cindy had also just been medicated and wasn't fully present.

The nurse quickly explained that Cindy's mouth was stained from grape juice. Alice pivoted and went straight to the nurse's station, and although semi-conscious, Cindy could still hear her yelling, "Why are you letting her drink so much grape juice? She's purple! That can't be good for her body!"

The head nurse replied, "It's what she wants. It's the only thing we can get her to drink."

"Well, you need to figure out *why* she wants it. What is it her body needs that's making her crave it? This is unacceptable!"

The staff assured her, saying, "Okay, we'll try to limit her grape juice to one or two glasses a day to prevent her from turning purple." Alice returned to the room with tears on her face.

Cindy knew her friend was upset at seeing her in this condition and quietly wondered if she had come down to make good on their pact. Cindy continued to suffer chronic pain and anguish. At that moment, she was willing to accept whatever verdict Alice came to. She trusted Alice to determine if she was going to make it or not, and Cindy put her life in Alice's hands. Not only was she too ill to stop her friend, she knew that Alice knew her deep down and would honor her wishes.

Cindy wasn't sure if Alice had come here with the medicinal dosage, and a part of her was afraid that Alice was going to use it, but another part of her trusted her friend to make the right decision. If she was that bad and she wasn't going to live, and if the doctors knew it but weren't telling her, she didn't want to suffer anymore.

Cindy faded to sleep while Alice was there. When she woke, Alice was gone. The fact that Cindy did wake up told her all she needed to know.

CHAPTER 20:
THE ANESTHESIOLOGIST

The regular anesthesiologist who worked with Cindy was named Dr. Porter, although everyone called him JP. He looked like a hippie with long hair and wore puka shell necklaces around his neck. Sometimes he'd come in dressed for the beach with his sandals on, and other times, he'd be dressed for surgery in his scrubs. Cindy had been reassured by the nurses that he was the best.

One day, Cindy confided to Nurse Elaine, "I think JP is trying to kill me."

Elaine was surprised to hear an accusation about someone as friendly as JP. "Why, Cindy?"

"After the surgery, he told the nurses to hold me down and put drugs in my IV. I don't want him to do my surgeries anymore. He keeps giving me these drugs, and I think he is trying to kill me!"

"Cindy, he's not trying to hurt you. He's trying to help you ..."

"No, no, I don't want him to do my surgeries anymore. He scares me."

When JP heard about Cindy's fears, he relented. "I don't want to do her surgeries if she's scared of me. You should find another anesthesiologist for her."

Cindy's parents were apologetic and knew Cindy's fears were unwarranted. "You're the best. The nurses have told us how lucky we are to have you. She doesn't know what she's saying."

Cindy's parents tried to convince Cindy that she was safe. And for a while, she let down her guard and agreed. But then she would see him again, and the fears and the certainty that he was trying to drug her would return.

Dr. Gray was an energetic young intern doing his residency at the burn unit, and he agreed to step in for JP. Dr. Gray worked with Cindy on her next two procedures before his absence made it necessary for JP to return.

JP made several visits to Cindy's room and sat and talked with her. Cindy liked his brown beard and mustache with flecks of gray, and she would watch the various silver rings on his hands dance as he talked. Cindy became comfortable with his easygoing style and clear explanations, and eventually, they became friends.

Cindy's parents said, "See? We told you he was the best!"

By then, Cindy had decided JP wasn't so bad after all, and she continued to let him work with her for the rest of her stay at Brotman.

CHAPTER 21:
I SMELL DEAD PEOPLE

In her recovery, Cindy's pain management included regular doses of morphine, which caused her to fade in and out of consciousness. One afternoon, as she drifted to consciousness lying on her back, she smelled an awful stench of decay and death. She was unable to move out of bed, but she knew that the pungent odor was coming from underneath her. Her stomach churned as she fought back the urge to vomit.

When Cindy's mom, Reota, entered the room, Cindy implored her mother while in her morphine haze: "Mom, I think they have me lying on a dead body. They put me on top of this dead person, and I can't stand the smell! Would you please get that dead body out from underneath me?"

Cindy continued to plead with her mom, believing that the staff was too busy to move the cadaver to the morgue.

Reota understood and agreed to help her, pretending to tug and pull at the sheets until the "body" came out.

"Thank you, Mom. Thank you so much," Cindy mumbled as she drifted back to sleep.

Reota stood against the wall as tears rolled down her cheeks, realizing that Cindy was smelling the rotting flesh from her own back, which continued to reject skin grafts. Her back was an open wound and had become infected, oozing creamy yellow and green pus.

Later in the early evening, Cindy woke again. "Mom, I can still smell the dead body, and it's disgusting. Can you see if they can move me to a new room?"

Reota explained the situation to the nurse supervisor, Cathy, a sturdy woman with chestnut brown hair, who, after consulting with others, agreed to move Cindy to a new room, knowing that psychological well-being and the will to live were essential factors in Cindy's recovery.

After the commotion of moving Cindy's bed, IV, and other medical equipment into the new room, Cindy felt better—until the next morning.

"Can you please have housekeeping clean under my bed? I can smell the dead person again," Cindy said.

"Of course, Cindy," Nurse Janet agreed. The young brunette bent under the bed and pretended to wipe around from the top to the bottom of the bed and then onto the other side. "I've got everything. That should be good."

Cindy nodded.

About two hours later, Cindy woke up again. "It still stinks. I can smell the dead body. It still stinks …"

Once again, the nurses pretended to clean out from under her.

Reota returned to the hospital the next morning, as she did every day, coming in around eleven o'clock and staying the afternoon alone with Cindy. Then, when her husband, Larry, got off work, he joined her, and they stayed together until eight o'clock. This went on for weeks. Cindy always felt relieved waking up to her mother's face.

"Mom, they keep putting dead bodies under me. I can't breathe," Cindy confided to her mom, reaching her hand out to her mom for help as strips of bandages hung off the back of her arm. She felt like a mummy wrapped in bandages.

Once again, Reota discussed the issue of the dead bodies with the staff, who graciously determined a plan of action to ease Cindy's concerns.

Nurse Robbie entered the room. "Cindy, we're going to give you a bath while Nurse Janet cleans out from under your bed." Cindy nodded her head in agreement. Anything to get rid of that putrid smell.

CHAPTER 22:
TV SPECIAL

Around mid-June, a TV crew came to the hospital to film a special clip about the dangers of fireworks and explosives that would air before the Fourth of July. When Reota came by the hospital for her usual visit and entered Cindy's room, Cindy asked her what all the lights and commotion were for in the hallway.

"A TV crew is here," Reota explained. "They're filming a special because they want to warn people to be careful with fireworks and avoid getting burned. Honey, would you mind if they came in here and filmed?"

"No. I don't want them here," replied Cindy firmly, shaking her head.

"Nobody would know who you are even. They would just show you as a burn patient and say, 'Look, this is what happens if you get burned.'"

Cindy replied adamantly, "No."

"Really? You're usually so willing to help people and teach people."

"No, I don't want anyone coming in here and seeing me like this."

Cindy was usually very willing to be helpful, but today was not a good day. Today, she felt miserable. The bright lights hurt her eyes, her head throbbed, and the noise bothered her. The stimulation was all too much. She didn't want anyone near her.

She asked her mom to shut the door and pull the curtain around her. She was in pain, and she didn't want anyone to see her like that—*especially* on the news. Doing PR was the last thing she wanted today. The pain was draining her willpower, and she was emotionally hanging by a thread. She felt thoroughly depleted.

Cindy asked to see Gary, an appointed social worker who worked as Cindy's advocate, helping to coordinate family visits, Jeremiah's and Cindy's care, and the kids' planned visits. Gary had initially befriended Ken and communicated any plans with him, but after he learned that Ken and Cindy were estranged, he backed off and started working with Reota until Cindy was better.

"Gary, I don't want to see the news crew. I don't want to be on TV. Make them go away," Cindy whined, exhaustion in her voice. "I can't do people today."

"No problem, Cindy," Gary reassured her. "I'll shut your door and let them know."

After he left the room, Reota sat in the chair in the dim room and watched her daughter sleep, a look of worry on her face.

CHAPTER 23:
CRASHING

After six weeks in the burn unit, Cindy continued to be in crisis. Her fever was 102°, and her blood pressure was low, 76/40. The EKG depicted *sinus tachycardia*, which meant her heart was beating fast and irregularly. Her pupils were unequal in size, indicating that she had developed *papilledema*, a condition in which increased pressure around the brain causes the optic nerve to swell. The increased brain pressure gave her blurry vision, a chronic headache, and a high fever.

The doctors ordered a cooling blanket to bring her temperature down. Ice packs were placed under her arms, along her thighs, and around her head. Flushed with fever and with cold packs surrounding her body, Cindy was miserable.

"I'm cold. I'm so cold," Cindy whispered. Between the pressure in her brain and the freezing bed, she felt like she was going to die.

"Cindy, your fever is running dangerously high. We have to get your body temperature down," said Dr. Goldberg, who had entered the room to discuss Cindy's recent condition with her parents. The doctors knew that if they didn't get the brain swelling down, Cindy would lose her vision. In a lucid moment, Cindy listened as Dr. Goldberg and Dr. Rush, the neurologist, reviewed her options.

"We can put a shunt in to drain the fluid and relieve the pressure. But if we put in a shunt and she gets an infection in her brain, then we will probably lose her." Dr. Rush paused. "Or we can let it resolve on its own and hope for the best. Regardless, with papilledema, she is probably going to lose her vision."

Tears rolled down Reota's cheeks as she listened. None of the options was optimistic. The doctors left the room so that they could discuss it in private.

"Should we have them put the shunt in?" Reota asked, looking at Cindy.

Cindy weakly shook her head no. She had been through enough.

"I don't want to risk her getting another infection," her dad said, supporting Cindy. He let out a big sigh. This was just one in a series of countless life-or-death decisions they had already made for her.

Larry summoned the doctors back into the room. "We've decided not to do the shunt."

"Okay," Dr. Goldberg said, looking at Cindy, "but you know that you could die from this."

Cindy nodded her head. She understood the consequences, but she was getting tired of hearing that phrase. Between the surgeries, the baths, her back infection, and her severe pain, she was losing the urge to fight. Her hip hurt, her leg hurt, her head hurt, her back hurt—hell, what didn't hurt? No matter what they gave her, it didn't control the pain; it only knocked her out for a while.

Only the day before, she had pleaded with the nurse to overdose her morphine, to give her extra pain meds so she could slip into a deep sleep from which she would not wake, slip away from the pain forever. Obviously, the nurse had not obliged.

"Please, please, just up my morphine dosage. I'm in so much pain," Cindy begged. Pride was not a factor. Her body was writhing in agony, the type of pain where she could not think of anything else.

"We can't, Cindy. Your respirations are low."

"I don't care. I don't care if my respiration stops. Just give it to me," Cindy demanded. "I can't stand it anymore!"

"Dr. Hoefflin said we can't increase the dosage," Nurse Cathy replied patiently.

"I don't care. He's fired. I want a different doctor. What's that other burn doctor's name? Dr. Hoefflin is fired!"

Early the next morning, Dr. Hoefflin entered Cindy's room with a smile on his face. "Good morning, Cindy. The nurses called me, and I understand you fired me last night?"

Cindy lightly nodded her head but said nothing. There was an intense throbbing in her head, and she could feel her pulse in her right eye.

"Well, I'm not going anywhere, Cindy, but we will continue to manage your pain the best we can," he said in a soft voice as he held her hand.

Cindy nodded.

"The nurses tell me your fever has spiked, so let's do some tests and see what's going on."

After further probing, poking, and tests, and putting Cindy on the ice blanket that afternoon, Dr. Hoefflin consulted her parents again about the decision not to put in the shunt. *Enough,* Cindy thought. *I can't take another surgery.*

After another thorough discussion, Cindy and her parents still declined the surgery, and Dr. Hoefflin respected their decision.

Cindy lay in bed and started praying: *Lord, I can't believe this. There is no way in hell You went through this much pain on the cross. There is no way You could have survived this. You ask too much of me. I know You carried the pain of the world, but that's just a metaphor. This pain is real. And You only had to go through this for three days; I've had to endure it for almost two months ...*

But Cindy knew in her heart that if Jesus could get through the pain, she could get through it too. She could survive this. *I can get through this ...* she thought. *Jesus, with your help, I can get through this.* And this became her mantra every time the Devil was tormenting her in agony.

CHAPTER 24:

ISOLATION

Cindy's papilledema had become a serious threat. Since she had refused to have the recommended surgery, the doctors felt her chances of blindness or even death from the infection were great.

While the papilledema didn't cause additional pain, the infection did affect her vision, causing fleeting blurred vision, double vision, and flickering. Also, due to the elevated pressure in her brain, Cindy suffered headaches, nausea, and occasionally vomiting. With all the other ailments Cindy was suffering, these symptoms did not necessarily stand out.

However, because of her infection, Cindy developed *sepsis*, a serious condition resulting from the presence of harmful microorganisms in the blood or other tissues, potentially leading to the malfunctioning of various organs, shock, and death. Cindy's life was in jeopardy. And to top it off, she was highly contagious.

Due to this, the staff moved her down the hall into the isolation ward for *resistant pseudomonas*—a common cause of healthcare-associated infections, including pneumonia, bloodstream infections, and surgical site infections—to reduce the risk of other patients getting infected. The isolation room was daunting. The doors were sealed shut, and anyone entering had to wear a mask, gown, foot coverings, and gloves so that no contaminants were brought into the room. Cindy felt cut off from the rest of the hospital, and the isolation took its emotional toll.

While she faded in and out of consciousness, she recognized her mom standing next to her bed, holding her hand with gloved fingers. Only immediate family were allowed visits, and the visits were for five minutes only. At this point, Cindy was responding to her name only on occasion, and her speech was slurred. The nurses also noted that she was lethargic, and her breathing was shallow.

Dr. Korda, a tall slim woman with short brown hair, was called in from the infectious diseases department, and she scheduled a CAT scan and ordered more blood cultures to be drawn from Cindy's jugular site. At times, Cindy became uncooperative and slept fitfully. She had a severe fever and complained of pain.

Nurse Elaine talked to Cindy in a soothing voice, and Cindy relaxed as if Elaine had waved a magic wand over her. Cindy appreciated that Elaine always took time with Cindy, never in a hurry like other nurses. It was validating to have someone talk to her and listen to her needs, displaying empathy toward her as a person. It made her feel like a human being, not just a body in a bed.

Dr. Korda had a friend at an LA hospital who had a new antibiotic in trials, and she arranged to give Cindy the choice to use it, since she was allergic to penicillin. Cindy's parents agreed to the trial on her behalf.

The doctors and Cindy's family were all on edge, waiting to see if the swelling would go down. Even if it did, Dr. Waxburg thought it was likely Cindy would suffer complete or partial blindness in her peripheral vision as a result, something he shared with Reota and Larry as gently as possible.

In moments of consciousness, Cindy lay in bed and wondered why she was fighting to live. Why didn't she just give in? Fighting every day was mentally and spiritually exhausting. But then Cindy thought of her boys. They needed her, and she had to live for them. She trusted her parents to provide a stable home for the boys, and she knew they would be all right with her parents ... *No*, she thought. *My boys need me. I need to fight for them.* She didn't want them to grow up without their mother. Without *her*. God would help her get through this.

As Cindy fought physically, mentally, and spiritually to endure, the medical staff was attentive to her body, giving her the drugs and the treatment she needed. She had to battle for her will to live, a desire that wavered with each day, each surgery, each painful procedure.

One day, as the nurses were giving Cindy her bed bath, she whispered to Nurse Robbie, "Please, just tell me the truth. I'm going to die, aren't I? I know how bad I am."

Making eye contact with each other, the two nurses paused in heavy silence, and Cindy took that as their response.

"Okay," she said, nodding her head. "Okay, that tells me things really aren't good," she whispered. "If I'm going to die anyway, why am I going through all this?"

She waited, hoping they would give her justification to let go.

Nurse Robbie quickly responded, "You are strong, Cindy. You can fight this. You have your boys to live for."

Cindy nodded her head in silence, tears streaming down her face. He was right. While Robbie's size and strength had intimidated Cindy at first, he was kind and good to her. Every time Cindy had a bout of weakness, he patiently reassured her. Cindy appreciated the nurses not only for their medical expertise but for the kindness that they bestowed upon her every day.

Dr. Waxburg stopped by regularly and checked her eyes with an ophthalmoscope to see if the pressure on her optic nerve was increasing or decreasing. Cindy's vision was blurry, but she recognized him by his nice cologne, which she smelled every time he leaned in to talk to her. He often hemmed and hawed while looking into her eyes, and Cindy could never tell if it was good or bad. It was usually bad.

On the tenth day, Dr. Waxburg sat back dramatically after examining her eyes. Cindy's fever was gone, and she was lucid and conscious, looking him directly in the eye.

"I can't believe this … You can see me, can't you?!"

"Yes," said Cindy. "I can see you."

"You should be blind. You should be blind, Cindy! I can't believe this. When you refused to let us put the shunt in, I thought for sure you would go blind. This is incredible. The inflammation has decreased significantly, and the infection is nearly gone. It's slowly improving, but it's a miracle it's improved at all." Dr. Waxburg stared at Cindy incredulously.

Cindy had been praying in her lucid moments, praying to keep her life and her sight. She'd asked God if she could live long enough to see her boys graduate from high school, to see them become young adults. Her will to live was driven to see that moment, and it gave her a fighting spirit. It was her marker in life to see them graduate. If she could just make it through this and live long enough for their graduation ceremonies, her life's purpose would be complete.

CHAPTER 25:
WHITE AS A GHOST

Even though Cindy's papilledema had improved, Dr. Waxburg ordered an MRI to check on the optic-nerve swelling along with the intercranial pressure in Cindy's head and the degree of her infection. She was still suffering from severe headaches. Because Cindy was still in isolation, the nurses needed to protect her from contamination and infection during transport and testing.

One of the nurses gently explained, "Cindy, we are going to transport you to a separate wing for an MRI so we can see the condition of the swelling. We need to protect your body from contamination to prevent infections on your skin, so we're going to place this sheet gently over your body and face while we transport you. You'll have plenty of room to breathe, and we'll be with you the entire time. Please nod if you understand."

Cindy nodded her head and looked at her mom. Reota nodded her head too.

The staff gently placed the sheet over Cindy and the gurney and began transporting her down the corridor, up the elevator, through the lobby, and into the next wing. Cindy felt her mom's gentle hand on her arm the entire time, and it helped relieve her anxiety.

Jim and Zena, local neighbors, had just arrived at the hospital to visit Cindy, who had always been like a daughter to them. They were rushing in to see Cindy because Reota had just told them that morning that Cindy had an infection in her brain, and they didn't know if she was going to make it. They knew they couldn't visit Cindy in isolation, but they wanted to be present for the family.

Jim and Zena walked through the hospital doors just as Cindy was wheeled by, covered in a white sheet. They saw Reota walking with the covered gurney, her hand touching the body in the white sheet, and Zena let out a cry of anguish as the gurney passed by.

"Oh my God, Reota!" Zena cried out. Her hand flew up to cover her mouth, and she held her breath as tears swelled in her eyes. Zena swayed like she was going to pass out. The anguish of Cindy's death was too much for her to bear.

Reota heard the cry and quickly looked over at Zena, and, upon seeing her face white as a ghost, knew at once what she had assumed.

"No, Zena! It's okay. They put the sheet over her to protect her from infection. We're heading over for a scan right now."

Reota didn't stop but kept walking with Cindy, as she didn't want to break contact with her daughter's arm.

Zena placed her hand on her husband's arm to steady herself and took a big sigh of relief. She met her husband's gaze with fear in her eyes. For a moment, they had lost their Cindy. Yet it struck her deep with the morbid reality that just because Cindy was alive didn't mean she was in the clear. There was a chance that Cindy might not actually make it through this.

CHAPTER 26:
THE STAIRCASE

Even after the staff moved her out of isolation, Cindy's health remained at risk, and she was in critical condition. She was still confused and disoriented but reacted to her name by opening her eyes. The nurses noted that she could not recall her husband's name or her children's names.

Cindy lay in bed, staring at the ceiling. When the nurse asked what she was looking at, Cindy replied blankly, "Nothing." She seemed to be awake but was not necessarily conscious.

Waking from a slumber, still feeling tired and in pain, Cindy weakly opened her eyes to see a group of friends in her room. There was also a circular staircase before her. Lining the staircase were people she knew, people from her past. As Cindy slowly rose from the bed and took the steps one at a time to make the ascent, her friends greeted her. Cindy confessed to them wearily, "I'm sick. I'm so sick. I just can't do this anymore."

And they replied, "We know, Cindy. We know."

Using all her energy to take each step, Cindy slowly climbed and pulled herself up the staircase, which curled around and around in a never-ending upward journey. Cindy saw the friendly faces of people she knew as she ascended and felt reassured that they were there.

She saw her friend John, who had drowned at Lake Gregory when they were in high school. John had dived into the cold lake and never resurfaced. Later, when they found his body, they said he'd had a heart attack—at age seventeen. Cindy was supposed to go with him and their church club that day, but she had canceled at the last minute. She had always liked him, and they'd had a date to go out the following week. It was good seeing him now.

More people Cindy knew and recognized surrounded the staircase, but she didn't focus on them. She felt herself being pulled up the circular staircase. She felt mesmerized by the warmth and love she felt emanating around her.

As Cindy rounded the bend, she saw her uncle Norman, whom she loved dearly. He was always one of Cindy's favorite family members, with his bright red hair and laughter that filled the room. Norman had been a police officer and died many years ago, but that did not stop him from wearing his uniform as he greeted Cindy on the stairwell.

"Uncle Norman! Oh my God, it's so good to see you!"

Cindy knew that he was no longer with the living, but he looked alive as he stood in front of her with his big smile. She sensed he really wanted to hug her, but something was holding him back. While Cindy couldn't touch any of the people who were welcoming her, she could talk to them.

"Your grandmama is right around the corner," he told her, smiling.

Hearing this, Cindy was overwhelmed with happiness, as she had always been very close with her grandmother. They were kindred spirits.

"Oh, I want Grandmama so bad. I need to see her!"

"Okay, come on up!"

Cindy took a couple of steps, and then her uncle turned.

"But you need to know, if you go see Grandmama, you can't go back down the stairs."

Wait, what? Cindy felt dismayed.

"But I want to see Grandmama! I need her!"

"You *can* see her. You just need to know that if you do, you can't go back."

Cindy stood on the stairs and started crying. She was in such physical and spiritual pain, and she wanted to be in the comfort of her grandmother's arms so badly.

Growing up, Cindy had always felt connected to her grandmother. Her grandmother had been gifted with a sort of ESP when things were going to happen. When Cindy was young, her grandmother looked her in the eye and said, "I know that you have the gift. This means, too, that I'm going to be able to talk to you when I'm gone." And she had. She had given Cindy clear signs throughout her life.

As Cindy stood there on the stairwell, she felt that spiritual connection to her grandmother and was drawn to her. She took a couple more steps. She could feel her grandmother's presence getting stronger, and she longed to be with her. She could feel Grandmama's spirit right there with her.

"Grandmama! You're right there! I know you're there!"

Cindy's grandmother spoke clearly: "I'm here. I'm here, Cindy. I'm right here!"

Cindy sucked in her breath, longing to take the next step up the spiral. Suddenly, she sighed. She had to make a choice. She knew if she went with her grandmother, she couldn't return. She then thought about Michael and Jeremiah and realized definitively that she couldn't go any further. "Grandmama, I can't. I love you so much, but I can't go with you."

"It's okay, Cindy," her grandmother replied understandingly. "I'll be here. I'll be here when you're ready."

Cindy turned and started her descent, tears running down her face. The girl in her longed for a hug from her grandmother more than anything. Well, almost anything. She wanted hugs from her boys even more. She chose to live.

CHAPTER 27:
NEXT-DOOR NEIGHBOR

In the next room over, there was a lot of commotion as a new patient was being brought in. It was just enough distraction to help Cindy break focus from her anguish and longing for her grandmother. She listened to the familiar hospital noises of the ICU.

"I have a new neighbor," Cindy whispered to the nurse. It took energy just to talk.

"Yes, you do. He's pretty bad."

Cindy knew not to ask more questions, as they would protect the patient's privacy and would not reveal his name or status. She was just thankful to have a distraction.

"Don't worry about him, Cindy. Let's focus on making you feel better and getting you your meds. You need some rest."

Cindy's body felt weak, and she slipped into the comfort of sleep. When she awoke again, she heard a commotion in the room next door. There was a rush of nurses and doctors, and she could hear the wheels of a crash cart, which held the emergency equipment and supplies for a patient who was in cardiac or respiratory arrest. Cindy lay in bed praying for him, visualizing what was going on in the next room.

The staff worked on the man for quite some time, and then it became quiet. It was a scene Cindy had been in too many times before, working late nights in the ER. Cindy knew with somber certainty that he had died.

When Nurse Cathy came in to help her get comfortable, Cindy asked, "The man next door died, didn't he?"

"I'm sorry, Cindy, I can't violate patient confidentiality." Cathy looked Cindy in the eye with sadness.

"It's okay. I'm a nurse. I can feel these things," Cindy said sympathetically. "I'm sorry he died."

Death was visiting the hospital, and a gloomy fog filled the corridors. Hospital staff held a common superstition that Death invaded on full moon nights and often in threes. The staff understood there would be more deaths that night.

CHAPTER 28:
NOT YET
June 29, 1982

In the middle of the night, Cindy woke with a startle. A man was standing over her bed, looking her in the eye. "Come with me," he motioned, extending his hand.

Just then, Cindy realized he was floating next to her bed, but she was not scared by this. She knew without words that this was the man from next door. "Come with me," he said.

"Why?" Cindy questioned.

"I don't feel pain anymore. Come with me. There's no pain. We can go together."

"I can't. What about my boys? I need to take care of my boys. They need me."

"They will be taken care of," he replied with certainty.

Cindy suddenly felt a pulling sensation from her abdomen and a distinct pop as she separated from her body. She was floating up alongside him now, and the absence of pain created an immediate sense of peace within her. Her pain had abruptly ended as she left it in the body below.

"Look down," he told her.

Glancing down, she could see the staff running around her body, and she could tell they were now working to keep her alive. She avoided looking at her own face. She did not want to look at herself.

With a sense of calm, Cindy and the man floated up into a dark space, like a tunnel, that kept rising. They could see each other but couldn't see anything else until a door opened, revealing a silhouette. As if through telepathy, Cindy heard a voice in her head.

"You weren't supposed to bring her," said the voice.

"She wanted to come. She was in so much pain," the man answered.

"No. It's not her time. She can't come yet."

Cindy nodded and internally understood. *I'm okay. Whatever you want me to do, I'll do it.*

The Lord looked toward Cindy. "You have to go back. You are not done."

Cindy immediately felt a sensation of falling, a whirling feeling in her stomach that felt like vertigo.

She opened her eyes and woke back up in her body, feeling flares of pain. The medical team surrounded her bed, and she was intubated. The beeping of the heart monitor filled the room.

"Her eyes are open!" the nurse called out. "Cindy, you went into respiratory arrest, but you're going to be okay," the nurse assured her.

The medical team breathed a sigh of relief, recognizing that she had returned to life.

Cindy never forgot this life-changing experience. The peace and wonderful feeling that Cindy had felt when she was out of her body and speaking with the Lord made it so that she would never again be afraid to die. She now knew without a doubt that there was someplace else to go and that it emitted the utmost sense of peace and warmth.

Heaven awaits.

CHAPTER 29:
JUST BREATHE

A couple of days later, Cindy woke up to find herself still on the ventilator, and she felt herself crushing the hard polymer blockers with her molars. The staff had put bite blockers in her mouth because she had been biting her ventilation tube. She lay in bed with her entire focus on biting each side in half. She wanted the staff's attention, and she wanted the blockers out of her mouth.

Nurse Cathy realized what she was doing and said, "That's why the machine keeps going off! How do you keep biting through those? You can't keep biting them!"

Unable to talk with the tube in her mouth, Cindy indicated with her hand that she wanted something to write with. Cathy brought her a pen and a pad of paper, and Cindy wrote, "I don't need it."

Cathy looked at her. "You don't need bite blockers?"

Cindy shook her head no and shook the note again.

"You don't need the machine?"

Cindy shook her head, indicating she did not need artificial respiration. She wanted them to take the tube out of her throat so she could breathe, talk, and drink. She felt so helpless and restless just lying there. Plus, she knew that she could breathe on her own. She thought to herself, *I'm awake! I'm alive! I feel fine. I'm fine!*

Cathy went out in the hall and consulted with Dr. Goldberg, and he agreed. They then consulted with Bob, the respiratory therapist who had been giving treatments to Cindy several times a day, and he also agreed. All three returned to her room. "Okay, Cindy," Dr. Goldberg said. "We're going to turn it off. And you breathe. Just breathe. Show us that you don't need it."

Cindy nodded that she understood.

Cathy flipped the switch off, and the machine became silent. Cindy lay in bed, enjoying the silence and then more silence. She waited for her chest to rise, to inhale the delicious air. Yet her chest stayed motionless. She looked over at Bob, a tall Columbian who always had a stethoscope around his neck, for his reaction. Cindy's body lay there and made no attempt to breathe on its own. Cindy felt confused and then panicked. Her eyes became wide with fear. No matter how hard she willed it, she did not have control of her own body.

The doctor nodded. The nurse switched the machine on again, and Cindy's lungs filled with oxygen. She looked at them with understanding and apology in her eyes.

Dr. Goldberg stepped forward and looked her in the eye. "Cindy, you still need it. Your brain is not telling your lungs to breathe yet. You've had a respiratory arrest and swelling in your brain. Try to be patient while your body heals."

That night, when Cindy was alone in her room, she wrestled with fear and thought about her encounter with the Lord. *I did die, but He sent me back. He said I had more to do. I'm going to be okay. I'm going to get better.*

Gail was going to church every day and praying for Cindy, saying a seven-day novena to the Blessed Virgin Mary that Cindy would get better and get off the ventilator.

On the seventh day, Gail's prayers were answered.

When Cindy's body began to breathe on its own, seven days after her respiratory arrest, the nurses took the ventilator tube out. Now she could finally talk, and she waited until she had the right moment and the right person to talk to. Her soul was burning to share what she had experienced.

Her brother, Larry, came to visit the next evening. She had always felt close to him.

"Larry, I need to tell you something," she whispered.

He looked attentive. This was the first time since the accident that Cindy had seemed capable of a sincere conversation.

"Larry, I ... I died. And I floated out of my body."

"Really?"

"Yes, and there was this man. He was Hispanic and really thin, and he had a little mustache. I don't know what his name is, but he woke me up, and he brought me with him."

Larry looked surprised. "Are you sure? He was Hispanic? That sounds just like the man in the picture that's out in the waiting room! I guess he had severe burns from some kind of explosion at work. What happened?"

Cindy replied, "I think it was the man who died in the room next to me. He tried to take me with him."

"His picture has been in the waiting room for the past few days, but there's no way *you* could have seen it." Larry threw his head back. "Whoa ... I just got chills. So what happened?"

Cindy then described the spiritual experience and what the Lord had said to her. That she had more to do. That He had sent her back. That she knew with every fiber in her being that it was real.

Larry sat in awe as he listened to Cindy's experience. And then he thanked God for not taking his sister.

Cindy never did learn the name of the patient who was in the room next to her, but she knew in her bones that it was him who had woken her up. She had been on the brink of death, but the Lord had sent her back. And while Cindy never did learn the man's name, she's always wanted to let his family know that he was at peace and that he had gone to Heaven.

CHAPTER 30:
A SPECIAL VISITOR

One night, Monsignor Lirette, a priest from their church and a good friend of the family, stopped by to see Cindy as he had done several times in the past many weeks.

He stood at her bedside, lightly picked up Cindy's hand, and placed it in his own, preparing to pray as he had always done.

Cindy's eyes fluttered open, and she immediately recognized Monsignor Lirette.

"Hi ..." she said in a slow whisper. Her eyelids felt heavy.

"Hi, Cindy," he said in a gentle voice, nodding affirmingly.

Cindy slowly shifted her gaze over to her mother, who stood against the wall. She realized with sudden certainty that they had called him in because she was dying.

"Mom, is he ... is he here to give me my last rites?" Cindy felt confused. God had sent her back, but Monsignor Lirette was here giving her last rites. *What happened?*

"No, honey," her mom said. "Monsignor Lirette just came to pray for you."

"Just tell me," Cindy whispered, looking from her mom to Monsignor. "If I'm going to die, just tell me the truth. Please."

She trusted Monsignor to be honest. She had known him since seventh grade, when he first came to Sacred Heart Church; he was called Father Lirette then, before he became a Monsignor. The day after she met him, he went to her parents' house and asked if Cindy could work for the church in the front office, as she had such a great personality. That was her first job, and Cindy always felt close to Monsignor for having faith in her and recognizing her potential.

Outside of church, he used to come over to her house in everyday clothes, drink a beer, and watch the game with her dad, who wasn't even Catholic and didn't go to church with the rest of the family. Cindy loved how down-to-earth he was.

As a young adult, she had confided in him that she didn't partake in confession. "I don't believe in confession. I think I can go to God directly. I don't think I need to go to you or another priest and tell them what I've done wrong so that God will listen. I think I can just … go to God."

"Well, then, just go to God," Monsignor replied. "You're fine! Honestly, some people have to be accountable and have to have that extra support. But if that's what you believe, Cindy, then just be true to yourself."

Cindy had always appreciated that he didn't lecture her about the importance of confession. Instead, she felt supported in her relationship with God and felt that Monsignor understood and accepted her.

Later, after he officiated her wedding in their church, she brought each of her baby boys down to LA from Truckee so that he could baptize them.

Once, she had asked him why he became a Catholic priest, and he'd joked with a twinkle in his eye, "Priesthood has the best benefits!"

Cindy loved that he was always down-to-earth and straightforward, and she turned to him now for honesty.

"Please, tell me if I'm dying …"

Monsignor looked her in the eye with compassion and assured her,

"Cindy, I'm just here to pray for you. I wanted to see you and do it in person. I've been here, praying for you, almost every day this past week."

Cindy looked at his hand and saw that he held rosary beads. With a deep exhale, she closed her eyes as she heard him say, "Our Father, who art in Heaven, hallowed by Thy name ..."

As she drifted back to sleep, the steady murmur of his voice soothed her like a peaceful lullaby, and for just a brief moment, she felt the light touch of his finger on her forehead.

CHAPTER 31:

AWAKE

July 10, 1982

Cindy woke up to the sound of Nurse Elaine opening the curtains and letting in the sunshine. She surveyed the room, wide-eyed and alert. Something felt different. Even though she hadn't yet had a morphine dosage, her pain was subdued, and her mind felt clear. Her head no longer ached. It was as if she had woken up to a different chapter in her life.

"Good morning, Cindy," Elaine said, asking routinely, "do you know where you are?"

"Yes," she replied assuredly. "I'm in the hospital. I'm in the ICU burn unit."

Nurse Elaine turned and looked at Cindy closely, cocking her head. "You're ... you're different today. I'm going to call your doctor ... It's like, you're *awake*."

"Yeah." Cindy nodded her head in agreement. "I feel different."

Elaine went out to the desk and excitedly told the other staff members that Cindy had "woken up." She paged Dr. Goldberg and Dr. Hoefflin. Some of the nurses came in to see for themselves.

When Nurse Cathy came in, she had a big smile on her face. She and Elaine had gone through every step with Cindy in the ICU, and even though staff members typically kept an emotional distance from patients, they felt a special kinship with Cindy.

Then, Dr. Goldberg popped into Cindy's room with a big smile on his face and took Cindy's hand in his own.

"Cindy," he said and then paused, looking into her eyes, nodding his head. "You're going to make it."

Cindy gave him a puzzled look, and he began to recount in detail what she had gone through in the last two months.

"Cindy, you've been through quite a battle. You've had well over a dozen surgeries. We've given you rounds and rounds of skin grafts. Most have taken, but some have not. You've had fluid on your brain and eye papilledema. Of course, there are cardio problems too, including the bigeminy, and then, most recently, you went into respiratory arrest. You've given us quite the scare on several occasions. It's been touch and go..."

Cindy listened attentively, letting the weight of it all sink in.

"However, I do believe," he added with an assuring smile, "that you're past the critical stage!"

Next, Dr. Hoefflin came to see Cindy as soon as he got out of surgery, and he was obviously pleased. He recounted all the surgeries she had been through during her road to healing.

He also told her that it was not over, that she still had the battle of recovery to fight. He explained that she still needed more surgeries to cover the burn areas and that they still had been unable to get the skin grafted onto her back.

Cindy could see clearly that she was in for a lot more trauma, and she understood that Dr. Hoefflin was trying to mentally prepare her for an ongoing battle. She had come out from the darkness, but it was not going to be sunshine and rainbows.

The staff also called her mom and dad, and they both came to see her. With tears in their eyes, they recognized how alert Cindy was. Her glassy eyes were gone, and she was looking them in the eye. They had their daughter back.

Now that Cindy cognitively understood how bad she was, she was afraid of something happening and having her health regress. Prior to this day, her will had been vacillating between wanting to die and wanting to live, but her boys were her beacon of light that had gotten her through. She knew she had been given a second chance at life, that this was the beginning of a new chapter, and she intended to use it wisely.

She understood now that she still had a lot to go through in order to get well again, and that meant going through a lot of physical pain. Even though she feared the pain, Cindy knew deep inside that she was going to get through it. After all, she was *awake*, and God had sent her back to live, and that meant there was no turning back.

CHAPTER 32:
BEAR HUGS

The next day, Michael and Jeremiah stopped by the hospital to visit Cindy, bringing her both a black-and-yellow snake firecracker—which, when lit, grew like a worm—and some sparklers, which they waved unlit in the air.

Cindy heard them coming down the hall and asked the nurse to help her sit up in bed so that she could see them better. She needed to hug her boys, a real hug—a bear hug. She had not hugged or kissed her boys in two months.

Michael and Jeremiah entered the room with Cindy's mom and sister right behind them.

The boys, seeing their mother sitting up, immediately ran over to her bed.

"Mommy, we saved these for you!" they both exclaimed.

Cindy wrapped her arms around them and hugged them tight. Warm tears of joy wet her cheeks as she held them. The room filled with emotion as Cindy's mom started crying too, and then Cindy's sister started to cry, followed by Cindy's physical therapist, Babe, who was helping to hold her up so she could hug her boys.

Cindy thought, *Oh God, it feels so good to feel their arms around my neck and to hug their little bodies. Thank you, Lord! What a glorious day to hold my children again!*

Cindy looked up and saw all the nurses from the nursing station clustered in the doorway with Kleenex in their hands. Even Dr. Reiss, Cindy's pulmonary doctor who stopped by regularly to monitor her lungs, seemed to have a lump in his throat. The boys clung to their mother, and not one person felt the need to be anywhere else.

CHAPTER 33:
THE PROMISE

Ken continued to come to town and stay with Cindy's parents so he could spend quality time with the boys. While some of Cindy's family thought Ken was innocent, others were certain he had started the fire. Still, everyone in Cindy's family agreed it was important to shield the boys from anything about the investigation and to remain cordial with Ken. If he had wanted, he had the power to file for custody of the boys, declaring Cindy incompetent since she was in the hospital and in recovery. That wasn't what Cindy wanted, and it wasn't what her parents wanted. They wanted to raise the boys until Cindy was able, so they made sure to keep the peace.

Ken often stayed with the boys at Cindy's parents', but sometimes he brought his friend Jim with him, and they stayed at a nearby hotel. Jim was unmarried and was always open to a road trip, and he had always been a good friend to Ken, offering moral support.

Ken didn't come down often, but when he did, he focused on the boys. In midsummer, he said he wanted to take the boys to Coleville to visit his parents for a couple of weeks.

Cindy's family was concerned about Ken taking the boys away, and Reota privately asked Cindy what she thought during her daily visit, but Cindy felt confident the boys would be taken care of at his parents' house. Still, she asked for Ken to come see her in the hospital.

"So, my mom tells me you want to take the boys for a couple of weeks?" she asked.

"Yeah. I thought I would take them up to see my folks and do a little fishing, try to enjoy some of their summer break with them," Ken replied.

Cindy nodded her head. "I know you want to take them, and you can, but you *have* to bring them back in two weeks." Cindy tried not to let the fear whisper through her voice. "I need you to promise me you will bring them back."

"I will," Ken nodded. "I promise."

In the end, Ken brought the boys back early because Jeremiah was having issues with his arm cast, and they needed the doctor to take a look at it.

Cindy felt the fear ease up in her chest when she heard they were back. She hated feeling so helpless and vulnerable, stuck there in the hospital room. She trusted Ken, but her greatest fear in life was losing her boys, and this fear sometimes overcame her logic. Ken had kept his promise, though, and it was one less thing for Cindy to spend energy worrying about.

CHAPTER 34:
MORE MORPHINE

Every nerve in Cindy's body was yelling at her. She had sharp nerve pain that was constant and sometimes debilitating. The more time passed from the date of the fire, the more pain Cindy endured as her nerve endings recovered.

In her daily therapies, with the pain of stretching her ligaments and stretching her fingers, it felt like the therapists were breaking her bones. She could feel every little snap. And the pain didn't let up. It never let up. It was relentless. It felt like she was still standing on the third floor, caught in perpetual flames. She was caught in an eternal hell.

Cindy had a burning sensation all the time. As her nerves started to recover, and she was more lucid, the pain was even worse. It was sometimes unbearable. Cindy would clench her teeth. She would often cry out when the pain was bad, and the nurses would give her *morphine*, a pain reliever derived from opium.

Cindy was grateful for morphine. While it didn't really take away the pain, it helped her have an I-don't-give-a-shit attitude. She could still feel the pain, but her brain didn't care. There was nothing she could do but ask for more morphine to help her mind float away out of the room and into another space, her mind drifting through rivers of dreams and memories.

When the morphine kicked in, Cindy often found herself snuggling on the couch with her boys in their house in Truckee. They would be reading *Sam I Am* and *Green Eggs and Ham*, or sometimes Bible stories. The sun was warm outside, and the snow glistened in the light. She could look out the window and see the beautiful view of Donner Lake below the mountains.

Or she'd be hiking and climbing rocks on the way to her favorite little lake. She imagined herself swimming in the cool water. She could feel the wind gently blowing across her face. It was relaxing and peaceful. This was her little piece of paradise. This is where she wanted to be.

The morphine gave her relief for maybe an hour, and if she was lucky, she fell asleep. But then the pain would start creeping back. It was just a dull throb at first, but it would build and build until it was excruciating again. Yet it wasn't time for more medicine. If they gave her too much morphine, it could stop her breathing.

She had to endure first the prickly pain as it escalated to an obliterating pain that left her writhing for at least an hour—or what seemed like two—until they gave her more pain meds, and the cycle, which ebbed and flowed steadily like the tides, started all over again. The never-ending cycle of pain made her want to crawl out of her skin.

Even though Cindy was in a perpetual cycle of pain and purgatory—her definition of hell—she never felt like the pain was something God was inflicting on her. She never asked God why he was doing this to her. Instead, she felt like bad fortune had happened to her, and it was God who was helping her through it. God was her salvation.

I can get through this. I can get through this.

Several nurses took turns administering her morphine depending on the shift, and Cindy was acutely aware when they came in to offer her relief. There was one particular nurse, a new one named Sherry, who gave Cindy her pain meds on a regular basis, but each time, Cindy felt like this nurse didn't give it to her right. Her pain was noticeably higher whenever Sherry gave her meds compared to the other nurses. By the end of the cycle, Cindy was begging for more pain relief.

"Please give me more, please give me more, it hurts. I hurt all over ..."

The next time Sherry went to give Cindy her meds, Cindy said, "You're giving it to me different from the others or something. Go check my orders to make sure you're giving me the right amount."

As a nurse herself, Cindy felt confident ordering the nurses around and making demands.

Cindy's sister, who was standing nearby, was surprised at Cindy's brashness. "Cindy, don't talk to her like that!"

"It's okay," Sherry replied sympathetically. "I understand."

"Go check my orders. I need more," Cindy repeated.

Later, when Nurse Elaine was in the room, Cindy said, "You know, when Sherry gives me my pain meds, it doesn't work very well. I want you to bring it and not anyone else. It works when you give it to me."

Elaine heard Cindy's concerns and notified the supervisor, Cathy, who came in to talk to Cindy.

"Hi, Cindy, I understand you think you're not getting pain relief when Sherry gives you your meds?"

"No, it doesn't last as long when she gives it to me. I think she's reading the order wrong," Cindy insisted.

"Well, because you're a nurse, I'm going to tell you something. We've suspected she may be stealing drugs. Would you mind if she brought it to you one more time? And then maybe we can catch her."

Cindy agreed to help. She wanted to get to the bottom of this too.

"Thank you. We'll be right in after she gives you your next dose."

The next time Sherry was on shift, Cathy asked her to give Cindy her pain meds. Sherry brought the meds into Cindy's room, administered them to her, and left. Right after, Cathy came into the room and gave Cindy a small dose more.

Later that night, Cathy came into Cindy's room and said, "We got her. We caught Sherry stealing your morphine."

Cindy listened incredulously as Cathy explained that Sherry was giving part of the vial with some solution to Cindy, and then she would take the rest into the bathroom and give it to herself. They followed her into the bathroom and found the vial and a syringe hidden in the trash can.

Cathy asserted, "We gave her a drug test, and she's been fired."

Cindy was stunned. She had simply thought that Sherry was misreading her chart. She knew that she was not getting a full dose and could feel the difference between Sherry's dosage and other nurses'. But in fact, Sherry had been *stealing* her morphine. Imagine stealing pain meds from a burn patient!

"Thank you for helping us. We've suspected she was using drugs for a while but could never catch her. Usually she would get rid of the vials, but this time, we caught her in the act. She's obviously never working here anymore," Cathy assured Cindy. "We fired her and reported her, which means she will lose her license and be on the drug-abuser list. We couldn't have caught her without you, so thank you."

Cindy was pleased they had caught Sherry and was thankful she had a nursing background to know that there was a difference in her medicinal dosage. She wondered how many patients had also been affected but didn't realize what was going on or didn't know how to speak up about how they felt. Cindy was mostly thankful that she would be getting regular dosages of morphine again. And at that moment, she was ready for the next one.

I can get through this ...

CHAPTER 35:
HAPPY BIRTHDAY
July 21, 1982

Cindy graduated out of the burn ICU and was transferred to the general burn unit on her birthday. Cindy knew she should be excited, but she felt scared. The burn ICU had been her home for over two months. During intervals, she hadn't been breathing on her own, and she knew it was a miracle that she was alive. Less than a hundred years ago, before respirators were invented, she would have died.

Cindy was frightened that she wasn't ready to be moved upstairs. She thought, *What if I stop breathing again? If they move me upstairs, how will they know if I stop breathing in the middle of the night?*

Cindy confided her fears to Nurse Elaine.

"Cindy, I will stay with you until this evening," Elaine assured her. "You'll be right across from the nurse's station. You'll like the nurses upstairs too. They're all really nice!"

"Okay," Cindy finally relented, "but wait until my mother comes. I want her with me when I'm moved."

"No," said Elaine, "let's move you now, and you can call her from upstairs and surprise her. I promise to stay with you until she arrives!"

Cindy was eager at the thought of using a phone again. She hadn't used a telephone in months!

The staff wheeled Cindy in her bed down the hall and into the elevator with a few bags of her belongings. Up on the next floor, the nurses pushed her into her new room. The staff put her bed in position so Cindy could pick up the new phone by her bedside to call her mom.

"Hi, Mom! It's me! I'm in my new room. You can come over now!" Cindy was excited to have access to her friends and family again with her room phone. She had always been a people person, and this renewed social access sent dopamine coursing through her body.

Her parents, the boys, her sisters, and her brother all arrived together. When they entered the room, they started singing "Happy Birthday." Cindy smiled wide, thankful for her family. She looked at Jeremiah's and Michael's faces, and they were both beaming. They seemed to understand that their mom was getting better and that this was an important occasion.

"Oh, my gosh," Cindy said, tears welling in her eyes. "This means so much to me!"

Her brother set a colorful bouquet of birthday balloons in the corner.

"We have a present for you, Mommy!" Jeremiah gushed, thrusting a large birthday bag onto her lap. Cindy took out the tissue paper to discover a large white teddy bear.

"I love it, boys. Thank you!" She wrapped her arms around each one and kissed them repeatedly on top of their heads.

Her mom had brought a birthday cake, white frosting with pink roses, along with little cake plates and forks. Written on the cake was *Happy 30th Birthday, Cindy!* After her mom cut it into squares, her sister Gail passed out pieces to the hospital staff, who were grateful for the sugar rush.

Dr. Hoefflin popped into the room to wish Cindy a happy birthday. Cindy looked at him as he spoke and realized she had never truly done that before. When he left the room, Cindy blushed as she said in a hushed voice, "I never realized how good-looking he was!"

The room burst out in laughter as Joy exclaimed, "Wow! You *are* feeling better!"

Cindy smiled, taking in the moment. This was the best day she'd had in months. She felt uplifted in her new surroundings. Unlike her room downstairs in the basement, Cindy's new room had big windows and was brighter.

Cindy admitted to herself that this was not how she had imagined celebrating her thirtieth birthday, and in truth, she hadn't wanted to celebrate her birthday that very morning. However, now she was feeling thankful to make it to another birthday, and moving into her new room had been the perfect way to celebrate.

CHAPTER 36:
THE BOOGER

Up until Cindy was transferred out of the burn ICU to the burn unit, she had only gotten out of her bed for the baths: she had not walked at all or eaten any real food during the last ten weeks. She still had a TPN IV and an NG tube, bringing liquid food and medicine directly into her system. She still had a long struggle on her road to recovery before she could function normally and be discharged.

On her first day upstairs, Nurse Rose, a skinny, curly-haired brunette, told her, "This is where the real work begins."

Cindy stared at her and thought, *What?! I've been going through hell! After everything I've just been through, it's going to get harder?*

One day, after yet another skin graft surgery, Cindy woke up a little groggy from the anesthesia and felt intense pressure in her nose. She felt like she had a giant booger in her nostril, although it was really her NG feeding tube.

The booger felt so large it was uncomfortable, but she didn't want to ask the staff to pick her nose for her. Instead, Cindy reached in and picked her nose, pulling out a long, stringy booger.

This is the longest booger I have ever seen! she thought, and she continued to pull it out until suddenly, there was a large balloon at the end.

Just as Cindy ripped the booger out of her nose with a *pop,* Nurse Rose walked through the doorway into her room.

"Oh, Cindy!" she cried out.

Cindy looked down and saw the NG tube with drops of blood on her sheets, and even in her medicated state, she realized what she had done.

"I thought it was a booger!" she lamented in pain.

Rose shook her head. "Well, we're going to have to put it right back in." She looked closely at Cindy's nose. "That one might leave a scar!"

Cindy's nose throbbed, and blood dripped out of her nostril. The nurse rolled up some gauze and gently filled her nostril to absorb the blood and stop the bleeding.

Rose then consulted Dr. Goldberg. He stood by Cindy's bedside and said, "Cindy, we can put your NG tube back in, or you can try to start eating food. It's up to you."

Cindy nodded her head in agreement, still in disbelief that she had done that. She wanted to try real food.

The staff started bringing Cindy liquid food, including protein shakes. Cindy's stomach had shrunk so much in the hospital that she became full quickly. She had entered the hospital weighing 260 pounds and had dropped to 230 in the two and a half months she had been there. The dietician started visiting Cindy regularly to make sure she was taking in enough nutrition.

When Cindy first tried to feed herself a shake, she had a tough time bending her arms to put the shake up to her mouth. Babe, her physical therapist who spoke with a Southern accent, started working with Cindy to make sure she had flexibility in her arms. Each new physical accomplishment led to another area on her body that was impacted and needed to be worked on. It was a never-ending chain reaction of recovery.

CHAPTER 37:
EAVESDROPPING

Cindy could hear Dr. Tamir, her orthopedic surgeon, talking to her mom outside in the corridor. Dr. Tamir had worked on both Jeremiah and Cindy, and Cindy appreciated that he always explained what he wanted to do with their fractures and the difficulty of putting casts on burned areas. Dr. Tamir and her mom had lowered their voices, but Cindy's hearing had always been exceptionally good, and she could still hear them talking about her.

"We're going to try to start getting her up and moving around," Dr. Tamir said. "I'll be honest; at this point, we don't know if she will be able to walk. We don't know if she'll need a walker or a wheelchair. The fractures in her hips and pelvis were really bad, and we did the best we could, but we won't know until we try to get her moving."

Cindy flashed back to the early days downstairs when she had been in traction while her hips and pelvis healed. She could still visualize her leg as it was elevated by a pulley, with the weight on the other end of the bed pulling her hip bone down to where it was supposed to be.

"I don't know," the doctor continued. "She may get up and not be able to stand, and you should be prepared for that. You also need to be prepared that she might not be able to work as a nurse again."

Cindy did her best to project her voice: "I'm gonna walk." But neither of them heard her. She said it again. "I'm gonna walk!"

Just then, her mom came into the room.

"I'm going to walk," Cindy said indignantly.

"Oh, did you just hear the doctor? I'm sorry, honey."

"I am going to walk." Her voice was firm.

Reota nodded her head. "I know you are, honey. I know."

"I'm going to be able to work again too," she added, addressing Dr. Tamir's comments. "I'm going to be able to work again, Mom."

"You know what, honey? I believe you will."

Cindy appreciated what a positive person her mom was—her dad too. They were both positive influences in her life. Perhaps it was because of this that Cindy knew with certainty that the doctor was wrong and she was going to recover. She felt herself become emboldened with determination.

CHAPTER 38:
BABY STEPS

Little by little, Cindy started moving more. Even feeding herself and sitting up in bed were accomplishments. She had to relearn many physical functions because her body had new limitations. She had restrictions on stretching, bending over, and standing straight. Despite the daily in-bed physical therapy sessions, moving out of bed was entirely different.

Despite multiple attempts, Cindy's shoulders continued to reject the skin grafts, and eventually, they started healing on their own, but now she had scar tissue on her shoulders, which was tight and affected her posture. The doctors wanted to go back into surgery to remove all the scar tissue and do another graft, but Cindy refused. Emotionally, she had met her limit, and if any surgery was not deemed absolutely necessary, she was opting out.

The first time Cindy stood on her own, putting her full body weight onto her feet, she screamed in pain. When she tried to stand flat on her feet, her Achilles hurt so bad that she had to walk on tiptoes. With the help of her physical therapist, Babe, Cindy learned to put her foot flat down when she walked. Even still, she was walking wrong, with her tiptoe first.

Cindy had difficulty walking because she needed more stretching and because her right foot was numb from her hip fractures. She had nerve damage and couldn't really feel that foot at all. Still, she needed to learn to walk again. Before the fire, Cindy had promised her sister Joy that she would be her matron of honor during her wedding ceremony.

"You're going to be my matron of honor at my wedding, and you're going to walk down the aisle," Joy said confidently. "And no wheelchair either!"

The wedding was in October, less than three months away, and Cindy made it her goal to be able to walk independently. The nurses pinned a custom calendar made from a hospital pillowcase on the wall. Nurse Rose drew a two-month grid with a big black marker, counting down the days until October, and it motivated Cindy to do her exercises every day. She visualized herself walking down the aisle in her long burgundy dress, Gail waiting for her at the end of the aisle, followed by Joy, the bride. It was her dangling carrot.

Learning to walk again made her feel like a child, and she resented it. Her mind knew how to walk; she recalled how easy it was to walk her rounds in the hospital ER and hike in the Sierra Mountains. But her body had forgotten. Its memory of how to function without conscious thought had been lost in the fire. Cindy had to retrain her body how to move and take one baby step at a time.

When she attempted a step and crumbled against the physical therapist's body, she could hear the echo of Dr. Tamir when he said she might never walk again. She refused to accept that. During Cindy's most frustrating moments, she looked at the calendar and counted down the days to the wedding. She just needed her brain to tell her feet what to do. Mind over matter, and many, many prayers. *Toe, heel. Toe, heel. Toe, heal!*

One afternoon, Cindy got out of bed to work on her steps. The nurse held her arm for guidance, but Cindy rejected it.

"No. I want to do this on my own. I need to do this," she asserted. She looked over at her mother, who was standing in the corner of the room.

"I'm going to walk over to Mom and give her a kiss!"

The nurse counted as Cindy took each precarious step. "One, two, three, four, five …" Cindy was halfway there. The nurse stepped next to Cindy in unison in case she needed support. Her mom stood in the corner with a hopeful smile on her face. Cindy focused on lifting her foot and moving it forward and down, toe first.

"Six, seven, eight, nine, ten!" Cindy stood before her mom and could see the tears brimming in her blue eyes. She had made it!

Cindy leaned forward and gave her mom a kiss. She felt herself smiling with pride. No one was going to tell her she would never walk again.

"Okay, now to make it back," she said. Cindy pivoted with the help of the nurse and began her slow journey back to her bed: toe, heel, toe, heel.

CHAPTER 39:
THE LOVE OF FAMILY

Cindy's younger sister, Joy, was working full-time and didn't come to the hospital often; she was never one for the smell of hospitals and avoided the experience if she could. She was also getting married in October, and the wedding planning was keeping her busy.

During a rare visit, Joy entertained Cindy by talking about the wedding planning, sharing details about printed napkins and floral bouquets, all while encouraging Cindy to get better before her wedding date.

Cindy looked at the calendar on the wall. It was near the end of July, and the wedding was less than three months away. She had been in the hospital for two and a half months already, and it was hard for her to imagine life outside those white walls.

"I've already picked out your dress, Cindy, and you're going to look so beautiful!" Joy was Cindy's best cheerleader, assuring her she was going to be up and walking again.

Cindy's brother, Larry, the only son of the four, would come at night to visit Cindy and flirt with the night nurses. Cindy was afraid to be alone, and he would hang out in her room, talk to Cindy and the nurses, and spend time with her. When they gave Cindy her pain meds, she fell asleep, but he would stay in her room and study for the Board to get his contractor's license.

The nurses titrated her meds, adjusting the dosages according to her individual response, and typically, they gave her an IV push over a five-minute period. Larry teased the nurses to give the morphine to Cindy quickly. "Give it to her fast! Let her get the rush!" he laughed.

One time, Cindy relented and agreed, "Okay, give it to me fast."

The rush was quick but felt like a nauseating roller coaster ride. She didn't like it.

"That was terrible!" Cindy exclaimed the next time he visited. "I didn't like it at all."

Larry laughed. "I wish I could have some!"

Cindy's father also spent time at the hospital, keeping Cindy company. He and Cindy's brother were both named Larry, but they didn't go by *senior* or *junior*, and this confused the nurses at first.

After the fire, her dad had put his business on hold to be at the hospital every day with her mom, but after four weeks, he needed to return to work to resurrect his business and provide income for the family. He spent his days working for his own business, Edwards' Backhoe Service, digging ditches for various clients, while Cindy's mom spent the entire day at the hospital. After work, he came to the hospital and spent evenings with Cindy and her mom.

One Sunday, Cindy's dad came alone. "Cindy, your mom stayed home today." Her mom had been coming to the hospital relentlessly every day for two and a half months.

Cindy nodded. "She should stay home and rest. She deserves a day to herself."

Cindy thought about all that her mom had done for her, staying by her side every day. They hadn't been close when she was younger, which made her mother's devotion that much more meaningful. When Cindy was younger, everyone knew her dad was her hero.

Although they didn't see eye to eye, Cindy had always admired Reota. Whenever she left the house, she was always dressed nicely, and her makeup was flawless, including her signature blue eye shadow.

Cindy's mother was given her unusual name, Reota, after she was born in an REO house car while her parents traveled through Wisconsin. Reota Monroe's childhood was spent traveling with her parents as her father, a Cherokee Indian, shared Indian dances and history at various schools and theaters across the state. He was known by most as *Chief Hailstorm*, but Cindy simply called him *Papa*.

In his autobiography, her grandfather wrote, "One of the purposes of Chief Hailstorm in presenting this part of his life story to his many friends and relatives is to point out to them the necessity of having courage, stamina, and conviction to keep right on going no matter how dark and gloomy things may look at times." This mindset of positivity and perseverance was passed down through the generations, and it was in this way that Cindy was brought up by her parents—to keep going no matter what.

In adulthood, Cindy's mother had swung in the opposite direction of her vagabond parents and focused on creating a stable home and keeping all the children close. She kept their home neat and tidy, but even so, she tended to worry a lot. Having company over caused a flurry of worries over whether the house was clean enough, if the good dishes were out, and if the bookshelves were dusted. Cindy recalled, as a child, how her job was to dust the wrought-iron railing every week.

As an adult herself, Cindy had in turn swung in the opposite direction of her mother. She didn't fuss over her house like her mother did. Having a spotless house wasn't that important to her, and she tried not to stress over trivial details like that either.

However, the strong love she had for her family was something she got from her mother. And her mother always had something positive to say about everyone, which Cindy tried to emulate. The older Cindy got, the more she appreciated her mother. Especially now.

Her dad stayed all day and kept her company as she faded in and out of sleep. Cindy had always been a daddy's girl and loved his company and attention, which she often had to share with her three siblings. She enjoyed this rare opportunity to have him all to herself. Cindy smiled. Through everything, she never doubted her family's love.

CHAPTER 40:
DEPRESSION

Throughout her hospital stay, Cindy was hooked up to various tubes, including a catheter to catch her urine when she had no bodily control. As she started recovering, Cindy told the nurses, "I have to pee. I have to pee!"

Nurse Rose responded, "It's okay, Cindy. You have a catheter. Let it do its thing."

This time, Cindy said, "No, I have to pee. I'm peeing around it. I can feel it!"

Sure enough, when the staff checked, Cindy had leaked urine on her hospital gown and on the sheets. The nurse said, "You are! You're wet. Let's get you changed."

The nurse assistant quickly changed the bedding and Cindy's hospital gown, and then the nurse took out her catheter in order to replace it. The doctor stepped in before the nurse did so, however, and said, "No, leave it out. If Cindy thinks she can urinate on her own, let her."

The next time Cindy felt the urge to urinate, they slipped a bedpan under her, and she was able to relieve herself on her own. She had never felt so happy to pee! To have some control over her body gave her hope.

Thereafter, Cindy called for the bedpan when needed, or they brought the potty chair next to the bed and eased her into it.

One day, while she was walking with assistance across her room, she asserted, "I'm ready for the toilet. I want to use a real flushing toilet."

Holding on to her arm in case she fell, Nurse Marilyn, a petite blonde, assisted Cindy toward the small bathroom in the corner of her room. Cindy turned the corner and flicked on the light switch, and for the first time since the fire, she saw her reflection in the mirror.

Cindy inhaled and held her gaze. She was shocked. "Oh my God, I'm a whole different person."

Cindy barely recognized herself. The last time she remembered looking in the mirror, she had long blonde hair, a tan face, and a healthy glow.

She turned her head and looked at both sides of her face. Her short, dark gray hair had sprouted into little curls, the change in color due to stress and the lack of nutrition. Her skin was pale white with red blotches all over. Past the hospital gown, she had scars all over her arms. She swallowed the lump in her throat. *Wow, what a change*, she thought.

The nurses had been asking her if she wanted to look in the mirror and assured her that her face didn't look bad. She was fortunate there was very little scarring on her cheeks or forehead. Up until then, she had always told the nurses she wasn't ready to look. And now she was staring herself in the face. Her heart sank. Her identity as she knew it was lost.

Cindy urinated in the toilet and asked to be put back in bed, where she wanted to stay. Depression soon spread through her like a heavy weight, pulling her under and drowning her in a sea of darkness. She could only handle so much …

Depression began to zap her energy. She was sad and frustrated that she still had a hard time doing the simplest things, like eating. Every day, the staff kept her busy with the routine of physical therapy and baths, and she felt exhausted. Nothing seemed easy, and she just wanted a break. Cindy felt her spirit drop.

Several days went by, and the staff could tell Cindy was depressed. It was important that she regain her morale, or her health progress could decline.

One afternoon, Nurse Marilyn raised Cindy's bed and said, "It's time for you to get up. I want you to visit someone down the hall."

With her assistance, Cindy begrudgingly got out of bed and slowly walked across the room to the wheelchair. "We're going to take you down the hall to see somebody. This gal has been here six months, and she had 70 percent burns too. She is still not ready to go home yet. I want you to see her and then tell us if you still want to be here six months from now."

Cindy entered the dreary room and introduced herself. She sat quietly in the somber space and listened to the patient's story. Her name was Anna, and she had been a counselor. One of her patients had had a crush on her, but she had thwarted his advances, explaining that she was happily married and had just adopted a baby girl.

Extremely jealous and irrational, the patient broke into her home one night and started a fire. Anna, her husband, and their daughter were all fast asleep. Fortunately, firefighters were able to get there in time to break the window into the baby's room and get her out safely. They also broke Anna's window and got her out along with her husband, although he had burns on 90 percent of his body and died within a couple of days.

Even though Anna had burns on 70 percent of her body like Cindy had, Anna was severely scarred. Her entire face was burned, and her nose was decimated. Her hands were mutilated in the fire, and they'd had to cut off her fingers. Anna lay in bed, and it was clear she was severely depressed.

Cindy sat and talked with Anna until Marilyn came to get her to bring her back to her room. She thought, *I am not going to be like that. I am not going to be in that bed looking pathetic and feeling sorry for myself in another three months. I'm not going to let myself.*

After that, Cindy pushed herself to get better. Whenever she was doing her walking exercises and passed Anna's room, she would say, "Come on, Anna. Let's go. Let's take a walk together."

Anna started taking walks down the hall with Cindy, and it didn't take long before it was their routine, and they became good friends. They were a good incentive for each other and encouraged one other when their spirits or energy was low.

Anna eventually got better and was finally discharged shortly before Cindy was. Cindy learned that Anna's sad story had continued after she left the hospital. Since she was now single and injured, the adoption agency wanted to cancel the adoption and put Baby Susie in a different home. Anna's parents encouraged her to give up the child, saying that she was having a challenging time taking care of herself, let alone a baby. Anna, however, insisted she could take care of herself and Susie and that she would get help if she needed it.

Anna learned how to clothe herself and change Susie's diapers, all without fingers, and in the end, the agency allowed Anna to keep her. Once they recognized her ability and agreed to let her keep Susie, Anna's outlook on life changed. Susie gave her something to live for.

Cindy and Anna kept in touch over the years, having lunch in LA when Cindy was visiting family. They even went to a Christmas party together at Dr. JP's house one year, and they saw many of their doctor friends. During the party, Cindy recognized a doctor's voice from the ER and suddenly turned to her, exclaiming, "Oh my gosh! I know you! I know your voice!"

The doctor, in turn, replied, "And I remember you! Wow, I thought you had died!"

Anna even took Susie up to Truckee for a visit when Susie was three. It was the first time in the snow for both of them, and they loved the cold, white powder. Cindy and Anna's friendship was a bond that could not be broken.

In the hospital, Cindy quickly realized that she had to learn to be a new version of herself. She wasn't the same person she had been just a few months earlier, and not just because of her looks. Everything she'd gone through had changed her. She was just different. She would always be different, affected by the fire in ways others couldn't understand.

Cindy also had to relearn how to use her hands and her fingers after the fire, including the simplest things, like dressing herself. Her fingers stumbled with buttons, for example. One time, after she had moved back to Truckee, she had to call her neighbor Nancy to come over to help her button a shirt.

When Cindy finally got out of the hospital, she looked around at other people's lives and realized that they had gone on living without her. They'd lived their days as if nothing had happened. Meanwhile, she had endured torturous pain and tragedy that affected her every day. She was no longer a carefree civilian. For a long time, she felt like an outsider looking in.

These were things that Cindy and Anna had in common. They called each other and shared victories, big and small. Anna would exclaim, "Hey, I learned how to hold a milkshake today using the palms of my hands!" Cindy was grateful to have Anna, who understood the intricacies of acclimating back into society and everyday life.

Cindy met other patients who became part of an inner circle of support in the hospital, including Jeanne, who received 30 percent burns after pouring gas on a barbecue. They shared their stories, cried together, and talked about recovery. This support group of sorts helped Cindy rise from the ashes and find her inner strength. After that initial meeting with Anna, there was no looking back.

CHAPTER 41:
AN HONEST REPLY

Cindy's mom and Gail started bringing the boys by for regular weekly visits. It was important for the boys to see their mom getting better, becoming more alert, and engaging them in conversation. More importantly, the visits helped boost Cindy's morale and gave her something to look forward to.

During one of their visits, Gail announced, "Miah had a nice conversation with a lady at the store the other day."

Cindy looked at her questioningly.

"We were in the checkout line, and this woman saw Jeremiah in the wheelchair with his three casts and asked him what happened. Without missing a beat, Jeremiah tells her factually, 'My mom threw me out of the third-floor window.'"

"You should have seen the look on her face!" she exclaimed. "I was mortified! She looked at me wide-eyed like *I* was his mom who threw him out the window. I quickly explained, 'She threw him out of the window to save his life from a fire.' You know she ran home to tell that story!"

Cindy started laughing, understanding Jeremiah's innocence and imagining the woman's surprise. Her mom and sisters laughed with her, their laughter echoing in the hallway.

Cindy could not remember the last time she had laughed freely like that. She used to laugh almost every day. People had always called her *joyful*, and she missed it. In times like these, the family accepted humor wherever they could find it.

CHAPTER 42:
ATTENTIVE STAFF

There were many doctors and nurses who had a hand in Cindy's care. For the first few weeks, as she phased in and out of consciousness and her eyes were swollen shut, she couldn't really see them or identify them physically. Without her sight to rely on, Cindy's sense of hearing grew more acute. She found she could often identify the staff by their voices. Some were soft and gentle; others were deep and low. Some staff stood far away as they spoke to Cindy; others leaned in close.

Cindy's sense of smell also became acute. While she was accustomed to the smell of disinfectant while working in the ER, she had a reprieve when she went outside and went home. Now that she was a patient, there was no break from the sterile smell. Only the occasional whiff of the staff's cologne or perfume gave her olfactory receptors a break.

Many of the nurses who worked with Cindy followed her from the burn ICU in the downstairs basement to the burn unit upstairs. Cindy had become familiar with these nurses—Cathy, Elaine, Janet, Anna, and Danny—and she felt comfortable in their hands. As Cindy improved, she got to know them not just as staff members but as people.

Elaine was Cindy's favorite nurse. She was chatty and friendly, and she spoke directly to Cindy as she took her blood pressure or temperature. She was pregnant in her second trimester, and watching her stomach grow made Cindy feel good inside.

While debriding Cindy's wounds and taking out staples, Elaine would distract Cindy by getting her to talk about working in labor and delivery, and her experiences in the OB helping deliver babies—all while asking questions about what to expect.

Elaine's questions both distracted Cindy and reminded her of her purpose on Earth. She absolutely loved helping to deliver babies. Being on this side of a nurse's care, Cindy quickly realized that a kind word was just as important and healing as physical care was.

Another night nurse, Danny, was friendly to Cindy, but at first, she had been afraid of him, perhaps because he was tall and foreboding. High on morphine, Cindy had terrifying dreams that he was sexually abusing her, and whenever he came around, she pulled away in fear. In her drug-induced nightmares, Danny spread open her legs and sexually assaulted her, and she was powerless to stop him.

One day, she finally confided her fears to her mom, who had gotten used to Cindy's hallucinations. "Mom, I know Danny is a good nurse, but I have dreams that he comes into my room at night and sexually abuses me." Reota quickly relayed Cindy's visions to Cathy, the head nurse.

Cathy thought back to some of the initial sponge baths and perineal care that Danny had given Cindy during the early phase when she was heavily on morphine and realized that Cindy's unconscious had internalized the negative experience. *Perineal care*, or peri care as many of the nurses called it, involved cleaning the private areas of a patient known as the *perineum*, the area between the anus and vulva in a female. Peri care had to be maintained at least once a day to avoid infection, which could be caused by unintended bacteria. Danny and other nurses had taken turns with this responsibility, but Danny's stature was domineering.

Cathy entered Cindy's room and held her hand, explaining that it was not unusual to respond to her experience that way since she had been so medicated. Since Danny had been nothing but proper and nice to her when she was alert, Cindy felt relieved after talking to Cathy—especially since, as a medical staff member, it logically made sense to her. As time went on, her mind became clearer, and she felt bad for being so scared of him, especially because he was such a pleasant, no-nonsense kind of guy who was just doing his job.

Another nurse who stood out to Cindy was Carla, a big black nurse who worked nights. Since Cindy had worked the night shift in the ER and OB for years, she was used to being up at night and asleep during the day, so Carla kept her company, often bringing in her knitting and sitting with Cindy in the quiet of the night while the other patients slept.

Carla also helped with the mouse problem. Cindy had been seeing a mouse running into and out of her room for several days. She even complained to her mom: "Mom, there is a mouse in my closet there. I told my nurses, and they've looked, but they keep missing it."

Reota looked into the closet and said, "Cindy, I don't see a mouse in there either." This pacified Cindy until she saw it again.

One night, Carla entered the room on a mission. "Okay, so you think there is a mouse in your closet?"

"Yes!" said Cindy. "I keep hearing it …"

"Okay, I think we need to clean that closet tonight, from top to bottom. We're going to do a spring cleaning!" Carla opened the door and started taking everything out. Cindy's medical supplies were in there, including dressings, a foot drop to flex her feet in bed to avoid Achilles problems, booties to prevent her feet from getting bedsores, and other supplies. As Carla worked, she turned on the TV to give them something to watch, stopping at the game show *Jeopardy*. Occasionally, she came across something that they had used on Cindy weeks before, like respiratory equipment, and said triumphantly, "We can get rid of this!"

After all the supplies were sorted out, Cindy's closet stood empty. "Okay, Cindy," affirmed Carla. "Look. There is no nest or mouse in here."

Cindy nodded, believing finally that the mouse was gone.

During another episode of morphine madness, Cindy swore there were blue daisies growing out of the wall and asked her mother to pick them for her.

"Sure, honey," Reota said understandingly. She walked over to the corner and started simulating picking flowers one by one in front of the wall. Cindy was so thankful her mom understood, and she knew, before falling asleep again, that her mom would put them in a vase by her bed.

Even upstairs on lighter doses, the morphine continued to play tricks on her.

CHAPTER 43:
THE SMELL

While Cindy was initially self-conscious about having a male nurse conduct peri care and was embarrassed that she had accused Danny of sexually assaulting her, Cindy had become comfortable under Danny's care, and she trusted him. He had always been completely professional. In Truckee, Cindy had worked alongside many male nurses who had provided nothing but high-quality care to all their patients.

One afternoon, Danny and two female nurses approached Cindy's bed tentatively.

"Cindy, I know we've talked about this before, but there is an intense smell coming from your perineum, and we can't figure out what it is. It's been there for weeks now, and it seems to be getting stronger, and I'm concerned. We've got to find out what this is," asserted Danny.

Cindy nodded her head in agreement. She was embarrassed by the smell and had heard the nurses talking about it, even when she was downstairs, and both Danny and the female nurses had tried to figure out where the smell was coming from. Cindy only noticed it during peri care when her perineum was exposed during a sponge bath. As a nurse, she understood the repugnant smell likely meant some sort of infection.

"We've got to find out where the smell is coming from in your perineum," Danny continued. "There is something causing the smell. It's like something has died inside you," Danny smiled, using humor to make the situation a little more comfortable. "As you know, we have been trying to figure this out for weeks now, and today, I had an idea. Were you, by chance, on your period when the fire happened?" Danny asked earnestly.

Cindy thought back to the day of the fire, to that morning when she stripped down and crawled into bed, and remembered. "Yes! Yes, I was on the last day of my period!" With all that had happened to her, her period hadn't been on her mind at all. She hadn't even had a menstrual cycle since she'd been in the hospital, which was common for trauma patients.

"Oh my God!" Cindy suddenly realized where Danny was going with his question. "Do you think I still have a tampon in there?"

"I'm thinking maybe," Danny replied, nodding. "If you had a tampon in on the day of the fire and it was never removed, it's likely still in there causing the smell. If so, we need to get it out as soon as possible to avoid toxic shock syndrome."

Cindy nodded her head and looked at the female nurses, who were looking at her with compassion. They all understood what an uncomfortable but important revelation this was.

"Cindy, what I'd like to do is this: I'd like to get a pair of forceps to see if there is something in there," Danny said, asking Cindy for permission.

"Yes," Cindy agreed. "Do it."

Danny left the room, leaving the two nurses with her as they helped get her ready, pulling back the curtain to ensure privacy and gently pulling off the blankets from the bed. Cindy bent her legs the best she could and opened herself up to the nurses so they could cleanse her perineum with a warm washcloth in preparation.

Cindy heard Danny reenter the room before he pulled back the curtain. He held a tray with sterilized forceps in his hand, which looked like long flathead tweezers on one end and scissor handles on the other. Cindy's heart raced.

"Okay, I'm ready," she told him.

Danny first felt with his gloved fingers for the string but had no luck.

He then used the forceps to try to find the tampon. After several attempts, he caught the dark red tampon and quickly pulled it until it was removed. The room immediately filled with a rank smell, and they all turned their heads in the opposite direction.

"We got it!" confirmed Danny. Cindy could see the triumphant look in his eyes.

Cindy felt a mixture of mortification and relief, knowing that had Danny not figured it out, she could have died from septic shock.

As Danny disposed of the rotten tampon, the other nurses provided peri care again. Once she was redressed and composed, Cindy asked for Danny.

"Danny, you might have just saved my life. Had you not thought of it, I could have died from septic shock, and no one would have known. They probably would have blamed the burns. Thank you," Cindy said with sincerity, tears coming to her eyes. "I mean it, thank you so much."

Danny smiled and looked down, embarrassed by the attention. "It's okay, you're welcome. I'm just pleased it's over. I wasn't going to let it go until I figured it out!"

He puffed up his chest jokingly, and Cindy laughed. Once again, the medical staff had saved her life.

CHAPTER 44:
FIRE STARTER

Cindy didn't ask a lot of questions about the cause of the fire until she was out of the ICU and in a frame of mind to be able to ask questions about the external issue. One day, during her mom's visit, she inquired, "Mom, did the police ever figure out what happened? What started the fire?"

Her mom picked at the lint on her shirt and gently said that they really didn't know, that it might have been electrical or something else.

She could tell her mom was nervous. "Mom? What happened?"

Reota hesitated. She took a deep breath and then confessed the truth. "The investigators have discovered that this was an arson fire. Someone set the house on fire with gasoline."

Cindy stared at her mom but didn't hear the next few words. *Arson?* She looked down at the white tile floor. *Someone lit the house on fire—on purpose?*

She looked back at her mom, who was still talking.

"… been looking at Ken and have named him a suspect, but honestly, honey, I don't think he did it. I don't think he would do this."

Cindy sat there in shock, her mind racing. *Who would've done this? Why would they do that to her?*

Cindy's mind suddenly jumped to a vague memory of that day before she woke up to the smoke. She remembered hearing someone downstairs and hearing someone unzipping her purse. She had thought it was Ken coming back for more gas money. She had even gotten out of bed and looked out the window but didn't see his truck, so she climbed back into bed, thinking maybe she had imagined it.

Now, she was certain she hadn't.

Cindy didn't know what to think. But she didn't think Ken would do this. Not to her, not to Jeremiah, whom he absolutely adored. His boys were everything to him.

But then that meant a stranger had been in her house while she was sleeping.

Cindy's mind raced. *Who would do this? Who was upset with her? Who had she pissed off?* Maybe a patient to whom she hadn't given meds they wanted or whose rudeness she didn't accept? Cindy had never been afraid to speak her mind. She knew she was outspoken, but she couldn't imagine upsetting someone so much they wanted her dead.

Was there really someone out here who hated her so much they were willing to commit murder?

CHAPTER 45:
INSURANCE POLICY

A few days later, as Cindy's mind was still spinning, she exclaimed, "Wait, we have insurance. Have we gotten any money? You guys can use that money to help take care of the kids!"

Her mom and dad shook their heads. "No, we haven't dealt with the insurance at all. Maybe Ken is dealing with them."

"Well, I need to talk to Ken and see what's going on," Cindy replied.

Her parents gave each other worried and knowing glances.

"Cindy, there's something we need to tell you. We didn't want to say anything because it might upset you, but now …" Reota confessed. "You know the sheriffs aren't sure what caused the house fire, but some people think maybe Ken did it. But we don't think he did it," she said quickly, glancing at Larry for moral support. "But the insurance companies are waiting for the investigation to be over to make sure it wasn't insurance fraud or anything else."

"No," Cindy said, shaking her head. "I don't think Ken would do that, Mom. He knew I was home asleep and wouldn't have …" Cindy paused, momentarily entertaining an evil thought. Shaking her head again, she continued, "No, he knew Jeremiah was home with me, and he'd never intentionally cause us harm."

That afternoon, Cindy called Ken on the phone and asked about the insurance money.

"The insurance company doesn't want to deal with me," Ken said.

"They're waiting to talk to you and for the sheriff's investigation to be over."

Feeling frustrated, Cindy called the insurance company from her hospital room.

"I'm inquiring about the open claim on our house insurance policy. What's going on? Our house burned down, and I'm still in the hospital. It's been months. We have bills, and we need money. What do we need to do to move this forward?"

"I'm sorry, ma'am, but the cause of the fire is still being investigated, and we can't provide a payout until the cause is determined," said the insurance representative.

"I don't understand," said Cindy, getting agitated. "What difference does it make what started it? It's burned down! I need living expenses for my kids. My kids are being taken care of by my parents, who aren't working because they are here with me. My kids need new clothes and school supplies—everything burned in the fire."

"I'm sorry, ma'am. We can't send a policy payout until the investigation is concluded, but we can send you a monthly check for living expenses until it's settled."

"Fine. That will help. I've been in the hospital for months now, so you'll have to backpay me too. My parents have gone pretty broke trying to take care of my boys and me."

In truth, Cindy's parents were in financial jeopardy, her dad having taken countless days off from his business to be with Cindy and her mom spending every day at the hospital. Her sisters were busy taking care of both the boys. Fortunately, the Truckee community had held a spaghetti-dinner fundraiser on Cindy's behalf and sent money to her parents. Other friends in Truckee donated money directly, as did local friends in West Covina. It was the donations from their friends and communities that were helping them stay afloat.

Cindy's next phone call, the following day, was to the Truckee sheriff's department. Sheriff Harrison picked up the phone.

"Phil, can someone please tell me what's going on?" Cindy implored. "What caused the fire?" She wanted answers, and she wanted someone to be straight with her.

"I'm sorry, Cindy, but it's still under investigation. What I can say is that this is considered an arson case based on the hard evidence. The fire was caused by a flammable liquid ignited with a match."

After talking with Phil, Cindy put the phone back in its holder and sat in silence, shocked by his certainty. She felt a knot in her stomach. Her mind did not want to accept the evidence. Then, the fear started to creep from her core like octopus tentacles.

Someone had set her house on fire on purpose. Using gasoline. Someone had literally tried to kill her. Who would want to murder her and Jeremiah? And why?

CHAPTER 46:
COUNSELING

Cindy began getting regular visits from Dr. Feldman, a tall man who stopped by to see her every couple of days to provide counseling sessions as she lay in bed. Cindy's depression fluctuated daily, even hourly. When she felt depressed, his visits were particularly annoying.

Dr. Feldman came into her room and stood above her bed, looming over her. Quietly, he asked, "How are you?"

Cindy's initial response in her head was, *How the hell do you think I am?* But instead, she muttered out loud, "I'm all right."

Probing for more response, he looked at her through his glasses and asked in his deep voice, "Well, what did you do today?" or sometimes, "When you lay there, what goes through your mind?"

Confined to her bed, Cindy relayed the daily procedures she was enduring, the staff members who came in, and the pain she was in.

"You know, it's not good for you to think about what's going on in here all the time. It's good for you to think about your life outside of here."

Cindy looked at his salt-and-pepper hair and his gray mustache and beard as he spoke, but it seemed like he was speaking a foreign language. *Did he really think she wasn't thinking about her life? About how her house and all her belongings had burned to the ground? That she and Ken were estranged?* And she didn't even want to entertain the idea that he could have started the fire. *Would she ever be a nurse again? How would she make money?* No, these were thoughts that Cindy tried to push to the back of her mind. She *had* to focus on the here and now—on healing.

"Look, doctor, I hurt. I've been through a lot. My life has changed. I just found out my house was set on fire. That it was arson." Cindy shook her head. She felt her blood pressure rising.

"You know what, Dr. Feldman? You don't need to come see me anymore. You keep telling me not to think about my pain. Do you really think I can lay here day after day and not focus on all that I'm going through? Not think about my pain? I try not to. Sometimes, I'm thinking and pretending I'm at the beach. I'm pretending I'm back in Hawaii when Michael was born, and I'm playing on the beach in Oahu and feeling the warm sand between my toes. That's what I think about when I close my eyes."

Cindy took a deep breath. "But the pain is still there. The pain does break through. But I'm not *trying* to think about it. I try very hard *not* to focus on it when I can." She paused. "I really don't need you to come see me anymore."

"I understand, Cindy," said Dr. Feldman, "but I need to come and check in on you. It's my job. I'll come back in a couple of days, and we'll see how you're feeling."

Two days later, he entered her room. Cindy glanced from the television to him standing in the doorway and then looked back at the TV, watching the end of *One Life to Live*.

"Do you want to just watch TV with me?" Cindy asked, looking straight ahead. "I don't need you or need to talk."

"Sure. I'll just stay right here." Dr. Feldman took a seat in the chair next to Cindy's bed and silently watched *General Hospital* for the next hour. Cindy knew he was waiting for her to talk or was there if she needed to talk, but she was firm in her resolve that she didn't need him.

After his hour, he bade her farewell and left.

Two days later, he was back again.

"Are you here to watch *General Hospital* again with me?" Cindy smiled.

"I just want to make sure you don't want to talk to me, Cindy."

"Thank you, but I'm okay," she replied firmly. Cindy simply couldn't listen to his garbage anymore. *Don't think about it. Do this. Do that ... What the heck did he think she was doing?* His suggestions were not helpful whatsoever. If anything, his patronizing advice aggravated her.

The next day, she told Dr. Goldberg that she didn't want Dr. Feldman to come around anymore, and he stopped coming. It wasn't that she didn't like him personally ... well, not really. He just wasn't what she needed right now. There wasn't anything that anyone could say to her that would make getting through this any easier.

As Cindy lay in bed, she knew that deep down, she had to make the decision if she was going to be an invalid. It was up to her to decide if she was going to get up and learn to walk or if she was going to be in a wheelchair for the rest of her life. She had to decide if she was going to learn to use her hands again or not. Every step of the way, Cindy struggled with her choices, but she knew each choice was up to her.

The thing with Cindy is that once she made a decision, she went for it and fully committed.

Cindy called Dr. Hoefflin into her room. "I want to go home by Labor Day," she said firmly, knowing it was a month away. "And I want to have a barbecue."

"You want a barbecue?"

"Yes, I want to have a family barbecue," she said with certainty.

"Well," he replied with a twinkle in his eye, "when you can dance with me in the hallway, you can go home."

Cindy was filled with determination. She did her exercises and her steps, but then she would have another skin graft surgery that set her back a couple of days, and she would have to start all over again. Whenever she felt frustrated, though, she looked at the pillowcase calendar on her wall, imagined the barbecue in her parents' backyard, and kept moving.

CHAPTER 47:
DAILY ROUTINE

During the recovery stage upstairs, Cindy had a robust schedule, which included a lot of physical work and a lot of pain. Because she was more conscious now, she was more apt to complain.

Early in the morning, she had physical therapy in her bed. While the burns had brought on an onslaught of health issues, being bedridden for almost three months had taken its toll on her body as well and had led to physical complications not related to the fire. Cindy's muscles had quickly lost strength and endurance from disuse, and her muscles were at risk of *atrophy*, a serious and often permanent decrease in muscle mass due to extended immobility. Her muscles were literally wasting away.

Further, she faced joint issues. A permanent tightening of the muscles, tendons, skin, and nearby tissues, called *contractures*, had caused her joints to shorten and become stiff. Being confined to a bed long-term added to the likelihood of developing an increased heart rate, decreased cardiac output, hypotension, poor circulation, and blood clots. As if these weren't enough, her bones risked osteoporosis from disuse.

These were many of the health issues Cindy faced from being bedridden—in addition to her fractured bones, burned skin tissue, and skin grafts caused by the fire. There were also risks to her internal organs. In some cases, the doctors were not yet sure if there had been damage.

Babe, her physical therapist, stopped by Cindy's room twice a day on rotation and helped stretch Cindy's feet, legs, hands, and arms. The stretching and movements were painful, and she vocally whined throughout each session. Next was her Betadine bath, which took a couple of hours.

After they dressed her wounds and got her back in bed, it was time for her second physical therapy session of the day.

Many times, Cindy lay there during the sessions with her eyes closed—tears streaming down the sides of her face. One time, she opened her eyes and looked up to see Sarah, her occupational therapist, stretching her hands and fingers with tears trickling down her cheeks. Cindy looked Sarah in the eye as they silently acknowledged each other's pain, one physical and one emotional.

"Don't stop," Cindy said. "Do it. I know you need to do it, no matter how much it hurts."

Sarah nodded, and together, they pushed through the pain. Assisting burn patients was a traumatic experience for the staff too. Cindy could see how the staff turnover in a burn unit would be high.

The nurses generally drew blood every day. Cindy was given regular blood tests and arterial blood draws. Because of her burns and scar tissue, it was often difficult for the nurses to locate a vein or artery that they could draw from, and it frequently took several tries to find a viable vein. To assist with this, Cindy had cutdowns in her neck so they could place a catheter for easier access to her veins. They sewed it in place so they could draw from it several days in a row until the vein collapsed, and then they found a new location.

First, they put in a port, and then it would collapse, and then they put the cutdown in, and then it would collapse. And so, the cycle continued. Later, they started drawing from her feet, which were more sensitive, so they gave her pain meds before drawing blood through her foot. Sometimes, her body did not have enough fluid in the spot to draw from.

The respiratory therapist also did arterial draws for blood gas to see where her oxygen level was, and they needed to go through an artery to do this. They looked at her groin for one and poked around until they found a viable artery. Sometimes, they used her wrist.

Some therapists were better than others, and Cindy asked for those she knew were better at it, like Tom. At times, she got someone new who poked and poked until Cindy had had enough and told them to go away, saying that she wanted someone else. As a fellow nurse, she knew it took practice, so she tried to be patient, but when everything on her body hurt and her tolerance was low, sometimes Cindy didn't have any patience to give. The novice would leave and send in someone else.

On more than one occasion, she tried to have a nurse removed from her care for incompetence. Cindy was certain that down at the nurse's station, they were rolling their eyes and taking bets on who had to go deal with that Ames lady. But as she struggled in her recovery, her tolerance and patience were often at a bare minimum.

The constant poking and probing left Cindy permanently scarred. She would have scars on her neck from the cutdowns and scars in the veins on her arms for the rest of her life. Even her feet were scarred. In an ongoing battle, for the rest of Cindy's life, nurses struggled with drawing blood, since her veins were littered with scar tissue.

After the medical tests, it was time for Cindy's second bath of the day, which was another two hours. Sometimes, she pretended to be asleep, so they left her alone. Sometimes, she just needed a rejuvenation break, and on a rare occasion, they gave it to her.

By now, it was dark, and the hospital staff was helping to prepare patients for sleep—but since she had been on the night crew for so many years, Cindy naturally felt awake at night. Sometimes, she turned on the TV to watch Johnny Carson on *The Tonight Show*, but often, she was in too much pain to focus. Every three and a half to four hours, the nurses gave her pain meds, which helped her sleep for an hour or two, and then she woke up again.

Because Cindy had been a night nurse, the night nurses often came in to visit and share stories about patients they had encountered, all without using names to protect the patients' privacy. The nurses made Cindy feel normal and encouraged her on her journey to healing. It was during these quiet hours of the night that Cindy talked to the nurses and got to know them.

Gladys and Rose became her favorites. Gladys was a black nurse with a sweet demeanor; she would come in and stroke Cindy's hand and do all the trivial things that Cindy asked her to do, like she had with the imaginary mice that Cindy saw run across the floor, and sweeping imaginary spiders off the wall. Gladys was a true caretaker, the best in the burn unit.

Rose, a tiny little thing with a calming aura, was the second-floor head nurse at night. She made sure Cindy had the pain meds she needed and gave Gladys extra time to pamper Cindy. She made Cindy feel like the nurses were looking after one of their own.

One night, Gladys asked Cindy, "Well, now that you have made it through this, what are you going to do about it?"

Without much thought or hesitation, Cindy answered, "I am going to write a book. Nurses and doctors need to know what goes on in a patient's mind when they are in bed for so long and are really sick. They need to know that their kindness impacts a patient and how important their touching and physical contact is." Cindy paused. "They also need to know how rudeness affects the patient and how ignoring them makes them feel."

Cindy thought about Pam, a young nurse in her mid-twenties who was annoyingly chatty. She always talked to the other nurses in the room and ignored Cindy as if she wasn't there. Pam would carry on a conversation about how she had just seen the movie *E.T.* or about her dating life, and she excluded Cindy, which Cindy felt was disrespectful.

One time, when Cindy was downstairs on the ventilator, Pam entered the room and started talking to another nurse about her date the night before. As Pam rolled Cindy onto her side to change her bedding, she continued talking to the nurse while ignoring Cindy. As she rolled Cindy back over, a kink formed in Cindy's ventilator tube, although Pam didn't notice.

Cindy waited for Pam to acknowledge her and to notice the kink, but she didn't. Cindy waved her hand to get Pam's attention, but the other nurse finally noticed and fixed the tube. As a nurse, Cindy was always mindful to include her patients in conversations and treat them as people, not objects in a bed.

"But mostly," Cindy continued, responding to Gladys' question, "I want to write it for myself and for families of burn patients. I want them to know how their support can impact their loved ones' lives."

"Well," Gladys responded, "that's a lot to write, but for a lot of good reasons. I think it's a great idea."

Cindy lay in bed thinking about her book. If there was one good experience that she could take from this, it was to help others understand what it was like from the patient's point of view, from the burn victim's perspective.

By morning, around four or five o'clock, Cindy started to doze off and slept a little after her second dosage of pain meds. When she was having a super-restless night, a nurse gave her a sleeping pill with her pain meds, giving her the best night's sleep, although short-lived. Around seven o'clock, the day shift entered the room and woke her up only to begin the daily routine again. Some days, it was exhausting to be alive.

CHAPTER 48:
THE CIRCLE BED

Even though Cindy had "graduated" to the upper floor and was on her road to recovery, she still faced a number of skin-graft surgeries. One of the biggest concerns the doctors had was her back, which remained raw and oozing.

"Cindy, after numerous attempts, your back is not healing like we'd hoped," said Dr. Hoefflin. "We're going to have to put you on a circle bed."

"No! Oh, no!" Cindy cried out, disheartened. She knew what a circle bed was from her own patients, and she knew from her patients that they hated it. The monstrosity was also known as a Stryker bed.

"Unfortunately, your back isn't healing, and we can't let you go home until it does. The circle bed will help you. We're going to get you off your back and put you on it for ten days so it can heal."

Cindy felt dismayed but trusted Dr. Hoefflin to know what she needed. The Stryker bed consisted of two large hoops about seven feet in diameter with a horizontal surface through the middle. There was an electric motor on the base that helped rotate and flip the patient over from back to stomach. The horizontal surface was the mattress that the patient reclined on in order to sleep. A stretcher-like device was attached when rotating the patient onto the stomach.

Before turning, the patient was tightly sandwiched between the top and bottom frames, which often caused claustrophobia. Once in the prone position, only the floor would be visible. This face-down placement, which was unobtainable with a regular hospital bed, would give the skin on Cindy's backside a chance to air out and heal.

Cindy's entire back had received third-degree burns, and despite a dozen attempts, it was refusing to heal and was riddled with infection. At first, they'd placed dressings on her back to cover where the dead skin had been, and they'd changed the dressings daily. As they pulled back the dressing, it peeled off her dead skin, which was stuck to the dressing. This was incredibly painful, especially when her nerves started healing. The nurses silently noted the green ooze on Cindy's chart. This became her daily torture.

Then they started using BioBrane, which was a biosynthetic wound dressing much like skin, and they put it on her back to protect her from infection. Unlike the dressing, they could leave the BioBrane on her back for several days. Still, every time they pulled it off, it felt like her skin was being pulled off too.

Eventually, her skin started regenerating under the BioBrane and healing itself, but that's not what the doctors wanted. When skin heals itself, it's often thicker with scar tissue, including thick and bumpy keloids. This was a serious issue, because backs need to bend and stretch for mobility, so the skin must be pliable and flexible. Instead of allowing her back to scar on its own, they wanted to graft skin from Cindy's buttocks and put it on her back.

Over the next ten days, Cindy endured a series of skin graft surgeries from her buttocks and legs onto her shoulders and back. When they put Cindy on the circle bed, she had to lay face down all day long, and she could only see the ground. The staff and her family would talk to her, but she couldn't look at them. Instead, she began to recognize people by the shoes they wore. Some of the shoes were really gross. Vaughn, a young black day-shift nurse with an upbeat personality, wore once-white Oxfords that were nasty.

"Eww, your shoes are so dirty!" she called out to Vaughn's feet below her.

"Well, honey, I'd be working!" Vaughn retorted with a laugh.

Most of the nurses wore white nursing shoes, and Cindy cringed whenever she saw a pair of black shoes because she knew it was the respiratory therapist who would be poking her with a needle, usually in the arm or wrist.

Eventually, the pressure from the bars cut off her circulation, causing her arms and hands to become numb. When she wanted some water, she couldn't do it herself; a nurse would have to hold a glass with a straw under her head. Not only was it debilitating, but she was bored out of her mind staring at the plain white floor—and the occasional pair of shoes.

Several times a day, they rolled her over so that she could be upright to take in fluids. She dreaded being turned over because it made her whole body hurt. During the process of turning her over, they put a rack on top of her and screwed it in place to lock her in. They sandwiched her between two racks before circling her upwards to a standing position. Being screwed in with both racks made her feel claustrophobic, but it was the only way she could be upright to eat.

Cindy's appetite had disappeared in the fire, and she had yet to eat solid food in the hospital. Being on a liquid diet for the last twelve weeks had caused her to lose 35 pounds. Adding the 30 pounds she had deliberately lost during her separation from Ken, Cindy now weighed 65 pounds less than the year before.

Even though she had no appetite, Cindy continued to like juice, particularly grape juice. It wasn't just any grape juice, either; it had to be Welch's grape juice. Sometimes, the nurses tried to trick her and bring her another brand in stock in the kitchen, but Cindy always knew. She could taste the difference, and she didn't like the taste of the other brands. Welch's grape juice became her Dom Pérignon, her favorite drink.

Since the hospital was often out of Welch's, Cindy's family began to scour grocery stores all over Culver City and brought the juice to her hospital room so she had a private stash. Cindy liked to have it in a cup with crushed ice and served to her with a spoon. The irony was that Cindy couldn't remember ever drinking Welch's grape juice before the fire, and she didn't know where the craving was coming from. It was a little thing, really, but it tasted so good to Cindy, and it gave her something to look forward to day after day as she lay in misery on the circle bed. Even so, the staff tried to set limits to her grape juice intake to prevent her from having permanently purple lips.

Because her back was oozy and exposed to open air, the fluids drained onto the sheets, causing them to smell. In order to change the sheets, the nurses pushed an automated button to elevate the bed to a standing position. Robbie, the tallest of the nurses, stood behind Cindy so that she could lean back onto him from the standing position. He placed his hands on her arms and his knees against the back of her thighs, holding her in place. He was always careful not to touch her back, and he kept her steady while the nurses quickly stripped the bed and put on fresh sheets. Leaning her body against Robbie's for this period of time was an act of trust.

The circle bed and her oozing back frustrated Cindy because she felt that every time she took one step forward, she took two steps back. She started to feel better and then regressed. The journey to recovery was not a smooth one, no matter how hard Cindy willed it. She thanked the heavens when the circle bed was finally removed. It was one move forward in the game of Life.

CHAPTER 49:
MIAH'S SLEEPOVER

Jeremiah was coming to the hospital for a one-night stay, and Cindy was eager with anticipation to spend some time with her sweet boy. Although Jeremiah's cast had been removed around her birthday, his arm and face were scarred from his burns, and while he hadn't needed skin grafts, the scars on his arms had formed lumpy, fibrous keloids, and Dr. Hoefflin wanted to tend to them.

Last week, when the boys were spending time with Ken at his parents' house, Jeremiah's arm had split open while they were playing outside. Scar tissue, in general, didn't stretch, and this was a concern for a growing boy. During the follow-up doctor's appointment, Dr. Hoefflin suggested putting Jeremiah under anesthesia so that he could perform dermabrasion, where he would sand down the scar tissue on both Jeremiah's arm and face to smooth it out. This would also make the facial scar less noticeable. It was a common and minor plastic surgery.

Although Cindy's room wasn't meant for two patients, the staff had agreed to squeeze in a second bed for Jeremiah so that he could stay with Cindy in her room.

Jeremiah came bounding into the room with Michael and her mother not far behind. "Mommeee!" Jeremiah shouted. It was obvious he was excited for their sleepover. "Mommy, I'm going to stay the night!"

Cindy smiled as she ran her fingers through his head of blonde hair. She was thankful that he didn't have a fear of hospitals, especially after seeing her in her early stages there. Then again, he had seen her get better in the hospital, so that probably helped. *I can't believe my baby just turned five*, she thought. The family had held a little birthday party for him a couple of weeks ago.

"Hi, sweetie!" Cindy replied, a big smile spreading across her face. "Hi, Michael!"

She looked at her eight-year-old, who seemed like he had grown up so much since Truckee. Michael was tall for his age and looked older than he was. He was also quieter than his younger brother. Michael walked over and gave her a hug. She winked at him, and he winked back.

"Hi, honey," said Cindy as she kissed the top of his head. She noticed his hair had turned a lighter shade of blonde during the summer, which blended nicely with his freckles and blue eyes. Both her boys had gotten her eye and hair coloring.

"Thanks, Mom, for bringing them over." Cindy realized she had so much more to thank her mother for, but this would do for now.

The group stayed for almost an hour, and by then, it was time for Jeremiah to get settled in and for the two of them to get ready for the night. The group did their kisses and hugs goodbye, and then it was just her and Jeremiah.

"Jeremiah, do you want to watch some TV?" she asked.

"Yes, please!" he replied with delight. He picked up the white teddy bear he and Michael had given her for her birthday and held it tight.

Cindy patted the bed, and Jeremiah came over with the bear, hopping up to sit on the edge of the bed next to her. Cindy put an arm around him and pulled him close. She missed snuggling. She used to always snuggle with her boys—on the couch, in bed, on the beach, wherever she could.

They watched an episode of *The Wheel of Fortune* until a commercial came on.

"Mommy, are you thirsty?" he asked as he hopped off the bed. He picked up her water cup off the side table and held it toward her face, pointing the straw her way, his little face beaming.

"Thank you, Miah," she said, feeling her heart swell. He then hopped back up on the bed, snuggling up next to her until it was time for lights out.

During the show, the nurses came in to take their vitals and prepare Jeremiah for the early morning surgery. The nurses gave him lots of attention, and he gobbled it up.

Jeremiah's procedure the next morning went smoothly. Dr. Hoefflin came in afterward and explained that the keloid had been sanded down and it shouldn't build back up. The doctor also did some light work on Jeremiah's face and told her he would have minimal scarring on his right cheek. For now, his right arm and the side of his face were bandaged to protect the wounds as they healed.

"He'll probably have to come back in ten years when he's a teenager," said Dr. Hoefflin. "As he grows, the skin on his arm will need to stretch, and it won't be able to. But we can help him with that."

Cindy nodded and thanked Dr. Hoefflin, who had been so good to both of them.

"We'll discharge him later this evening, and he can head home with your family," said the doctor.

Cindy's friends Cathy and Joe planned a visit with Cindy's parents and offered to bring dinner: pizza from their restaurant for the entire family to enjoy. Michael loved pizza, so he was more than happy to go back to the hospital with Grandma and Grandpa. This time, it was Michael who came into the room excited to see his mom and little brother. Cathy and Joe's daughter, Catherine, was buddies with Jeremiah, and Jeremiah was excited to see his friend when they arrived. There was a lot of talking and commotion as everyone caught up.

The pizza tasted amazing to Cindy. She thought pizza had never tasted so good! Even though her taste buds still weren't normal—her sense of taste was diminished due to her trauma and medications—they were starting to come back. The tangy tomato sauce and spicy sausage were an amazing reprieve from the bland hospital food. It was great having everyone there, and for a moment, Cindy almost felt normal.

After they all left, the room felt quiet and lonely, and Cindy fought the momentary urge to cry. Jeremiah had been so sweet and loving, doting on Cindy, and it refueled her desire to get home, and to get there as quickly as possible. She wasn't sure if it was because the boys needed her or she needed them, but she knew with all her heart that they belonged together.

CHAPTER 50:
FOR COLLEEN

As Cindy kept her eye on the calendar, she continued walking up and down the hall, gaining her strength. Her mom often walked with her and kept her company.

One day, the nurses from the burn ICU downstairs approached her and asked if she was willing to visit critical patients to encourage them and show them that they could get through it. They wanted her to be their inspirational representative, and Cindy was happy to help others.

Since Cindy wasn't walking that far yet, the nurses helped her into a wheelchair and took her downstairs. They wheeled her into patients' rooms, where Cindy would stand up, sometimes sit in the room chair, and say, "Hey, I've done it. You can do it. It's painful, but you *will* get through it."

Often, Cindy just sat and talked to the patients, keeping them company. These visits helped her to recognize how far she had come.

One day, they wheeled her into a new patient's room: a young woman named Colleen. Colleen had been in an explosion and suffered burns on her upper torso: on her chest, her face, and her head. Her hair was patchy, partly singed in some places and in others partly gone. She was newly admitted and thus far had only had one surgery and some debridement. Her family was on the East Coast, so she didn't have anyone to visit her. Cindy offered a friendly smile and talked with her.

"Colleen, you're going to be okay. You're going to get through this."

"No. My face …" She looked imploringly at Cindy, fear and despair in her eyes. "My whole face …"

Cindy looked at Colleen's severely burned face, which was exposed and looked like it had been melted onto her skull. Her mouth was shrunken, and she barely moved her tight lips as she whispered. Her skin was discolored red, cracking and peeling. Her eyelids were swollen, and her eyelashes and eyebrows were gone.

She wore a bandaged headband, and Cindy could tell that her bangs had been burned off and the rest of her reddish blonde hair was singed and would need to be shaved off. Her chest was dressed in bandages, and her breathing was labored.

"I … don't … want to do this," she said between labored breaths. "I don't … want to live … like this." She turned her eyes toward the ceiling. "My scars … I was beautiful. I'm only twenty-five. And I'm alone. I don't have … anybody." She paused, and Cindy waited in the heavy silence. She looked back at Cindy. "How … did you do this?"

"My kids. My boys helped me a lot. And I have family who visit every day."

"I have no one."

"Don't you have any family?"

"They're … on the East Coast. I never … see them. I never … hear from them." Colleen paused. "I can't do this."

"No, you *can* do this. Trust me, you can."

Colleen returned to the surgical room the next day. When Cindy went to see her for a visit afterward, her throat was swollen, and she couldn't speak. Cindy continued to talk to her and held her hand, and Colleen squeezed back, acknowledging that she knew Cindy was there.

In the next couple of days, Colleen developed respiratory issues from inhaling smoke during the explosion, and she had to be put on a ventilator. During her visits, Cindy talked aloud to Colleen and continued to reassure her.

After three days, Colleen was taken off the ventilator.

"How are you doing today?" Cindy asked.

Colleen shook her head while whispering, "No, I can't."

Cindy knew she didn't want to live. "Just do what you can. Keep trying …"

After a week had passed since her admittance to the hospital, Colleen's mom and sister flew in to see her. Cindy didn't stop by her room that afternoon to give the family time to visit, but the family came upstairs to see Cindy. The staff had told them Cindy had been stopping by regularly, and they were hoping Cindy could shed some light on Colleen's condition.

"She's … I know she's bad," Cindy began. She wasn't going to tell them that Colleen didn't think she could make it.

"But she's only burned 30 percent," her sister contested. "You were 70 percent, and you're doing good."

"She's 30 percent," Cindy interjected, "but it's all from here up." She gestured toward her chest and face. "Her chest. Her whole face. Her identity—everything." She shook her head. "You've just got to be there for her and let her know you'll be there to support her."

"She's not doing good. It doesn't look like she wants to live. She had better live!" exclaimed her sister.

The next day, Cindy went down to visit Colleen, and compared to their last visit, Colleen had worsened. She wasn't very responsive, and she didn't acknowledge Cindy or squeeze her hand. Cindy held her hand and spoke to her softly. "Colleen, you have to be true to yourself. You have to do whatever is best for you." She paused. "I will keep praying for you."

Colleen died two days later.

Before Colleen's family left the hospital for the last time, they came upstairs to say goodbye to Cindy. Cindy walked slowly to the floor lounge to see them.

"Cindy, we just wanted to thank you for everything you tried to do. We know you tried to help her," said her mom. "We just can't believe this happened."

Her sister seemed angry. "She could have lived. If she had wanted to, she could have gotten through this. She could have lived."

Cindy spoke softly. "But if she had lived, she would have been disfigured her whole life. Could she have gotten her face back again? I don't know, but she never would have been the same as she was before. Her life as she knew it was gone."

Still, Colleen's family walked away frustrated at Colleen for giving up, and it made Cindy's heart ache. They would never understand how difficult it was to endure anguish and suffering as a burn victim. How hard it was. And all the pain. How difficult it is going through it all. It takes strong support from the family and something to drive you, whether it's a husband or kids or whatever. She would never wish this upon another person.

Cindy felt grateful that she was through the worst of it. But if she had to go through it all again, she wouldn't. If she were ever in a fire again, she knew with certainty that she would sit down and allow herself to burn to death. She didn't blame Colleen one bit for letting go, and it was her decision to make. People shouldn't be angry if their person doesn't live. For some, death is a blessing.

CHAPTER 51:
THE DANCE
August 30, 1982

After Cindy made it her goal to be discharged by Labor Day, she got out of bed every day and slowly walked up and down the corridor while gently holding onto the arm of a nurse's aide. At first it was ten steps, then twenty. Now she was up to forty. She also practiced standing up out of her rocking chair, which was another part of the discharge agreement.

The day finally came when Cindy was ready. She called Dr. Hoefflin into her room. She rocked the rocking chair to gain momentum and then stood up.

"Okay," she smiled. "Let's dance."

Cindy took his arm like a formal escort, and they walked together out into the hallway, where the nurses gathered to watch in anticipation. *Oh, he's tall!* Cindy thought to herself, realizing for the first time that Dr. Hoefflin was probably six foot one.

With his right hand lightly around her waist and his left hand in hers, they slowly sashayed in a circle. Cindy smiled at Dr. Hoefflin as they danced slowly from side to side to imaginary music. She admired his brown hair, his long mustache, and his big smile. She couldn't tell what color his eyes were behind his glasses. She had always appreciated his soft, gentle voice.

The nurses cheered her on as they whooped and whistled, calling out, "Yeah, Cindy!"

Cathy stood clapping with a huge smile on her face. Marilyn, the blonde nurse's aide, was awestruck.

"Okay," said Dr. Hoefflin. "I guess you're ready to go home!"

Cindy's heart swelled. She felt excited—she couldn't wait to get back out into the world! But she also felt scared that no one would be looking after her any longer, which meant she would have to monitor herself.

"I'll start working on the discharge papers," he told her. "If all goes according to plan, you'll be discharged Friday, September 3, so you'll be home for Labor Day."

Cindy couldn't believe it. Labor Day weekend was only a week away. It had been fifteen long weeks since the fire.

Cindy went into her room and looked at the pillowcase calendar on her wall. The nurses had been marking each passing day with a big *X* and had written *Homeward Bound* on the bottom before pinning it back up. Now Cindy circled Friday, September 3, on the pillowcase. It could not come soon enough.

CHAPTER 52:
DISCHARGE
September 2, 1982

Cindy could not believe her discharge day had finally come. After spending the last seventeen weeks and three days of her life in the hospital, she was finally allowed to leave. After twenty-one surgeries and countless procedures, her body had recovered enough from the burns that she was being discharged to her parents' care and daily outpatient appointments.

Cindy reflected on her journey these last four months and everything she had endured. She did not look like the same person from four months ago; her body was scarred like a patchwork quilt. Nor *was* she the same person. She had summoned strength that she didn't know she had to survive. She had found clarity about her life's goals and purpose. Her family circle had been there to support her like never before, and their love had helped her survive.

And she knew without a doubt that she wanted a divorce. If this experience had taught her nothing else, it was that no day was ever guaranteed, and she refused to spend any of them in an unhappy relationship. From now on, her life would focus on healing, her children, and joy.

Dr. Goldberg sat down and faced Cindy, looking her straight in the eye. "Cindy, when you were first admitted, 70 percent of your body was burned, and three-fourths of that was third-degree burns. You were admitted with a slim chance of survival. In fact, your mortality rate was –30 percent. You stopped breathing and left us once, and we brought you back, and you've been on the cusp of dying several times. It was touch-and-go for weeks.

Your survival required transfusions of eighty-one pints of blood, not to mention the two dozen surgeries you've endured so far."

"Oh my God," Cindy said, feeling humbled at her own predicament. She hadn't been able to realize the full context of the situation until now. She was moved by Dr. Goldberg's honesty and vulnerability. He had actually been scared. Cindy knew with certainty that God had intervened.

"At one time, your lab values were ..." Dr. Goldberg shook his head as he looked for the words. "I slept here for three nights because your lab values were that of a nonexistent person. There was no reason you should have been living. Your blood labs were way off. Your sodium, potassium ... everything was off. You should not have been able to survive. And yet you were still breathing."

He took a deep breath. "For three nights, I slept here and waited because I was certain you were going to code and that you were going to die ... and then a week later, you did. You went into respiratory arrest. Shortly after that, you just got better. Like the snap of a finger. And then I was able to go home. But until I knew you were going to live, I didn't want to leave."

Cindy's eyes welled up with tears. She blinked as they slowly rolled down her cheeks.

"You know, even though I am Jewish, I don't know how I feel about God," Dr. Goldberg admitted. "But after seeing you go through this, I believe now. Because it wasn't us that kept you alive. It was *not* us."

Cindy felt a sense of surrealness as tears flooded her cheeks. She was so grateful to the medical team who had helped her tirelessly and never gave up on her. She could never convey how much she appreciated the doctors and nurses who were by her side twenty-four hours a day, seven days a week. And she was so very thankful to her family for always being there for her and for taking care of Michael and Jeremiah for her.

She knew the fire had affected not only her life but her family's lives.

Her family had put their lives on hold to tend to her needs. She was grateful, too, to Ken for respecting her wishes, staying away and only coming down to visit the boys, giving her the physical and emotional space she so desperately needed.

In the first few days after she had been admitted, the hospital staff had told her family that their support would make a significant difference in Cindy's recovery, and they made sure they were there as often as possible. Many burn patients die because they do not have emotional support and have no one there to boost their will to live. It can be hard, too, for family members to watch a loved one endure pain as a burn victim. Cindy couldn't imagine what her parents went through watching their child go through that—to watch their child suffer. She knew it must have taken a toll.

Other statistics are not good for a burn patient going through recovery; the process often leads to divorce because of the emotional strain on the spouse and the strain on their marriage. Burn patients often change, too, because of their experience, and after recovery, they make life-altering decisions about the direction of their lives that may or may not include their spouse. Or the burn patient may look different or seem different to their spouse after recovery, causing the couple to grow apart.

Then there was the psychology of it all. Burn patients suffer from anger, resentment, anxiety, low self-esteem, depression, post-traumatic stress disorder, and more. Emotions ebb and flow like the tides. Cindy glanced over at the counseling brochure sitting on top of her bag.

She knew that she was alive in part because of her family and their devotion. They made sure they were there for her as often as possible. They gave her something to look forward to and motivated her to recover with their encouragement. She owed them her life.

CHAPTER 53:
FAREWELL
September 3, 1982

Cindy was discharged on Friday of Labor Day weekend, just in time to be home for her Labor Day barbecue. Before she left, Cindy insisted on going down to the operating room and recovery room to see the nurses. The staff got permission for her to enter, which is normally forbidden to non-staff, and she was wheeled down to the OR in a wheelchair.

Cindy was wearing a new white shift dress with a floral pattern of little pink and blue flowers. Even though Cindy couldn't yet reach her arms to the top of her head, the nurses had helped her put her short hair in a bun and placed a headband on her head. She wore pink lip gloss for the first time since the fire. She felt decorative.

When Cindy got to the room, the attendant put on the wheelchair brakes, and Cindy slowly pushed herself up to a standing position and gingerly walked step by step toward the counter.

Dr. Hoefflin knew Cindy was coming down and greeted her enthusiastically. He looked around at the attending staff.

"Do you guys remember who this is? Do you know who this is?" He held out his hands to Cindy and shook his arms in the air, as if he were exalting her.

One of the nurses looked confused but was clearly curious. "Who is this?"

"This is Cindy Ames!" Dr. Hoefflin exclaimed.

The air in the room got sucked in before exhalations filled the void. "Oh my gosh! Cindy! Wow!"

The nurses swarmed around Cindy and rejoiced in her recovery. Dr. Hoefflin then had her walk into one of the surgical suites that had just finished a surgery to show her off to the OR nurses in there. "This is Cindy Ames! Do you remember doing her surgeries?"

The nurses couldn't believe Cindy was the woman who initially had a −30 percent chance of survival.

Cindy remembered them vaguely, faces in surgical masks and surgical hair caps. She recognized some of their eyes or their voices.

Everyone was so joyful and amazed at her recovery. The OR staff often didn't find out if the patients lived or died or get to see them again after they left the OR. The praise filled Cindy's heart, and she simply said, "Thank you, thank you" over and over. There weren't any words for the gratitude she felt in her heart for all they had done for her. Each one of them had played a part in her recovery, and she would forever be thankful.

"I just want to thank you. All of you," she said, feeling tears well in her eyes.

"I can't believe you lived!" they exalted. "I can't believe you're walking!" They were so pleased and happy for her.

Cindy recognized the amazement in their eyes as a mirror of her journey, her victory over death.

The attendant then wheeled Cindy down to the therapy department, where the experience was repeated: joy and praise and Cindy's "thank yous" filling the air. She knew from her own experience that seeing a patient you had worked on or treated post-recovery was one of the best rewards of the job. It was an affirmation that their work had purpose, and for that reason, she wanted to be sure to personally thank as many hospital personnel as she could.

About forty minutes later, they moved on to the next round in the burn ICU.

Cindy had the attendant stop in the hall before the closed doors; this time, she wanted to walk into the room to see the nurses.

"Here I am!" Cindy's smile filled her face, which was beginning to hurt. "I'm finally going home tomorrow!"

The nurses again swarmed around Cindy, looking her up and down. Was this really the same woman who was brought in unrecognizable just four months ago?

"I wanted to thank all of you in person before I leave. I am so grateful for all your hard work. Each of you played a part in my recovery, and I wouldn't be here without you."

The ICU nurses were humbled as misty eyes filled the room.

"I can't believe …" Nurse Cathy started. "You were one of our biggest challenges. And look at you now. Amen!"

As an attendant wheeled Cindy back to her room, her heart felt warm and fuzzy.

That afternoon, the hospital held a farewell party for Cindy in the conference room that lasted two hours. Someone brought in a pink round cake that read, *We'll Miss You! Congrats, Cindy!* There were balloons and signs decorating the room. A steady stream of visitors came by; all of her therapists, the social worker, and even her nutritionist came to say goodbye.

Other patients whom she had befriended, including Jean, came over. Anna even came back to the hospital to give Cindy a goodbye hug, and Cindy recalled attending Anna's own farewell party. Babe, Anna, Sarah, Bob, Danny, Elaine, Cathy, Marilyn, Vaughn, Robbie, Janet, Gladys, Rose—all of those beautiful humans had entered her life at Brotman and were a part of her journey. They had made an imprint on her life forever.

Cindy's parents and her boys were there, too, along with Joy, Gail, and Larry. Even Ken traveled down from Coleville for the party. Everyone took pictures, and Cindy felt renewed wearing a pretty dress instead of a hospital gown.

After the party, Cindy took a moment to look around her hospital room, her home away from home for the last four months. It had been 116 days since the fire. There were at least fifty cards taped to the wall, sent by loving friends and family. Artificial red roses brightened the room; fresh flowers were not allowed in the ICU. The big white teddy bear the boys had given her sat in the corner chair. A boom box and a few audio tapes sat on top of the cabinet. The band Air Supply had gotten her through many afternoons of recovery.

She would not miss the hospital smell, the smell of disinfectant-like sickness in the air. She would not miss the hospital bed. Sleeping in a normal bed, sans the sounds of the hustle and bustle from the hospital corridors, was one of the things she looked forward to the most on a long list of what she missed. Hugging her boys was at the top of her list. Extensive snuggles and cuddles were in store in the evenings—along with her mom's country-fried steak and her famous crepes, all the things that she used to take for granted.

She had endured so much in this hospital. She had done it. She was a survivor. It was exciting that tomorrow, she would be discharged, and she could start to rebuild her life and put the pieces back together. It was also scary knowing that so many things would be different now and that she had so much to learn as part of her recovery. For now, she relished all the joy and love from her farewells. Tomorrow was another day.

The next morning, her mom walked with her to the hospital entrance as her dad went to get the car to pull it around. Even though Cindy wanted to walk her way out of the hospital, hospital policy was to wheel patients out in a wheelchair due to legal liability. Attached to the wheelchair were bags of clothing, the stuffed teddy bear, and the cards that had filled her wall. Cindy held the vase of red roses on her lap.

The nurse pushed her steadily through the large sliding doors into the blinding light outside. Cindy felt like she was breaking out of prison. She had not seen the sun or felt its warmth on her skin for seventeen weeks. It was a beautiful day in September with clear skies—perfect LA weather. A cool breeze washed over Cindy's sensitive skin. She felt reborn.

Once near the curb, Cindy sat in the chair for a moment and took it all in. The brightness hurt her eyes, which were now filled with tears. The world stood still in those breathtaking minutes. She was experiencing a perfect moment. *I'm going home*, she thought. *I can't wait to go home and be with my family. Thank you, Lord!*

CHAPTER 54:
WHITE NOISE

As part of Cindy's discharge from the hospital, it was agreed that she would stay at her parents' house in West Covina. Her mother would drive her to physical therapy three times a week, a forty-minute drive to the hospital. Traffic in LA could be horrendous; if they left too late, it could literally take hours to get home, so they planned her appointments around the commuting schedule.

Cindy's dad volunteered to move out of the master bedroom into the spare room so Cindy could move in. Her parents had a hospital-type bed that was split in the middle, so either side could be moved up or down, and they separated the sides so Cindy could sleep in one and her mother in the other, allowing her to keep an eye on Cindy throughout the night. Cindy would often need help during the night because she could not get out of bed without assistance, and she was scared to sleep alone, scared she might need help and no one would be there. The sleeping arrangements worked for the first couple of months.

On her first night home, as Cindy lay in bed, she realized it had been months since she had slept on a regular mattress. The thick foam and the springs cradled her body, and the soft blankets caressed her skin. She lay in bed, relishing the simple things that she used to take for granted.

Even though the bed was comfortable, Cindy was not. Her body was in pain, and she felt distraught. She lay in the silence and waited for sleep to overcome her, but the house was too quiet.

She realized within minutes that she missed the steady comforts of the buzzers: the heart monitor's *click, click, click,* and the IV alarm signaling it was almost dry and needed to be replaced. When Cindy's breaths had become too shallow, an alarm went off, and the nurses came into her room and instructed her to take deep breaths to get her lungs working to their greatest capacity.

Her air bed had periodically inflated with air and then beeped and went back down. Cindy could also hear alarms and beeping going off in other patients' rooms in the ICU. The dripping and clicking and beeping became a kind of music that soothed Cindy to sleep, noises that reassured her that others were monitoring her and, honestly, that she was still alive.

Now, as she lay in her parents' home, wondering when sleep would come, the deafening silence made her feel scared and insecure, fear preventing her from closing her eyes and allowing sleep to consume her.

CHAPTER 55:
LABOR DAY
September 6, 1982

Labor Day was a beautiful day in LA. The weather was in the low eighties, and it was a perfect day for a barbecue. Even though Cindy's arms were bandaged and she wore a gauze vest to cover her crusty back underneath her shift dress, she felt good. She felt alive. The light breeze felt glorious on her face. It was bluebird conditions: not a cloud in the sky. Cindy felt like she was in paradise.

Her parents had invited friends Zena and Jim to the barbecue along with her cousin Eric and his family. Otherwise, it was a simple family affair, just as Cindy wanted it. Cindy sat on the outside patio with its pretty lattice cover watching Michael and Jeremiah swim in the dough boy pool, splashing in merriment. Listening to their sounds of play made her smile and made her heart swell. She had missed this. Missed *them*.

Cindy's dad was busy in front of the barbecue, the scent of juicy hamburgers wafting through the air and filling her nostrils with delight.

"Who wants cheese?" he surveyed.

Cindy's mouth started watering. In addition to burgers, her dad had also prepared barbecued ribs and would be making hot dogs for the boys.

Cindy could hear her mom bustling about the kitchen while listening to the radio. Casey Kasem was her favorite DJ, and he was currently playing "Abracadabra" by the Steve Miller Band. Reota was putting the finishing touches on her famous German potato salad and baked beans.

Gail was busy making a fruit salad. Cindy's stomach growled. This sure beat hospital food!

Cindy inhaled the sweet scent of freshly mowed grass. "Achoo!" she sneezed in that quiet little way that she always did. "Achoo! Achoo!" She held up her finger to her nose and let out a little giggle. She always sneezed multiple times in a row.

Just then, Larry brought her a strawberry wine cooler, her favorite. The cool, sweet liquid cooled her throat.

"Better than I remember!" Cindy smiled at her brother, the dutiful bartender.

Joy and her fiancé arrived, having stopped by the bakery to finalize their wedding cake order. They beelined to Cindy and gave her hugs. Now that the last guests had arrived, Cindy went to retrieve the seven-layer dip she had made—her specialty—and gingerly carried it from the fridge to the table, focusing on one slow step at a time.

Cindy scooped her chip into the dip and then took a bite. Chasing it with her wine cooler, Cindy noted how she had a new appreciation for the simple things in life.

"Joy, come tell me about the wedding! How is the planning going?"

The sisters walked back out to the patio. Joy held Cindy's arm and carefully helped her walk outside. They sat down at the patio table.

"Who wants a hot dog?" called out her dad.

"Me!" shouted both boys in unison.

Cindy was thankful her dad had closed his business for Labor Day. It meant so much to have everyone in the family together.

Just then, a car pulled up alongside the house, and out piled Zena's daughters—Diana, Karen, and Cheryl—to surprise Cindy. Cheryl, the third Musketeer with Cindy and Nancy, raced to the patio to give her a hug. Cindy was filled with warmth to have her second family there too. Her heart was full.

Cindy felt elated. She couldn't believe that after everything she had been through, all the weeks of crippling pain, the physical therapy sessions, the countless surgeries, here she sat on her parents' patio, surrounded by all her favorite people on a gorgeous day. At this moment, she was ignoring her pain, the Percocet helping to suppress it. She felt blessed and filled with gratitude that, at least for this afternoon, this brief moment, life was good.

CHAPTER 56:
A SECOND SKIN

Cindy was discharged from the hospital after having made several agreements with her doctors. One condition Cindy agreed to was to wear a Jobst body garment every day, seven days a week, twenty-three hours a day, for three years. The garment was only to be removed for bathing.

The Jobst garment was horrible. The medical compression bodysuit was custom-made to fit her body like a glove. No, a glove was too kind. A glove was made of luxurious leather that was buttery and soft to the touch, moving with your body. A Jobst garment ran the length of her body from her toes up to the middle of her neck—a turtleneck that made Cindy feel itchy. The top zipped up the front, and the legs and top Velcroed together around her waist. The garment was crotchless, which allowed her to use the restroom without removing it. The flesh-colored bodysuit became her second skin.

The importance of the garment was to place pressure on her skin so the burn scars healed flat rather than leaving her with bumpy, scarred skin. Its compression therapy interfered with the production of collagen and realigned the collagen fibers. Cindy understood the significance of wearing the compression garment, but because there was consistent pressure on her skin, she was constantly hot, which gave her hot flashes on a daily basis. And since her skin no longer had pores to sweat, her hot flashes felt like spasms.

Along with the bodysuit, Cindy had to wear compression gloves with only her fingertips exposed, which at least allowed her to touch and feel with her own skin. Although both hands had received third-degree burns, only her left hand had skin grafts in a successful attempt to keep her fingers intact, since her bones could initially be seen through the burn tissue. Cindy felt fortunate they had not been amputated and gladly wore the gloves.

Cindy had limitations with her physical movement, and because the bodysuit was so tight, she needed help putting it on. Every morning, her mom met her in the bedroom to assist. Cindy dreaded this time of day. She would sit on the edge of the bed nude, usually with a blanket wrapped around her for warmth, while her mother kneeled over to slip the bodysuit first over her feet and then up her legs. The suit would get tight around her calves, and her mom would have to start yanking it up her leg as Cindy stood to her feet.

Not only was the bodysuit tight and uncomfortable, but the whole experience was mortifying—feeling her body shoved into a sausage casing. Cindy knew she was a large woman, but this experience dramatized it and did nothing to boost her morale. Squeezing her arms into the top was uncomfortable, too, and it was this action that often caused her to have hot flashes.

There were some mornings when Cindy's patience was low, and she threw a little tantrum.

"I'm not going to wear this! I hate wearing it! It's so uncomfortable, and I hate it!" Cindy ranted and kicked her feet in distress.

Reota was usually patient and would take a deep breath, allowing Cindy the space she needed to express her frustration. Then, once it was over, Reota would continue yanking up the bodysuit.

This morning, however, after almost a month of the tiresome routine every day since Cindy came home, Reota had had it too.

"That's fine!" she said, picking up the bodysuit and throwing it in the corner. "Then don't do it!"

Reota had had enough. The wall she had created to shield Cindy from her emotions caved. She burst into hot tears of frustration and stormed out of the room.

Cindy rarely saw her mom like that, and in self-reflection, Cindy realized she had been acting childish. Her mom was only trying to help and had been there for her every day for the past five months. All of this—the fire, Cindy in the burn ICU, Cindy nearly dying several times, visiting her every day in the hospital, and now being her primary caregiver—was stressful on her mom. Cindy let out a deep sigh and stared at the loathsome bodysuit curled up in the corner.

About five minutes later, Reota returned to the room.

"I'm sorry," she said with a sigh.

"No, *I'm* sorry. I'm the one acting like a baby, throwing a little fit. I know you're only trying to help. I'm sorry I took it out on you."

"No, you're not a baby. You've been so strong, and you've been through so much. We just need to continue trying and get the garment on you." She paused. "Doctor's orders …"

Cindy smiled with a grateful heart as she sat back down on the bed, took a deep breath, and held out her foot in her mom's direction.

This wasn't the only time her mom expressed stress or felt frazzled from all the pressure. One day, she went to get Cindy's pain reliever—a couple of Percocet—and she entered the dining room with them in her hand. She stood at the table talking to Gail, and after a few minutes nonchalantly picked up a glass of water on the table and swallowed the pills.

"Oh my God!" she exclaimed, immediately realizing what she had done. "I wasn't thinking and thought they were my Excedrin!"

Cindy stared at her wide-eyed and then started laughing. "Well, you better go lay down and relax. You're about to feel really good!"

Everyone laughed at their mom's innocent mistake.

Cindy's relationship with her mom had become closer than they had ever been, and sharing a room and helping with daily tasks like dressing made it even more intimate.

Cindy continued to wear the bodysuit every day for the next three years. Sometimes, she took it off at night if she was feeling uncomfortable, but often, she left it on and slept in it. She knew that she would have a better outcome wearing the Jobst, and after wearing it for such a long time, she began to rely on the comfort of the compression; it made her feel like she was "held together."

While her skin tone and the skin grafts didn't look or feel good, her second skin helped her feel secure in her own skin. Sometimes, too, when she took it off, her body spasmed without the pressure. For all these reasons, Cindy learned to live in the bodysuit, and later, she recognized that her skin did heal flat, especially compared to other burn victims.

Even though both her arms were predominantly skin grafts, people sometimes commented that they couldn't tell she was burned. Only when they looked closely could they see her skin was textured like tight mesh. While she loathed wearing the garment year after year, she came to appreciate its effectiveness for the rest of her life.

CHAPTER 57:
TRANSITION

Cindy had to make other transitions in her daily life in addition to the Jobst suit. She had to learn to work with her body to make it mobile. She wouldn't have thought twice about normal body movement in the past, having done them a million times while taking her body for granted. Now, even watching TV while lying on the couch was an issue.

In order to get up, she rolled off the couch onto the floor and then did a knee pushup to get her body off the floor, which was difficult because her arms were weak. Then, she put her hands on the coffee table to push her upper body vertically. Since her back was not flexible, standing up from the kneeling position was an awkward motion until she was standing upright on her feet.

Cindy was thankful to have an emotional and physical support system. The boys had gotten used to living with her parents for the last four months and accepted them as authoritarians, which continued as Cindy gained her bearings. At times, though, when Cindy and/or her parents scolded the boys, there was conflict between who was in charge.

Eventually, she told her parents, "I have to be the mom again. You need to back off and let me be in charge. I appreciate everything you have done, but I need to be their mom."

Her family nodded in agreement and began to back off as they slowly transitioned to a normal family hierarchy. While Cindy's family relinquished parenting to Cindy, Ken moved back to Truckee to get work and make money. Truckee, however, was not a welcoming community, convinced that Ken had committed the arson. Stares and sneers followed Ken wherever he went.

Ken's previous words while sitting in the waiting room rang in her family's ears: "I could have done it. I learned all about making explosives in the military and could have rigged it up …" Cindy's family members had stared at Ken incredulously. Cindy's brother felt in his bones that Ken did it and, later at home, mumbled something under his breath about getting even.

Cindy's mother, though, had doubts. "I don't think Ken has it in him. He would never harm those sweet boys," she whispered late one night as they sat around the kitchen table while the boys slept. She didn't want to believe that a father could hurt his own children like that.

Cindy was confused. Everything the investigators had told her suggested Ken was a suspect. He was an angry drunk, and they were estranged, but she couldn't allow herself to think about it because it would make her sick in the pit of her stomach, thinking that her husband had tried to burn his wife and child to death.

Cindy blocked it out and focused on her recovery. She had faith that the Truckee Sheriff's Department would investigate and figure it out, even though it had been five months with no arrests.

CHAPTER 58:
A NEW BODY

After moving in with her parents, one thing became quickly apparent to Cindy: she needed a new wardrobe. During her stay in the hospital, she wore hospital gowns every day and sometimes a robe that her mom had bought her. Now that she was living at home, she needed something other than the Jobst garment.

Everything she had had burned in the fire. Her mom had bought her some cotton robes that she could put on and button up, but she needed clothes to go out in public. Cindy's sisters volunteered to go shopping and bring her home some clothes to try. They knew it was going to take some experimenting to figure out what worked with her new body.

One afternoon, Joy brought home a couple of dresses that would easily slip over Cindy's head, but when Cindy went to put on the blue one, they realized she was unable to lift her arms high enough due to the scars on her back. This was something Cindy was working on in physical therapy; one exercise required her to crawl her fingers up the wall to see how high she could go.

The scars under her arms, on the back of her arms, and across her back were very tight, especially on her back where the grafts didn't take, and it was difficult for her to raise her shoulders. The physical therapy helped to stretch her out and decreased the number of back spasms she had, but she wasn't yet able to raise her arms high enough to put on the dresses.

"Thank you," said Cindy in disappointment, "but this isn't going to work."

They found that she could wear loose T-shirts if she slipped one arm in, then another arm in, and then twisted her head through the hole, but she could not remove the shirt by herself. She needed help. In fact, she would need help dressing indefinitely, whether it was her mom, her sisters, or her boys. Her boys enjoyed helping her tie her shoes, showing off their knot-tying skills.

Cindy's mom continued to help her put on the Jobst garment every morning. The garment was stretchy enough for physical therapy but too difficult for Cindy to reach down and put on herself.

One day, after her sister had bought some pants that didn't work, Cindy sat on the edge of her bed in low spirits. Through all this, while she tried to remain strong and be positive, occasional waves of anger or depression swept over her. This particular wave was despair.

Cindy knew with absolute certainty that her body was never going to be the same. *She* was never going to be the same. She was never going to be able to dress how she used to because of the scars. Plus, she would always have the scars, and she would forever be self-conscious about them. They weren't really a physical deformity, but she knew strangers would likely gawk.

Cindy could never see herself wearing something sleeveless again, perhaps not even short sleeves. *How could I ever get in a bathing suit again?* she wondered. *Does this mean I'll never go swimming in the lake again?*

She missed wearing her favorite seventies "hippie dresses," which were long and flowy, but now she wouldn't be able to get them over her head. Even if her body could have worn them again, they had burned in the fire, and she wasn't even sure where she could find something similiar. The immensity of the cause and effect of the fire overwhelmed her as the ripples kept expanding.

As Cindy learned to dress her new body, she had to make compromises. She used to love scoop-neck tops that gave her a lot of breathing room, but now she was too self-conscious because they exposed her Jobst garment.

Sometimes, she got stuck in a shirt that she could not get out of and had to wear it until someone was home to help.

When she did find a garment that worked for her, she often bought a couple in assorted colors. Cindy ended up wearing a lot of big, baggy clothes that she was able to get in and out of, but in the end, they did nothing to boost her self-confidence because she didn't find them flattering.

After many failed attempts, Cindy's sisters finally convinced her to go shopping with them. One afternoon, they took her to the May Co. department store where Joy worked. This was Cindy's first outing in public since the fire, and she was nervous. She knew people were gawking at her burns and staring at her bodysuit as they walked through the store toward the women's section, but she averted her eyes and kept her head down to avoid eye contact.

Being in public made her feel vulnerable and uncomfortable, like she was naked and exposed. Joy and Gail helped Cindy pick out some clothes options and quickly whisked her into a dressing room, away from prying eyes. She chose a couple of long dresses in different colors with long sleeves that covered her arms, but she didn't want to shop more. She couldn't wait to get home.

Adjusting to strangers' reactions to her scars or her bodysuit took some getting used to, but eventually, Cindy became more comfortable in her new skin and accustomed to strangers' reactions. Cindy actually preferred that people were up-front and simply asked her about them so that she could explain, rather than just staring at her, which made her self-conscious and uncomfortable.

Unlike adults, kids were straightforward. One day in the grocery store, a young girl saw Cindy's bodysuit and asked, "Mommy, why is she wearing that?"

The mother responded, "Shhh, it's not polite to point or stare."

Cindy quickly responded with a sincere smile. "Do you want to know?

It's okay, I can tell you." With her parent's nod of approval, Cindy said, "I was in a fire, and the doctors made me better, but I have to wear this to help my skin heal faster."

Cindy could easily explain this to children, but the problem with adults is that they would typically stare rather than ask. Cindy wished they would comment to invite conversation, like "Oh, were you in an accident?" or "Did something happen to you?" Initiating a conversation took the mystery out of the situation and made her feel less like an exhibit at a freak show.

Another area in which Cindy became self-conscious was her face. While most people commented that they couldn't even tell her face was burned, whenever she drank alcohol, she noticed that her face turned bright red, and the white outlines of her burns became clearly visible. Like a coffee cup with a design that changes with heat, the pattern of Cindy's burns was visible on her face when she was flushed.

In addition to getting dressed and getting gawked at, another issue this new body presented was continual pain and discomfort. Because of her scars, her skin occasionally hurt, often with spasms or hot flashes. Because she no longer had sweat glands in her skin, she suffered from hot flashes as her body attempted to cool down. This often resulted in her face becoming flushed and bright red, making her self-conscious.

There were a few areas where her sweat glands were not affected, such as her neck and under her chin, so they sweated in overdrive. Anywhere that was grafted, however, no longer had sweat glands, and without that means of cooling down, her body fought to find another way.

In some ways, Cindy was amazed at her body's ability to heal and recover from the fire. The skin grafts in themselves were a miracle. Cindy silently thanked the Swiss doctor who had discovered skin grafts in the late 1800s. She would have lost the fingers on her left hand if it weren't for him!

The scar she disliked the most was on her left arm and on her elbow. She had a *keloid*—irregular fibrous tissue formed over a deep scar—which was thick and raised. Per Dr. Hoefflin's recommendations, she rubbed the keloid regularly to help break down the tissue, and the therapists rubbed it during physical therapy, but it hurt when they did.

Pain, however, was a part of her new normal. She learned that in order to get better, she had to hurt herself. If she didn't hurt herself, she wouldn't get flat scars. If she didn't hurt during her stretches, then her physical movements weren't going to get better.

For example, she had to stretch her arm and try pulling it over her head. For most people, that stretch might feel good, but for Cindy, it felt like a rope was being pulled all the way from her hip up her side, and it was painful.

And then there were the IV cut-downs, which had left a series of scars all over her body, especially her neck, scalp, legs, and ankles. Cindy could still see them and feel them on her skin as a reminder of all she had been through. While all these scars brought down her self-esteem, she knew that when it came to survival, there was no room for pride.

As if all this wasn't enough, Cindy also had poor circulation, mostly in her legs, a lot of it because of the fire and damaged skin. The poor circulation led to swelling in her legs and feet, and she always had to be mindful of circulation, much like a diabetic patient. She would have to have vein surgeries in the future, but it wasn't a high priority right now.

Her heart, however, was always a top priority, and her whole cardiac system was compromised. She would need to take medication, in fact, medication*s,* for the rest of her life.

And then there was her hair. She would forever miss the long strawberry hair she had loved throughout her teenage years and adulthood. The unusual hue had brought out her blue eyes. After the fire had singed off her hair, it had grown back a brownish gray. Her doctors explained that it was because her body had no nutrients.

Slowly, as Cindy started eating regular food again, her hair started turning a lighter brown, much like her sisters'. Her hair also grew out in tight little curls like she had gotten a perm. While she was okay with it being a curly brown, it was yet again a new part of her identity.

Cindy sat on the edge of the bed, stared at the new blue dress next to her that she could not put on, and sighed. This was all a lot to process, and she felt a wave of despair sweep over her. Cindy lay down on her bed and closed her eyes. Later, she had to go to her physical therapy appointment, but right now, it was a good time for a nap.

CHAPTER 59:
WEDDING DAY
October 8, 1982

Today was the wedding day—the date that motivated Cindy to get out of bed, take baby steps, and walk down the hospital aisle again and again. It was the date that had prompted the countdown on her calendar in her hospital room, marking a blue X as each day went by. She had promised her sister Joy that she would be her matron of honor and walk down the aisle at her wedding. It was a promise Cindy had made to Joy and herself, and finally, the day had arrived.

Cindy looked down at her bridesmaid's dress, a pretty burgundy satin with an empire waist, princess neckline, and long lace sleeves that both covered her Jobst compression suit and matched the bride's sleeves and neckline. There were six bridesmaids and groomsmen in the wedding party, and they all matched with style.

Large floral bouquets of lilies, carnations, and roses guarded the entrance to the nave, and their scent wafted through the air. The musical notes from the church organ playing the "Wedding March" filled Cindy's ears, and she knew it was her turn in the procession.

Cindy quickly turned and smiled at Joy, standing next to their father and looking beautiful in her white wedding gown. Then, Cindy stepped onto the aisle of Sacred Heart Church, peering down toward the altar, past the two hundred guests. Four hundred eyes were looking in her direction, all understanding how significant this moment was.

She had never been more nervous. *I wasn't this nervous at my own wedding*, Cindy thought. She took a deep breath and stepped forward, placing her foot carefully on the ground while balancing her weight from one foot to the next.

Gripping her flower bouquet, she looked ahead at her sister Gail, Joy's maid of honor, who had preceded Cindy down the aisle. Gail locked eyes with Cindy, giving her a smile and a nod of encouragement. Cindy took another careful step. She didn't want to fall, so she didn't want to rush. She had been practicing walking up and down the hospital aisle slowly for weeks and also at home, and she knew she could do it, one baby step at a time.

Two steps later, Cindy found her mom at the end of the front pew, looking at Cindy with tears in her eyes, a mixture of heartache and joy. Cindy smiled, fighting her own tears. She felt nervous, but her heart was filled with love: love for her parents, love for her brother Larry and her sister Gail, love for her sister Joy and her brother-in-law-to-be.

Cindy looked down the aisle and could see Michael and Jeremiah next to her mom, both looking at her with smiles on their adorable faces, and she felt her heart swell. This moment had been worth living for, worth fighting for. She took a deep breath and took another step.

Near the altar, she could see the chair they had waiting for her, so she could sit down once she got to the front. She knew she would not be able to stand through the long Catholic mass, and she was thankful for the accommodation. Cindy stepped forward again in her black ballet flats and took two more steps. She was nearly there.

As Cindy passed her mom, their eyes locked, and Cindy couldn't hold it in any longer. Her eyes brimmed with tears, and then large tears of joy rolled down her cheeks. Cindy glanced over at the groom and offered a smile before stepping next to Gail in front of the chair, her spot in the wedding party lineup.

She had done it! A feeling of triumph and satisfaction swept through her. All those hours of physical therapy and practice walking had prepared her for this moment, this day of love and celebration. Cindy turned around and faced the back as the bride stepped into the archway.

The organist started playing Wagner's "Bridal Chorus," and the wedding attendants all stood up. Cindy wanted to sit down but waited until Joy reached the altar and their father gave her away, lifting her veil to kiss her on the cheek. Cindy's family meant everything to her, and she wouldn't have wanted to miss this moment for anything.

CHAPTER 60:
DAILY DOSE

At home, Cindy continued to take a cocktail of medications daily to help manage her pain. The longer she took the medication, however, the less it seemed to work, so Cindy started taking more. Even when the increased dosage started having a lower effect, she continued to take the pills, needing refills earlier than recommended.

During her weekly checkup, Cindy's doctor looked at her prescription history and said, "I think we need to cut down on these pills. I see you're taking quite a lot, which suggests they're not working as well as they used to."

"Okay," Cindy nodded, knowing she was becoming immune to their effects. "Don't give them to me."

"No, we can decrease gradually," he assured her.

"No," she said, shaking her head vigorously. "If you don't think I need them, don't give them to me."

Cindy still had some at home that she could take to wean her off her dependency, but she didn't put in a request for a prescription refill. She essentially went off the meds cold turkey.

She was on other nonaddictive meds that helped sometimes too: Benadryl for all the itching, which made her sleepy; muscle relaxers for the muscle contractures she was having constantly; and Neurontin for the hand spasms and nerve problems, among many other vitamins and herbs to help build up her dangerously depleted immune system.

It didn't take long, however, for the pain to overcome her desire to be free of the pills. So Cindy started turning to alcohol as another way to numb the pain. Sometimes, she'd sip peppermint schnapps or Kahlua and cream. Sometimes, she'd have a glass or two of wine to relax and numb the pain. The libations varied, but Cindy's intake had slowly increased in the last month, and she was taking daily doses.

Usually, she could get through the mornings, but as the day progressed and the pain became less tolerable, she found an excuse to have a cocktail. Her brother Larry loved to drink, so when he got home from work, they had a couple of refreshments together. Her sister Joy was a wine girl, and she'd happily have a couple of glasses of white Zinfandel with Cindy. Cindy easily drank four or five cocktails in the evening. This went on for a couple of months.

One night, the entire family decided to have a Hot Apple Pie drink with Tuaca. Cindy had introduced them to it when they had come up to Truckee a couple of winters earlier. It was a great hot drink, and they all loved it.

As she was drinking her second one, Cindy's face suddenly became beet red, and her whole body began radiating heat. She sometimes had hot flashes due to the scars, but this was extreme.

Her mother became really worried and begged to take her to the emergency room. Although Cindy didn't want to go, she started to get nervous. She hadn't had a reaction like that before. She immediately stripped off the bodysuit to try to cool down. Then she began to drink cold water.

As she stood stark naked in the bedroom, Cindy looked back at her patterns and realized she had just traded pills for alcohol. *This isn't okay. I need to stop.* That experience was enough for her to realize she was drinking too much and that it could become dangerous for her.

With her stomach in knots, Cindy realized she had traded one substance for another, and if she kept on this trajectory, she could see herself easily becoming addicted to alcohol. After everything she had endured with Ken's drinking, her love for the boys and her self-respect would not allow her to continue down that road. Cindy made a conscious decision to stop drinking daily. She would find a way to get through this without substance assistance.

Only a couple of days before, Cindy's friend Rich had mailed Cindy a care package from Truckee, including audio tape recordings of Pastor Brian's sermons at Calvary Chapel and a book titled *Where Is God When It Hurts?* Rich had thought Cindy might appreciate the pastor's recent sermons of encouragement. One conveyed the message, "God is there for you, and you can lean on Him."

Both gifts felt like they were speaking directly to Cindy. It was exactly what she needed to hear at this moment in time. As she considered her dependency on pharmaceuticals and then alcohol, she knew she needed to lean on God to help her break away. These sermons were so meaningful that Cindy hung on to them for years.

A couple of days later, as Cindy felt pain washing through her body and found herself looking for something, anything, to help squelch it, she started praying and had an epiphany: *I'm going to feel pain. I'm going to have pain for the rest of my life, and I just need to learn how to deal with it.* And from that day forward, she learned to live with the pain.

CHAPTER 61:
CRASHING THE PARTY

It was late fall, and Cindy couldn't wait to return home to Truckee and see some of her old friends after being in LA for six months. This was her first return to Truckee since the fire, and she wasn't eager to make a grand entrance. Instead, she was sneaking back, but not without telling a few friends about her arrival.

Her friend Linda, a nurse's aide at the hospital, had been taking care of Cindy's car, the '82 Subaru she had bought just days before the fire. Cindy loved her new car, and she was thankful it had not been affected by the fire. Linda drove it to Reno to pick up Cindy and her boys from the airport after offering to let them stay at her house and to drive them around during their visit. As they drove through Truckee, Cindy admired the crisp white snow from a recent storm.

Cindy had called her friend from the hospital, Joanne, the day before she left, and Joanne couldn't wait to see her. "Oh, my gosh, Cindy! I'm so excited to see you! You have to join us for the hospital party tomorrow night. It's for the fifteen-year employees, and there will be a dinner. It's on the top floor of OB's. Meet me there!"

Cindy felt awkward crashing the party, but she knew she would be welcomed. She was looking forward to the chance to visit and reconnect with everyone.

That night, as she walked through the doorway into OB's restaurant, her eyes went straight past the tables and the antique décor to the back where the stairs loomed menacingly. After Cindy approached the stairwell, she lifted each leg one step at a time while holding on to the banister, only stopping once to catch her breath. The mountain air was thinner in Truckee, and she was feeling it. Linda stood behind her each step of the way, making sure she didn't fall.

Once she reached the top floor, she stood for a moment and scanned the room, looking for Joanne.

"Cindy!" Joanne came right over to join her. "Is it okay to hug you?"

"Of course!" Cindy replied as she felt Joanne's arms around her.

"Come sit over at my table. They're going to get started on the longevity awards soon."

Cindy and Linda followed Joanne to a table and sat down while Joanne went to get them a drink. Cindy's old neighbor Dee and her husband John spotted her and waved.

After the awards ceremony was over, a few people lingered to talk to Cindy, including Dee and John. Dee was a nurse at the hospital who lived down the street with her husband, John, and their four kids.

"Cindy, it's so good to see you! We were so happy to hear about your recovery. We're still in shock about the fire. We drive by your old place every day, which is just a pile of ash and rubble. Are you guys going to rebuild? The boys really miss Michael and Jeremiah, especially Peter and Danny. They miss running around the neighborhood with them! The boys will have to come over and spend the night!"

Cindy nodded. "The boys miss them too. Call me tomorrow, and we can plan it. We're hoping to move back next year sometime. We might rebuild the house, but it took Ken years to build it last time. Plus, Ken and I just filed for divorce, and so I'm not sure yet what we're going to do."

Cindy faltered, feeling a little overwhelmed by the immensity of it all. Today, her goal had been simply to get up the stairs.

"We heard it was arson! Did they ever find out who started the fire?" Dee inquired. "Have they found out anything? Do they have any clues? What would you do if you found them?"

Cindy felt her resentment rising as she thought about all she had lost—her house, her belongings, her health—and how there was someone out there responsible for it all.

"I don't know," she said. "What would *I* do? Personally, I couldn't do anything, but I would want them to serve the maximum time they could get because they put me through hell, and they tried to kill my son and me!"

Dee looked over at John, perhaps embarrassed by Cindy's anger, before looking back at her. "Well, it was good talking to you, Cindy. I hope they catch 'em, and we hope to see you and the boys again soon."

Cindy looked over and caught Joanne watching the interaction between her and Dee, as if she felt protective over Cindy, and it made her smile.

Cindy sat at the table for most of the night and felt tired by the end. It was emotionally draining being there just as much as it was physically. *One day at a time*, Cindy thought. *God, please give me strength to get through this one day at a time …*

CHAPTER 62:
WELCOME RECEPTION

The Tahoe Forest Hospital had always been Cindy's second home—a place where the staff was like family and where she felt a sense of purpose. However, the last time she was there had been trauma-filled, and Cindy felt a need to walk through the ER doors that she had been rolled out of six months earlier.

The day after the hospital party at OB's, Cindy did just that. She didn't let anyone know she was coming. She had Linda pull up to the ER doors, where Cindy got out of the car, took a deep breath, and took one gingerly step in front of the other all the way through the wide automatic doors. A big gush of air washed over her face, and Cindy reveled in the familiar sounds and smells. *Home.*

The ER nurses immediately swarmed around her.

"Oh, amen!"

"We've missed you, Cindy!"

"You look great!"

"Are you coming back?"

Cindy welcomed their questions with gratitude—gratitude that she was here in this moment, feeling their genuine compassion and concern.

Amid the hustle and bustle, Cindy spotted Steve's sandy blonde hair in the corridor. He was the doctor she was supposed to travel to San Francisco with before the fire. Cindy excused herself and walked after him, trying to catch up in the hallway with her little baby steps.

"Steve!" she called out, and he turned. His eyes widened when he saw Cindy, and a warm smile spread across his face.

"Cindy Ames!" he greeted her, walking back over to her. The nurses quickly dispersed to give them some privacy. Several knew the two of them had had some chemistry in the past, although it'd never had a chance to amount to anything.

"Oh Cindy, I am so sorry for everything that happened to you. When I heard that day that you were in the ER ... that you had been in a fire ... of course, right before our weekend too. I was devastated," he confessed. "I cried over you. My heart was broken ... We didn't know if you were going to make it."

He took a deep breath. "I'm sorry I never got a chance to visit you in LA."

Cindy's eyes welled up at his heartfelt honesty, and warm tears flowed down her cheeks. She looked into his eyes and saw he was crying too.

"Can I give you a hug?" he asked, and Cindy nodded, slipping her arms around him, feeling his warm arms and six-foot-two frame wrap around her. They stood in the hallway hugging, bodies pressed together, tears on their faces for several minutes, or hours. Time stood still. She breathed him in.

"I'm so glad you're here," he said as they pulled apart.

Cindy smiled. She knew someone like Steve would not stay single for long. He was a handsome doctor, and she was, well, a burn victim now. Even if he were still interested, she wasn't in a place in her life to date anyone. She couldn't fathom trying to add that layer to her life.

"Your friendship means a lot," she said genuinely. There was a pause.

"Some of the hospital staff are throwing a welcome reception for me tonight at Hilltop. Can you come?"

Steve shook his head no. "I wish I could, but I'm on staff tonight."

Cindy understood. As they parted ways, Cindy felt the dream of what-could-have-been slip away, and she returned to her nurse friends, who eyed her knowingly.

Cindy next went upstairs to visit the medical surgery ward and then the OBGYN ward. Word spread quickly that Cindy was back in town, and her hospital friends got busy planning the informal welcome-back get-together so her coworkers and friends could visit with her. Truckee was a small town where everybody knew everybody, and Cindy was the Town Miracle.

Not only was she a beloved nurse in the medical community at Tahoe Forest Hospital, but her house fire had made her infamous with the Truckee fire department and police department too. Everybody knew what had happened and that it was a wonder she was still alive, and they wanted the chance to see the Miracle for themselves.

Cindy and Linda dropped the boys off at Dee and John's house for a slumber party, and the boys were excited to see their friends after six months apart. Then, the women drove to the Hilltop Restaurant, which overlooked the historic Truckee strip, the train station, and the Truckee River. There were dozens of staff members standing around waiting for her arrival, some still in their scrubs.

Cindy stood in the doorway and surveyed the room as everyone surveyed her. She could tell by the look in their eyes that she looked different from what they remembered six months ago. Her long strawberry blonde hair had been replaced with a mop of short brown curls, and the bodysuit covered her burns. Still, she was the same person in her heart, and she smiled meekly at the crowd, grateful they were there to welcome her.

Cindy fought the urge to turn and leave, feeling self-conscious from the awkwardness in the air. A few people leaned forward like they would step near her but then hesitated, unsure how to approach her or if they could touch her.

Cindy's colleague, Jeannie, broke the ice, walking straight up to Cindy with a big smile and asking, "Can I give you a hug?"

"Yes, please!" Cindy responded, welcoming the intimacy and a break in the tension. Cindy had known Jeannie for a while, since she worked as an office manager for Papa Black, and they occasionally bumped into each other at the hospital or Papa Black's office. While Cindy didn't know her well, they had connected a week before the fire at the Northwoods Clubhouse in Tahoe Donner and had a couple of drinks together, bonding over single parenthood. They had become instant friends and vowed to hang out together. Then the fire happened.

Standing before her, Jeannie flung her arms open wide and hugged her, swaying slightly from side to side. Cindy felt her eyes mist up as she pulled away.

With the ice in the room now broken, everyone quickly followed Jeannie's lead, and Cindy welcomed hugs and encouraged them to touch her arms. "Yes, it's okay! It doesn't hurt!" she assured them.

The small groups rotated through the room one by one until Cindy was left with only a handful. After two hours of mingling, she began feeling tired on her feet.

"What's next?" they asked.

"I want to move back to Truckee!" Cindy exclaimed. Truckee was her home, and there was nowhere else she'd rather be. Being a small town, the people in Truckee were like family to her, and so many of her friends were dear to her heart. Cindy loved her job at the hospital, working with wonderful people and helping patients.

The kids loved it there too and were always outside playing with their friends. In the winter, they loved skiing, sledding, and having snowball fights with neighborhood kids. During the summer, they swam in the lake, went fishing and crawdadding, and rode bikes up and down the street.

Cindy enjoyed hiking with the kids and exploring trails, canyons, and hidden lakes in the Sierra Mountains surrounding Truckee. Going cross-country skiing in Carpenter Valley in Tahoe Donner was a favorite, but most of all, she enjoyed sitting on her deck and listening to the train glide across the mountain on the other side of Donner Lake, its whistle echoing across the water. There had never once been a doubt in her mind that she would return to Truckee when she could.

CHAPTER 63:
OB'S BOARD

The reception began to wind down, and people began leaving to go home, but Cindy felt like she was just getting started. It felt so good to be social, out amongst her friends. It was nine o'clock on a Saturday night, and the night was too young to end. The night owl in her was ready to hoot.

Her friend Jeannie sensed her energy. "Hey Cindy, do you want to head down to OB's Board? A few of us were thinking about heading over there."

Cindy smiled. She knew she always liked Jeannie, both single moms with the night off.

During the short drive to the bar, Cindy noticed it had started to snow, with snowflakes drizzling down from the sky. The glistening lights along the historic strip downtown made it feel like Christmas and painted an idyllic postcard.

OB's Board Pub & Restaurant—simply called OB's—was a lively tavern in the historic part of downtown Truckee off Donner Pass Road. Cindy had fond memories of the local haunt. Not only was it where all the locals went on a Friday night, but most tourist "turkeys" ended up there, too, so it was an interesting mix of people. It was a chilly night with snow falling on the ground, so there would likely be a large fire in the fireplace toward the back.

As they approached the brick building, Cindy heard soft music playing in the background mixed with the chatter of voices, and she felt excited.

She had missed this place. This town. These people. There's nothing like a small town where everyone knows everyone, and OB's was the place to be.

Cindy stepped in the doorway and took a moment to admire the eclectic Western decor: green plants, chandelier-type lamps, barn wood, stained glass, and an array of antiques. Just as Cindy entered, she saw the bartender handing Jeannie three Keoke Coffees, a perfect concoction of coffee, brandy, and Kahlua for a chilly night. Jeannie turned to hand one to Cindy and one to Linda.

"Welcome home! Cheers!" Jeannie toasted, spilling a drop of libation on the floor as their mugs collided.

They quickly walked over and grabbed an available table. Since it was still a little early, the tables weren't all taken yet. A few other people from the reception sat down with them, and Cindy sat back and listened as she caught up on hospital updates and town gossip, enjoying the chatter and music.

A couple of rounds later, Cindy needed to use the restroom. "Jeannie," she said quietly, "would you mind joining me? I might need help with my bodysuit."

"Of course!" Jeannie replied, happy to help her friend.

The two got up and wound their way through the people, since the bar had gotten crowded. The restrooms were located toward the back, near the fireplace and the lively dance floor.

Cindy's spirits were high; she hadn't felt this, well, *free* in a long time.

As she walked past a table of young, good-looking men, one called out to her, "Hey, ladies! Where are you headed? Are you two heading back to the fire?"

Feeling frisky on Keokes, Cindy couldn't resist and responded promptly, "No, I was just *in* one!" She threw her head back and laughed.

The group of men paused and noticed her compression suit, looking first at her arm and then at her face, their minds scrambling to put the pieces together.

"Are you ... are you Cindy Ames?" one of the men asked, making the connection. Her house fire had been infamous after all.

Cindy nodded, feeling confused. The flirtatious vibe in the air had suddenly turned serious. She had no idea that she had become known throughout the town as "the nurse whose house caught on fire." In fact, this was a reputation she would carry throughout her life in Truckee.

"Oh my God, Cindy! Is it really you? We're the firefighters who were on your fire! We put out the flames!"

Cindy looked at them in surprise, and they, in return, stared at her in astonishment. What were the odds?

"We all remember that day so vividly, and we talk about it all the time," the man went on. "We thought for sure you were going to die. It's incredible you survived the fire. That you jumped out the window. And look at you now ..."

Cindy beamed, feeling gratitude toward this group of men who helped on that fateful day.

"Please, sit down with us and tell us how you're doing!" The firefighters grabbed a chair and rearranged theirs to make room for her. It was rare to be able to talk to a burn survivor, let alone from a fire they had worked on.

"Yes, and let us order you another drink!" added another, looking forward to the conversation.

"I'd love to join you, gentlemen," Cindy paused with a twinkle in her eye, "but I'll be right back. I first need to use the Ladies!"

After an evening of libations and engaging conversation, it was time to go home. As the ladies paid their farewells to the firefighters and headed out through the bar, they spotted Dr. Chris Arth, a local pediatrician whom Cindy had worked with and was friends with, and they beelined in his direction. Chris hugged Cindy and asked, "How are you doing? Really?"

Cindy caught him up in medical terms.

"Chris, rub Cindy's hand," Jeannie said enthusiastically.

"What?" Chris asked, confused.

"Rub her hand!" she encouraged again.

Confused, Chris held Cindy's left hand in both of his as if in a gentle hand hug. Cindy flushed, knowing where Jeannie was headed.

"Do you know where that came from?" Jeannie asked, egging him on.

Chris shook his head no but continued to rub her hand gently.

"The skin on her hand came from her pubis!" Jeannie confessed, laughing. "Every time someone rubs her hand, it feels really good!"

Chris looked down at Cindy's skin grafts on her hand, and his face turned bright red. The entire group immediately erupted in laughter, causing others to look over. Cindy laughed so hard she had tears on her face, and her stomach hurt. She couldn't believe Jeannie said that!

From then on, it was a regular inside joke that Jeannie took advantage of whenever possible. Cindy would hold out her hand to an unknowing man, and Jeannie asked if he wanted to kiss her hand or told him that if he rubbed her hand, Cindy would *really* like it. It was always cause for blushing and laughter.

Bidding farewell to Chris, the trio left the boisterous bar. Outside in the cold night, Jeannie and Linda helped Cindy steady herself on the slick sidewalk as they walked to the car. Cindy watched as her warm breath filled the night air like white smoke and smiled. She had missed Truckee—its natural beauty, the friendly people, the small-town vibe. It was so different from Los Angeles County in every way. She couldn't wait to move back, although she'd miss seeing her family every day.

A new snow berm loomed in front of them from the recent snowplow that had come by, preventing them from accessing the parking lot. It was a long way to the next break in the snowbank, so Jeannie had the idea of climbing over it. With the help of her friends, one on each side, Cindy took a large step over the snow berm and immediately realized it was a mistake. Now she was stuck straddling a pile of snow in her crotchless Jobst garment.

Cindy quickly cried out, "Wooo hooo!" and explained her predicament. They all started laughing uncontrollably. Funny quips and female jokes quickly ensued. It felt good to be silly and laugh again. She always used to laugh. On this night, she felt like her old self.

It was a while before they could all settle down and get her other leg over the berm. It was the best feeling for Cindy to be enjoying life again with friends. It was a night she would never forget.

CHAPTER 64:
A DAY IN TRUCKEE

In the spring, the sheriff's office called and wanted to meet with Cindy in Truckee to interview her again about the fire. She had been on the phone many times with them already and answered all their questions, but they wanted to talk to her in person. After her last visit to Truckee, Linda had driven Cindy's car to West Covina, so when Cindy started to drive, it would be there.

When her sister Gail had her Easter break from teaching in the spring, they drove up to Truckee to look for places Cindy might be able to rent and to meet with the sheriff's office. The day after their arrival, Cindy drove to meet the sheriffs in their office. Sheriffs Phil and Ed explained that they were positive the fire had been arson and admitted the only suspect they had was Ken, although they had no evidence.

"Cindy, we have to ask you directly. Do you think Ken could do this? In your opinion, is he capable of this?" Phil inquired.

Cindy paused in reflection before responding. "I know he would go crazy sometimes when he was drinking, but I don't think he would do that, especially since he knew his son was in the house. I left him because he would threaten me with harm, but he never did anything physical to me. But then, the fire did happen before he sobered up and became a Christian ..." She paused. "Honestly, I have no problem asking him. I'm moving back up here in May and will ask him face-to-face."

Now Cindy had to confront him and would know the truth in her gut.

After the interview, she and Gail picked up a copy of the local *Sierra*

Sun newspaper to get some rental options. They then started driving to look at the properties' exteriors, even though the weather was freezing. The heater warmed them well in her new car, and she loved testing its limits, feeling confident with its four-wheel drive.

It was dark after a couple of hours, and they were driving on the slick roads in Glenshire. It had started snowing, and it was beautiful. Large snowflakes glowed in the headlights.

Cindy was driving around, showing Gail possible areas where she could live, when she suddenly hit an icy patch, and the car slid right off into a ditch. While unscathed, they had to dig the car out, and it had been a while since Cindy had had to do that herself—and never with her weakened body.

Due to the storm, the power suddenly went out in the area houses all at once. Now it was freezing and dark, with just the moonlight lighting the glittering snow. Since Gail was from the city and didn't know what to do, Cindy put Gail behind the wheel, got behind the car, and tried her best to push while Gail hit the accelerator.

The car did not budge. Cindy was wet to her knees, and her Jobst garment was not helping her stay warm at all. This experience was yet another reminder that she was not the person she used to be.

Dr. Arth lived less than a mile away, but it was too far for Cindy to walk uphill. She surveyed her options; houses were spread out across big lots. Finally, after getting warm, Cindy walked to a large house on the corner while traipsing through two feet of snow. She knocked on the door several times, but no one answered.

Cindy stood in the doorway and prayed to God. *Please let someone be home. Please. I don't think I can walk to another house, and we can't keep the heater on in the car. We could die of carbon monoxide poisoning.* As a last resort, Cindy tried yelling. "Hello! Is anyone home? I am stuck and need to borrow your phone to call AAA!"

Cindy was pleasantly surprised when a woman came to answer the door. Cindy quickly explained what had happened, as she could tell the woman was a little leery. The homeowner explained that her husband was still at work, and she was at home with her two small children during a blackout, so she had been hesitant to answer. A couple of minutes later, she opened her door wide and let Cindy in to use her phone.

After calling AAA, Cindy thanked the woman, walked back to the car, and waited for the tow truck with Gail. As they sat in the car, Cindy began to think about all the challenges that awaited her after she moved back, in addition to facing Ken.

Truckee was a beautiful place, but living there was a lot of work. The summers were gorgeous, but the winters could be brutal. Truckee frequently registered as the coldest place in the nation. Even getting enough firewood for the winter and having the cords stacked in the right place would be a feat.

Still, Cindy knew Truckee was her home, and the people there were kind. This was where she wanted to be. She didn't know how she would work it all out, but she knew God would provide. And even though she felt cold and frustrated waiting for the tow truck in her disheveled car, she knew she and her sister would laugh about this in the future.

CHAPTER 65:
RETURN TO TRUCKEE

Almost exactly a year after the fire, Cindy was ready to move back to Truckee with Michael and Jeremiah. The boys were excited to return to their old school and reconnect with their friends, especially before school let out for the summer, when it would be harder to see them all. Cindy thought it was especially important for Jeremiah to finish kindergarten in Truckee so that he would know some of his classmates come fall. After the fire, both the boys had received letters from friends and schoolmates, which helped them stay connected with the Truckee community.

Dr. Hoefflin allowed Cindy to move away on three conditions: 1) She continued to wear the Jobst bodysuit every day; 2) She had her physical therapy sessions lined up with someone he could keep in contact with; and 3) She made living arrangements where she would live with an adult or next to an adult who could help her if she needed it.

Nancy, a single mother and a nurse Cindy had worked with in the ER, had suggested Cindy rent the duplex next to her on Donner Pass Road, right across from the lake. The duplex had stairs Cindy would have to go up and down, giving her regular exercise, and it was right next to the road Cindy used to take up to her old house.

Nancy's son Michael was friends with Cindy's Michael, so the kids would have someone to play with. To top it off, Nancy had offered to help Cindy anytime she needed it. It was perfect.

"Doctor, if I rent this duplex, one of my nurse friends will be right next to me. I can pound on the wall if I ever need anything, and she'll be right over!" Cindy explained excitedly. Cindy loved her family, but she was ready to be independent again.

Cindy signed a six-month lease, uncertain what the future held. The location worked out well because Ken was also living in Truckee and renting a room from his friend Mike right down the street, and he would be able to spend time with the boys. Cindy and Ken's divorce had been finalized over the winter, and thankfully, it had been a cordial process.

While Cindy had been focused on her recovery, Ken had been on his own journey. Sometime after the fire, probably because most people in Truckee thought Ken was the arsonist—setting fire to his own family—and treated him with scorn, he had started binge drinking. It was his alcoholism that had forced his and Cindy's separation, but his drinking had since gotten even more out of control. That is, until he turned his life around that winter when he stopped drinking and became a born-again Christian. His friend Mike introduced him to the church, and they became close friends, supporting each other in their recovery and dedication to Christ.

With Ken living right down the street, he could visit the boys, help pick them up from school, or even have them overnight for a day or two. Mike, who had a son too, encouraged Ken to spend time with his own boys and be the father he needed to be. Cindy's move to Truckee was a win for everyone.

CHAPTER 66:
ONE QUESTION

It wasn't long before Cindy found herself alone with Ken, and she knew she had to summon the courage to ask him about the fire. She had promised the sheriffs she would inquire about the arson and gauge whether or not he was guilty. Many of the folks in Truckee had already labeled him guilty, and they were horrible to him: ignoring him, avoiding eye contact, or making rude remarks. It happened everywhere he went.

Cindy had heard rumors that people were calling him cruel and vicious names, names she could not bring herself to say out loud about the father of her children. One nurse in particular, a colleague of Cindy's but not a friend, had been particularly nasty and had spread unfounded lies about Ken around town.

That night, Cindy and Ken had dinner with some old friends in Tahoe Donner, and Ken had given her a ride. Afterward, on their way down the steep Northwoods Boulevard hill toward their homes on the lake, Cindy took a deep breath.

"Ken, I need to ask you something." Cindy paused. Ken glanced sideways in her direction, gripping the steering wheel. "Did you start the fire? The sheriffs know it is arson, and they're trying to figure out who did it, and I just need to ask. I need to know the truth."

"No," Ken replied firmly. "I swear to God I had nothing to do with it. But I understand why you are asking."

Cindy took another deep breath, feeling the apprehension leave her body. "I'm sorry ... I didn't think you did. You knew Jeremiah and I were home that morning, and I know you would never do anything to hurt him. I believe you. I just needed to hear you say it."

Ken exhaled deeply, the weight of the accusation lifting into the mountain air.

Cindy knew in her heart he was speaking the truth. She knew with conviction that he would never deliberately hurt their boys. He might have been a mean drunk, but he was not evil. And now he was clean and sober, a changed man, giving her an honest answer.

The next day, Cindy returned to the sheriffs' office and reported back to Phil and Ed.

"So you don't believe he did it?" Phil asked.

"No, I don't think he did. He understands why he's a suspect, though, and why he still is, but he didn't do it."

"Okay," Phil said. "Then we will just keep looking."

CHAPTER 67:
CLICK, CLICK, CLICK

For years after she was discharged, Cindy's hip hurt when she walked, but she never let that stop her from walking. The bottom of her right foot, too, sometimes lacked sensation or tingled with pinpricks. Even though it hurt, she could still get around.

Cindy hadn't realized how numb her foot had become until one day while walking around her kitchen, she heard a strange sound: *click, click, click.*

Cindy stopped and looked around her. *What was that odd noise?* She took a few more steps only to hear the faint *click, click* again. Cindy looked down.

Is the floor squeaking? Cindy wondered.

She turned around and looked behind her. She then lifted up her foot and, with a gasp, spotted the culprit: a flat silver tack stuck in her foot.

Cindy pulled the tack out with her fingernails, and small drops of blood dripped on the floor. *How did I not feel this? My foot is number than I thought!*

Cindy realized she needed medical help for the numbness and made an appointment with Dr. Jenner, a chiropractor, the next day. She started seeing him regularly, and after a while, the adjustments to her hip and spine relieved some of the numbness.

While better, the numbness was something Cindy would deal with for the rest of her life. She just learned to live with it like all the other physical impacts from the fire. Decades later, she still couldn't reach up like she used to or twist and turn her waist because the scars on her back were too tight. She had to learn how to comb her hair differently because she couldn't reach her arm all the way up. Little physical movements she had taken for granted were now difficult.

Some of the issues were a result of the scars, but some were because of her bone structure too. Simply laying in the hospital bed for so long had had a negative impact. Laying in the same position for four months affected her limbs' mobility; it was almost like rigor mortis had set in while she lay in the hospital bed and made them stiff. She would never be able to bend her arms or legs like she used to. Even though she had hated it, she was grateful the physical therapists had worked with her every day in the hospital because she knew the stiffness could have been much worse than it was.

Despite her physical restrictions and daily pain, she knew her situation could be far graver and chose not to focus on the negative. She was alive, and she was moving. She thanked God every day for that.

Every time she saw the head of a silver tack after that, she'd remember her foot and hear a faint *click, click, click.*

CHAPTER 68:
A SLOW NIGHT
June 13, 1983

In June, after Cindy felt settled in her new home, the sheriff's department called and asked her to come back to the station. Cindy was curious if they had new information but wasn't obsessing over the arson. With no leads, there was nothing to think about, and she was trying to move forward with her life.

Cindy stopped by the office the next day.

"Hi, Cindy, why don't you come into my office and take a seat?" said Phil. Cindy noticed that he closed the door.

"Well, here's the thing," Sheriff Phil started. "Periodically, we get these reports on our juveniles who are in a boys' group home in Grass Valley." Phil waved his hand over a stack of files on his desk. Cindy felt confused about what this had to do with her. She had heard of the group home, a residential treatment center that took in troubled teens and supplied counseling and treatment.

"The reports go to their caseworkers, their appointed probation officers. One night last week, it was a slow night, and one of our parole officers wasn't busy, so he decided to go ahead and go through them. In one of the files was a report about one of the boys who had performed a skit. Now, these skits or plays are based on scenarios that the boys create in which the boys make something up about what you would do or would have done in a particular situation and how you would handle that situation. They're called *psychodramas*."

Phil paused. "What the boys don't know," he continued, "is that what they choose to act out is recorded in their file."

Cindy adjusted herself in her seat, curious as to where this was heading.

"One of the boys acted out a scenario in which he started a fire, and a mother and son had to jump out a third-story window, and they were burned ... And then he asked the group what they would do in response to the situation."

Cindy inhaled sharply. *A boy? A teenage boy?*

"So our caseworker was reading this in the file and immediately made the connection to your case. He recognized right away that this was the Ames fire. This is a Truckee teen talking about starting a fire to a three-story house and a mother and son jumping out of the window and both getting burned. This is not a coincidence."

Cindy's mind raced, thinking, *Who would do that? Why? Why her?*

"Do you happen to know a teenage boy named Jude Fair?"

Cindy's mind raced again, thinking, *That name sounds familiar.*

"What about Dee Fair?"

"Dee? Yes, I've worked with her in the hospital. She just moved. She has four kids, and one of them is named Jude."

"But do you know Jude? Does he know you?"

"Yes." Cindy nodded her head, affirming the connection. "They lived just down the street. Sometimes he would come up to get my boys to play with his younger brothers, who were the same age. Sometimes in the snow, when it was really bad, I would meet him halfway, and he'd get the boys, or I'd bring his brothers up and watch them while the kids played together ..."

"Well," the sheriff continued, "Jude is the one who acted out this scenario, and we believe he's the one who started the fire."

Cindy looked Phil in the eye. Disbelief and shock overcame her body. She could feel her blood pressure rising, and her face turning red and hot, her patchwork quilt on display.

Jude. Her boys were frequently at his house and played with his brothers. They had played with them on countless occasions. He had been inside her house. She knew his family and was friends with his parents. She worked with his mom. Jude? He was just a boy, maybe fourteen or fifteen. Perhaps a troubled young teen, but this? Why?

Cindy imagined Jude walking toward her house, his tousled brown hair just long enough to touch his gray sweatshirt. She had known him since his family moved to Truckee the year before. He wasn't even her height yet, maybe five foot seven.

Cindy felt a range of emotions, first disbelief and then sadness. Her anger would come later. Cindy looked to the officers, her mind racing for answers.

"We're going to investigate this, Cindy," Phil assured her. "We're going to go down to Grass Valley and talk with Jude in person. But we wanted to connect with you first. See what kind of connection there was between the two of you. Meanwhile, no one can know about this. You can't tell anyone."

Cindy understood. She needed time to come to terms with this anyway. Jude, whom she had never shared a harsh word with. Jude, who had been around her boys and in her home on countless occasions. *What would make a young, innocent child do such a thing?*

CHAPTER 69:
MAKING CONNECTIONS

For the next few days, Cindy went on her way and pretended everything was the same. The officers had asked her not to tell anyone about the latest turn in the case, but it was all she could think about. During the next couple of weeks, friends stopped her in Safeway and in her church, Calvary Chapel, and asked if there was anything new about the fire, and she simply shook her head and said, "No," while inside screaming, "*Yes! Yes!*"

She still couldn't believe it was Jude, but she could not come up with any justifiable reason why he would make up such a scenario during his group activity. For the life of her—literally her own life—she could not understand why he would set the house on fire and/or want to murder her and Jeremiah. Did he even know she and Jeremiah were home?

Cindy started to piece together what she knew about Jude and what background the officers had given her about him. Apparently, Jude was a petty thief. He frequently stole women's wallets in Safeway and Longs, and this is what got him arrested. He would steal the women's wallets from their purses, take the cash, and toss them outside. Some wallets had been found in nearby garbage cans.

Apparently, on the day of the fire, the police found a neighbor's wallet in Cindy's driveway, a wallet that her neighbor Susan had reported stolen earlier in the day. After putting the puzzle pieces together, they knew how it had gotten there.

Cindy thought back to the previous spring and remembered there had been several break-ins in their neighborhood. It was a small town, and nobody locked their doors, but people noticed when things went missing. A neighbor had asked her once if she'd had any underwear stolen.

"Underwear?" Cindy asked. "I don't know. I'm not sure I would know, as mine are all just thrown into a drawer."

"Well, a whole stack of mine in my drawer went missing right after I did the laundry," she confessed. "It was so bizarre."

An elderly couple, the Goobels, had their cabin down the street broken into. After they reported it to the police, they told Cindy what happened, and she assured them she would keep an eye on their house for them.

And then, about a week before the fire, Cindy was downstairs, looked out the window, and saw two teenage boys at the next-door neighbors', the Hannas, standing at the door, holding the door handle like they were trying to get in. The homeowners had twin grandsons about that age, and while Cindy had never seen them come up on their own, she figured that was them.

Cindy had opened the door and called out "Hello!" and waved to them. They stopped, awkwardly waved back, and quickly went through the door. Minutes later, after Cindy had grabbed a load of laundry out of the dryer and was heading back upstairs, she saw the boys come outside. She figured they were probably heading to the lake and went on her way.

A couple of days later, Cindy saw the Hannas pull into their driveway and walked over to chat with them as they took groceries out of the car. "Hi! So good to see you!" She welcomed them with a hug. "Were the twins just up here? I thought I saw them at your door ..."

"No! They weren't! But we noticed this morning that someone had been in the house. They didn't take anything, but they moved things around in our front room, and we could tell someone had been inside. We didn't report it, though, since nothing had been stolen."

"Oh, wow!" Cindy relayed what she had seen: two teenagers, one with brown hair, one with dark hair. Now she realized they probably weren't just trying to get in—they were picking the lock.

Now that Cindy thought back, she realized the dark-haired teen was probably Jude.

Oh my God! Cindy was suddenly struck with a hair-raising thought. *Did he try to kill me because he knew I saw him breaking into the Hannas'?* The sheriffs had told her that Jude was put in the Boys Home because he had reached his third offense shortly after the fire occurred. *Maybe he was afraid I would report him for his third offense and that he would go to jail as a result. Maybe he's still afraid I might testify I saw him breaking in?*

For the first time, Cindy felt afraid for her life. Even though her skin could not form goosebumps, she felt her nerves light up. There was someone out there who actually wanted her dead, someone who had tried to kill her on purpose, someone who might still try to kill her.

All this time, she had thought the fire was some kind of accident. Even when they said it was arson, that someone had poured gasoline on her staircase, she still couldn't believe there was an evil out there with malicious intent who wanted her dead. Until now. Now, she had a motive.

Cindy called the sheriff and listened to the phone ring, her stomach tying up in knots. *Someone had literally tried to kill her.* When the secretary transferred her call to Phil, Cindy rambled on about her memory and how she had made the connection. Cindy felt scared, and Phil could hear it in her voice.

"Cindy, we're gonna get this kid. We're building a case around him. It might take a little while, but we *are* going to arrest him. Meanwhile, rest assured knowing that he is still locked up."

That night, Cindy could not get Jude's face out her mind—even after she tucked her boys into bed, even after she read the Bible and said the Lord's prayer, even after the clock struck two a.m.

CHAPTER 70:
ANGELS

After her lease ended at the duplex on Donner Lake, Cindy moved to Tahoe Donner, a nearby housing community, to share a house with her friend Meera. Thanks to Social Security, she received a $600 disability check each month, and it was just enough to get her by. This time, she signed a one-year lease, but all the while, she missed her old house and the breathtaking view of Donner Lake and the train tracks. She was continuing her physical therapy every week and had made progress. Little by little, her life was moving forward.

Since there was now an official suspect in the case, Ken was no longer a suspect and had been cleared. She and Ken weren't sure what to do with their old property. As a contractor, Ken wanted to rebuild the house, and Cindy wanted to live there with the boys if she could.

The night before, Jeannie and her daughter Andrea had come over to watch the new movie *Yentl* that Jeannie had rented on VHS, and afterward, she asked if Cindy had gone by the property yet. Cindy had been back in Truckee for seven months at that point and had even lived in the duplex near the old property, but she still couldn't bring herself to gaze upon the devastation.

"No," Cindy admitted. "I don't know if I want to, but I feel like I have to. I don't know what to expect, and I'm afraid of the memories that might come flooding back."

"Well, you're gonna have to if you're ever going to rebuild," said Jeannie, "and I'd be happy to go with you if you want moral support."

Cindy took a deep breath before agreeing to go on Saturday. That morning after breakfast, Jeannie, who also lived in Tahoe Donner, swung by Cindy's place and picked her up, and they drove down the long, steep hill on Northwoods Boulevard until they arrived in town. Then they headed west toward Donner Lake. After turning on Denton Avenue, they began the winding ascent to the highest part of the hill, where her property waited.

Cindy didn't realize she was holding her breath during the ascent until she let out a deep exhale when she spotted the mound of black, charcoaled timbers where her three-story house had loomed a year and a half ago. She could see the bottom of the house wall where they had jumped, and a few floorboards still slightly intact from the first floor. Jeannie pulled up and turned the car off as they both surveyed the charred carcass of her beloved home.

"Are you all right?" Jeannie asked thoughtfully. "Do you want to get out, or do you want to take a moment and just sit here?"

"No, I want to walk around," said Cindy assuredly, opening the Subaru door. She slowly walked up the steep driveway and then found herself staring at the foundation ruins. Even though she was wearing white Reeboks, Cindy started walking through the charred boards and molten metal. She found herself searching for memories among the ashes.

"Be careful," Jeannie said with concern. "There might be nails and sharp objects that you can't see." Jeannie followed close beside her, holding her arm to help Cindy walk on the uneven ground. This would not be a good place for her to fall.

Cindy approached the pine tree where Candy had been tethered that morning. She was so grateful the dog's barking had woken her up, giving her and Jeremiah time to jump out the window before the flames engulfed the house. *God sent us an angel*, Cindy thought. Candy had suffered mild burns but had recovered quickly while living with Ken. Cindy had gotten her angel back after she moved to Truckee.

At the very top of the property line, she could see the guardrail that separated their lot from Interstate 80. She remembered how two strangers had pulled over on the side of the freeway when they saw the flames from her house shooting through the pine trees and how they had hopped over the guardrail to find her scared and burned but alive, and had volunteered to drive her and Jeremiah straight to the hospital. *Yes*, Cindy thought, *God definitely sent His angels.*

Cindy then walked over to the large granite slab adjacent to the house, which had been built into the foundation and had been her and Jeremiah's landing pad once they dropped out of the window. She remembered not wanting to let go of the windowsill, knowing the granite rock would make a hard fall. *Kind of like the expression "between a rock and a hard place,"* Cindy thought.

She continued to explore the scorched remains. As she walked on the shaky boards, she could see the view of Donner Lake from what would have been her living room. She closed her eyes and tried to remember the happy times there. But at this moment, there was too much sorrow in her heart, and tears started streaming down her cheeks.

When she opened her eyes, she saw Jeannie was crying too. She took hold of Jeannie's outstretched hand and said how much she appreciated Jeannie bringing her there and supporting her through this. She had made amends and was now ready for the insurance company to haul the ruins away. It was time to give the property a fresh start.

CHAPTER 71:
LETTER TO THE EDITOR

It took months for the sheriff's department to gather evidence and build a solid case against Jude. Since this was a juvenile case, all details were kept confidential to protect Jude, a minor. Cindy was not allowed to talk about the case or about the suspect to anyone.

Eventually, after some persuasion, the sheriffs gave Cindy permission to make a statement about the case in a written letter to the local newspaper, *The Sierra Sun*, in which she was allowed to say that there was a suspect and it wasn't Ken. This finally dispelled the ugly rumors and ominous cloud that had followed him everywhere he went, and the small town rallied their support behind Cindy.

Letter to the Editor
April 1984

> Dear Editor,
>
> My name is Cindy Ames. As you and your readers may remember, I was involved in a major house fire at Donner Lake almost two years ago. I was asleep in a third-story room when fire swept through the two lower floors, blocking escape. It was necessary for me to drop my son out the window and jump after him to escape certain death.
>
> I have two important and specific reasons for bringing the matter up. At the time of the fire, a lot of rumors raged … Almost as severe as the fire did. The most

destructive one was that Ken, my former husband, was responsible, directly or indirectly, for the fire. Two years later, these rumors are still wandering around. There is NO truth to them. Ken was not there at the time and not in any way responsible, and the pain caused by these allegations hurt all of us deeply.

The fire was deliberately set ... This is a known and proven fact, agreed upon by all investigation agencies. There is a definite suspect in the case, but because of continuing investigations, Phil Harrison Investigator, from the Nevada County Sheriff's Department, is unable to release any further information at the present time.

Arson is just as possible here as it is in the cities, and I think it's important for the locals to realize that, and be aware this could happen to someone else.

The second reason for this letter is to sincerely thank the community for its continuing support. The love that was shown to me by the cards and letters I received was tremendous. The money donated helped to support the boys while I was in the hospital. It also helped with medical bills, many of which weren't covered by insurance. I also want to thank the Emergency Room staff at Tahoe Forest Hospital for the excellent care I received before being transferred to Brotman Medical Center in Culver City. Because of the severity of my condition, I know their care had a lot to do with my survival. I thank God for all of you. It's great to have such competent Nurses and Doctors.

Ken has placed his trust in the Lord and is now doing well after all he went through, watching his family suffer. He's working and living in the area and trying to forget the nightmare he went through. Michael, 10, is very happy to be back up in Truckee and enjoys school and his old friends again. Jeremiah, 6, is doing well, his broken bones have mended remarkably and loves being back. I am planning to go back to work at the hospital soon. I still have to see my doctors for little things but nothing major. I'm also enjoying the challenge of being co-owner of the Merry-Go-Round, downtown with Jeannie O'Brien.

God bless you all,

Cindy Ames

CHAPTER 72:
A GOOSE CHASE
June 16, 1984

It took exactly one year for the sheriff's department to build a strong enough case against Jude to act on it. Since Jude was serving a three-year term in the boys' home, they weren't worried about him going anywhere and took their time to gather evidence and to do it right.

Meanwhile, Cindy was trying to move forward with her life; she was anxious that the day of his arrest would never come. Despite the letter to the editor, the small town continued to whisper behind Ken's back, and sometimes even make snide remarks to his face. Cindy had confided to her parents that there was a juvenile suspect, and they had told her brother and sisters, but they were down south. Even though it felt good to be able to talk to *somebody* about it, she couldn't tell anyone in Truckee about Jude, including Ken, who knew he was no longer a suspect but didn't know who was. Not for a long time.

Meanwhile, Cindy tried to silence her frustration that the process was dragging on so slowly. That was until the day she finally got the phone call.

"Cindy, we're heading down to Grass Valley to question Jude."

Cindy felt herself rejoice. Finally, some action! These were the words she had been waiting to hear! They were going to interrogate him and see if they could elicit a confession. Cindy could be open with everyone that they had a suspect. And she wanted answers. She had questions that only Jude could answer.

When the sheriffs called the boys' home to let them know that they were on their way to interview Jude Fair for arson with great bodily injury, they received a shocking update.

"Um, Sheriff, I hate to tell you this, but I have unwelcome news. We released Jude this morning, and he is currently being transported to Reno, where he is flying to Florida to meet up with his parents."

Phil slammed the phone down. They had spent the last year building up their case knowing Jude was securely held in the boys' home with almost two years left in his term. Without their knowledge, his release date had been moved up.

Phil and Ed quickly moved into action. In an attempt to stop the transport shuttle and bring Jude in for questioning, Ed reached out to the driver on the CB radio, but within the Sierra Nevada Mountain range, there was poor reception. By the time they got through, the shuttle was already at the airport in Reno, which was in the state of Nevada. The sheriff's office only had power in California.

The sheriffs' hands were tied, and there was nothing they could do. The fact that he was wanted for questioning wasn't even mentioned to Jude as he boarded the plane to Florida. He had no idea how close he had come to being held back.

Cindy's heart deflated. She had thought this was finally going to be over, that somehow confronting Jude was going to give her answers and a sense of closure. And to have him get away so narrowly! Cindy got off the phone with the sheriff and broke down sobbing on the couch. *Was there no justice in the world? How could this happen? How could God let this happen?*

She could feel her vindication flying away on the plane to Florida, and she felt cheated. Hot, angry tears flowed down her cheeks and wet the hem of her Jobst bodysuit.

CHAPTER 73:
NORTHWOODS BOULEVARD

October 1984

Four months later, as Cindy drove down the long, steep hill on Northwoods Boulevard on her way into town from her rental in Tahoe Donner, she noticed the beauty around her: the aspen trees were turning yellow, and the sky was a brilliant blue. Still, she felt a heaviness in her heart that prevented her from appreciating the beautiful mountain landscape. As she drove, she tried to untangle her web of feelings.

Cindy felt the anger bubbling that she harbored inside, an anger that she kept to herself. She didn't want others to see how bitter she sometimes felt or to burden others with her ongoing troubles; she kept her dismal emotions buried inside as her personal secret. At times, she found herself feeling resentful that her life, once so full of joy, had become an ongoing series of difficult challenges.

She knew her heart was hardening, and she was grappling with dark emotions. Cindy prayed: *God, I don't like having this angry heart. I don't like the way I feel. I'm just so mad and resentful inside all the time. Please, oh Lord, help me through this.*

Will I always feel frightened that the person who tried to murder me is out walking around? Angry that he is walking around free? Where is the justice? She poured out all her fears and questions at once. *Will I always feel so alone in my struggles?*

Sometimes it's so hard being back in this environment. It brings back so many memories. I remember what I used to be like and the friendships I used to have, and it's sad to realize so much time has gone by, and people and places are not the same.

I'm different, and I realize that. I have scars—ugly scars. I'm divorced now, and I have a different life as a single mom. I am a different person than before the fire, and I need to remember that too. Yet I feel like the same person stuck in a bad dream—but it wasn't a dream, was it?

Cindy wasn't sure if she would ever feel normal again ... if she *could* ever feel normal again. She felt cheated and angry. She felt alone—no one could ever understand how scarred the whole ordeal had made her, both internally and externally. How hard it was to cope with life every day. Her traumatic experience isolated her from others. Cindy wondered if she could endure this for the rest of her life.

Once she allowed herself to acknowledge her emotions, they all came tumbling out. She thought about the root of her anger. She was angry for finding out that it was arson. Angry at Jude for starting the fire. Angry at God for allowing this to happen to her.

She resented having to learn to walk again and how to dress herself— really everything—all over again. She hated that she couldn't do all the things she used to do, like hiking and climbing rocks; she needed to relearn how to work with her new body and its restrictions. She was bitter about the constant pain she was in. She was sad she had lost the job she loved.

And she was sad that she couldn't be the mom that she wanted to be and that she was meant to be. She had physical restrictions that prevented her from being active with her boys like she wanted. She was angry that this had happened to her even though she had always lived her life helping people and lived a Christian life. She was a good person, a nice person, and that made her struggle with this anger even more difficult.

Dear Lord, I can't do this anymore. I can't feel like this anymore. I can't be so angry on the inside anymore. The weight is dragging me down.

Cindy knew she hid her anger from her friends and family, from the world. Everyone on the outside thought she was so sweet because she always seemed positive, but deep down she was festering inside. Like a slow poison, it was preventing her from truly healing.

Lord, please help me! Help me let go of this anger. Help me overcome these demons. Cindy took deep breaths as she prayed, keeping her eyes focused on the road.

Cindy drove down the long, steep boulevard, dropping in elevation. Near the bottom of the hill, Cindy suddenly felt a release inside, felt the weight lift off her chest. God had heard her plea. She knew she could handle whatever God put in her path.

By the time Cindy got to the bottom of the long windy drive down Northwoods Boulevard and pulled up to the stop sign, she'd felt God lift her anger away, and without it, she was able to look at her life and cope with it in a more rational way, understanding that what had happened to her wasn't personal and what she needed to do to move forward. It was a relief and a revelation.

CHAPTER 74:
RED TAPE

Getting Jude extradited and in court for the trial dragged on for months and then years. The legal system pushed Cindy's patience to the edge. In order to get the indictment, Sheriff Phil Harrison petitioned the local district attorney, Fred Holmes. The case sat there for six months. Some believed there wasn't enough evidence to make a case.

In her frustration, Cindy took the initiative and made some phone calls, and later wrote letters. Cindy spoke with the DA and informed him that she had talked to Nevada County District Attorney Darlington in Nevada City and requested that the case be moved there. Still, no progress was made.

In her frustration, in September of 1985, Cindy made another series of calls, this time threatening to go higher up and write to the attorney general of California. She was frequently told, "This is a juvenile case, and there is little evidence. It's not going to go anywhere…" Yet Cindy was not willing to give up until Jude was brought to court and justice was found.

Near the end of September 1985, Cindy received a subpoena to go before the California grand jury to represent her case the following month. Cindy was nervous to attend court—after all, it was the grand jury. She knew she had to convince them with facts that this case needed to be pursued. A grand jury focuses on preliminary criminal matters only and assesses evidence provided, and if enough is present, an indictment is issued.

Cindy entered the courtroom with her stomach in a ball of nerves. Then she looked over at the jury and saw the familiar face of someone she recognized from Truckee, and she realized these were just regular people who wanted justice in the world like her. Her conviction for justice gave her the courage to sit in court and describe all that she had been through, all that she had survived. As Cindy sat in the stand, she shared her detailed story and answering their questions.

A month later, in November 1985, two and a half years after the fire, the indictment was approved by the grand jury, asking the state of Florida to arrest and hand over Jude, who had been formally charged. Jude was finally arrested in Florida but then was let out on $25,000 bail. In order to get Jude to California, they continued to wait for the governor's extradition.

While waiting, the sheriffs in Truckee learned that the family moved to Louisiana, which started the paper process all over again. Finally, the Louisiana DA approved the extradition, although this entire process took another month.

When Jude's parents, Dee and John, were informed that their minor Jude was going to be extradited, they immediately hired a lawyer who recommended that Jude turn himself in to California authorities before he was arrested. Because he turned himself in the day before the extradition date, on February 28, 1986, Jude was released on his own recognizance, which meant he would not be brought to jail or have to pay bail to be released—he only had to sign a written promise to appear in court as required. Jude was able to walk around unaccountable for his actions and completely free.

Meanwhile, Cindy lived in fear. She had no idea what Jude was thinking. Was Jude angry at her for pressing charges or for some other reason? Would he sneak back to Truckee and finish the job he started? Should she fear for her sons' lives? She felt frustrated at the justice system, but most of all, she felt an ongoing sense of powerlessness.

CHAPTER 75:
THE THICKENING PLOT
February 28, 1986

The day after Cindy learned Jude had turned himself in on his own recognizance with his attorney in Nevada City, someone told Cindy they had recently seen Jude in town. Truckee was such a small town that no visitors went unnoticed.

Jude had a baby sister, Rose, buried in the Truckee Cemetery. He was seen at the cemetery, and Cindy's friend commented that maybe Jude would stop by to see Cindy now that she was back home in Truckee— thinking he might want to visit with an old neighbor and her kids. Of course, since Cindy had been keeping it a secret that he was the suspect, she could not acknowledge how much this news created fear in her heart. After two years of construction, she and the boys had recently moved back into their newly built house on her old lake property. Jude would know where to find her.

Cindy ran across the street from the hospital, where she had returned to work part-time, to the sheriff's office as soon as she heard the news. "Phil, is it true Jude is in town? Did you know? Someone told me they saw him in the cemetery. I'm scared to death!"

The sheriff assured her they knew and were keeping track of his whereabouts.

"We know, Cindy. And we're keeping an eye on him. We didn't want you to be worried about his whereabouts, but we've been tracking him."

Apparently, Jude had arranged for a visit to his sister's grave before flying back to Louisiana.

"Did you by chance look into the death of his baby sister?" Cindy felt a cold chill run through her body as she said it out loud. "They said she died a crib death, and Jude often babysat his sister. Just a thought, but are you sure he didn't kill his baby sister?" She sucked in her breath at the horrifying image. She felt guilty and horrible for even thinking it, but she couldn't shake the thought.

The sheriff quickly replied, "Yes, it did occur to us actually, and I assure you we already looked into it, but there is no proof that he did it."

Jude didn't go to school with the other kids, and because he wasn't in school, he helped watch the baby whenever his mom was working at the hospital. John, Jude's dad, was on permanent disability and was usually home, but sometimes he ran errands or took a nap and put Jude in charge of the baby. Cindy had once asked his mom, Dee, why Jude wasn't in school, and she said, "Oh, he has some problems and has been in trouble, so we moved here to give him a fresh start."

Cindy didn't press for details but noted that they had brought his problems with them to Truckee; whether they were mental problems or legal problems, she didn't ask. Meanwhile, he was around running amok while the other kids were in school.

Cindy still remembered the horrific day John came into the ER with their eight-month-old baby, Rose. Cindy and Dee had been on shift, and Cindy had interrupted a surgery to pull Dee out to be with her family. John had brought all the kids in with him, including Jude. Cindy remembered Jude seemed really distraught. His baby sister died two months before Cindy's fire.

And here he was, visiting his sister's grave.

I wonder if he feels remorse, Cindy wondered. She knew in her bones that Jude had set the fire. The more time went on, the more the evidence pointed in his direction. And now she was terrified that he might come to her house. He had been fifteen back when the fire happened, but he was nineteen now—an adult. As an adult, Cindy found him even more menacing. She needed reassurance from the sheriff's office, but she found there was little they could say to console her.

Shortly after she got home, Sheriff Ed called to tell her that Phil had agreed to put a security system in her new home free of charge. Phil had recently retired from the sheriff's department after twenty years and had opened his own detective service in Truckee while still working as a part-time sheriff. Even though Phil was no longer the chief, he was still Cindy's ally. While a security system eased her fears a little, Cindy knew she would not feel secure as long as Jude was walking around free.

CHAPTER 76:
THE PARENTS

Some things just gnawed at Cindy's conscience. She could never get Jude off her mind, not only that he had started the fire but how she had trusted her boys to his care and how he had known her and was still able to light the house on fire. The thought of it gave her chills—how she had let the Devil in through the front door.

And then there were his parents, Dee and John. Cindy recalled that last conversation she had had with them at the hospital party years before, the conversation running over and over in her mind like a reel on repeat. They had asked her a bunch of questions about the fire.

"Did the police find anything? Are there any clues?" John had inquired. "We heard it was arson?"

"What would you do if you found out who did it?" Dee had asked.

"What would *I* do?" Cindy had replied. "Personally, I couldn't do anything, but I would want them to serve the maximum time they could get because they put me through hell, and they tried to kill my son and me!" Cindy remembered her blood pressure rising as she felt her face flush red.

"Oh, yeah, of course, I imagine," murmured Dee and John as they nodded their heads in agreement and gave each other a look. At the time, Cindy was so caught up in her own anger that she couldn't place the look they gave each other, but later she realized they looked nervous.

Cindy had thought it was strange they were asking her questions mainly about the fire and not about her prognosis, her health, or her care in the hospital. After all, Dee worked at the hospital too. Instead, they were interested only in the investigation.

They knew! Cindy suddenly realized. *They knew or suspected what Jude had done and wanted to see if he was a suspect.* Cindy caught her breath. *No wonder they hightailed it out of Truckee all the way to Florida. They were trying to put distance between themselves and the fire.*

Now the conversation clicked into place. Of course they were only interested in the fire and the investigation. Whether they suspected it was their son or he had confessed and told them, she didn't know. What she did know was that before that spring was over, the family had suddenly uprooted and left town.

Cindy's decision that spring to move back to Truckee had been at the last minute. The boys wanted to move back and be with their friends, and Cindy had called the school to see if they could possibly make room for the boys. They said yes—they could fit the boys in before the school year was over. Cindy thought it was a good idea, so the boys could get acclimated to their old friends before school let out and it was summertime.

So, Cindy made a fast plan to move back with the boys in two weeks, around mid-May. Some people at the hospital knew, and word had spread. As the OR supervisor at the hospital, Dee had found out. Everyone thought she'd be excited, as Cindy's old neighbor.

However, the next day, as Cindy was told, Dee came back to the hospital and told the staff she had a job offer in Florida and had to leave in ten days. Everyone at the hospital was shocked. Dee had never expressed interest in wanting to leave the hospital or move away from Truckee, and Florida was on the other side of the country! The staff peppered her with questions:

"Are you sure?"

"So quickly?"

"Can't you stay a few more days to welcome Cindy back?"

"Won't your boys want to see their friends Michael and Jeremiah come home?"

Dee assured them she could not wait.

Dee and her family packed up and moved on a Friday. Cindy moved back home that same weekend. At this point, Jude was already in the group home, and baby Rose was in the cemetery, so they left with only their two younger sons.

Dee had been her neighbor, her colleague, and a friend, and she had betrayed Cindy to protect her son. Dee never attended any of the court hearings with Jude, and Cindy never saw Dee again after the hospital party.

Meanwhile, Michael and Jeremiah periodically brought up their old neighbors and friends and said they missed them. But what could Cindy do? She couldn't tell them that their friends' older brother, someone they had known and spent time with, had burned down their house and all their belongings, almost killing their mom and Jeremiah. Instead, for many years, Cindy did her best to protect them from the truth.

Over a year after Jude had become the suspect, Cindy reached out and wrote a letter to Dee:

Dee, what your son did has no bearing on our friendship. Michael and Jeremiah really miss your boys and have asked about them often. It would be great to hear from you.

It was an olive branch, and she meant every word. She didn't blame Dee for Jude's actions.

Cindy neither got the letter back in the returned mail nor heard a reply, but it was shortly after that, probably because they realized Cindy had their address, that the family moved to Louisiana. She never heard from them again.

CHAPTER 77:
THE TRIAL

March 17, 1986

When the court first held its primary session in Nevada City in March of 1986, Cindy wanted to go. It was important to her to face Jude. She wanted to face the teenager who caused her so much fear, the menacing teen who haunted her dreams. Cindy's mom, Reota, went with her for moral support along with a couple of friends, including Meera, her counselor-in-training.

Meera had been a great support for Cindy through this entire process. She was finishing up her schooling to be a counselor and had listened to many of Cindy's stories and helped her work through a lot of feelings—and would continue to do so for several years. However, only Cindy was able to go into the small courtroom.

Even still, the judge might force Cindy to leave the courtroom. Since Jude had been a teen at the time of the fire, this was considered a juvenile case, and the juvenile courts were closed to outsiders, including victims. Cindy hoped to appeal to the judge to allow her to stay. She felt she deserved that right.

Cindy entered the courtroom and sat near the front row. She glanced down at her lap and nervously fingered the black, red, and white skirt that her friend Cheryl had bought her, along with a white button-down blouse. Cindy was living off her disability checks and didn't have a lot of money, so Cheryl, who had a flair for fashion and sophisticated LA style, had taken Cindy shopping so her friend would look good and feel confident during the trial.

Jude and his lawyer were called in first, and they sat in the first row, right in front of Cindy. Jude had gotten taller since she had last seen him, and his shaggy hair was gone. His jawline had squared out. He was no longer a young teen but a man.

Then the judge was called in. Judge Frances established that this was a preliminary hearing to decide if there was sufficient evidence for a court case. This also allowed Jude to declare his plea. The judge clarified who was in the courtroom and what their roles were. Then he looked at Jude and asked him, "Is that your mother?" The judge nodded toward Cindy, sitting directly behind Jude.

"Who?" Jude asked, turning around and looking Cindy in the eye, realizing for the first time that she was there. As he looked at her, his deep brown eyes were emotionless, cold as steel. Cindy thought she might meet the young teenager she once knew, remorseful and repentant, but what she found was someone who was cold and conniving. He didn't even acknowledge that he recognized Cindy. Fear rushed through her body and made a home in her stomach as they held each other's gaze.

Before he could answer, Cindy looked from Jude to Judge Frances and replied firmly and loudly, "No. I am the victim."

"Oh!" remarked the judge before Jude's lawyer quickly said, "She can't be in here, your honor. She can't be in here. This is a juvenile setting."

"You know what?" Cindy asserted loudly. "He tried to kill my son and me. And I made it through. And I'm here, and I have a right to hear what he has to say, and the right to look him in the face."

The district attorney also asserted that the victim had the right to attend.

Judge Frances nodded his head. "I agree with you." He turned and looked at Jude's lawyer. "She can stay."

The charges were then announced: one count of breaking and entering, and two counts of arson with great bodily injury. Unfortunately, there wasn't enough proof to charge him with attempted murder, so the DA had filed lower charges, believing Jude would at least serve some time instead of risking him going free.

The judge asked Jude how he pleaded. Jude stood up and said, "Not guilty."

Cindy's heart sank. It would be a fight then. She would have to fight for justice. And she had to believe in her heart that justice would prevail.

Before the court was dismissed, Cindy addressed the judge again.

"Your honor," Cindy asserted, "this young man tried to kill my son and me. I'm not comfortable with him. I heard about him being in Truckee. I've heard about people seeing him. I shouldn't have to deal with that. I shouldn't have to live in fear."

Judge Frances nodded his head in agreement. "You're right."

Turning to look at Jude and his attorney, he said, "You are going to have to fly straight into Sacramento from now on. You cannot fly into Reno. You cannot go through or visit Truckee."

"But the flights are cheaper to Reno," Jude objected.

"It doesn't matter," replied Judge Frances. "You fly into Sacramento and come here. You cannot be within sixty miles of Truckee."

Cindy felt relieved, knowing that at least there was an official order to keep him away. Still, not a night went by that she didn't activate the security system in her home. She wasn't sure if she would ever feel safe in her sleep again.

CHAPTER 78:
THE VERDICT
May 1987

The trial began in the spring of 1986, four years after the fire, and lasted fourteen months. Jude was twenty years old when the jury reached a verdict. Sometimes sessions were canceled because Jude couldn't fly out from Louisiana due to the winter weather. Another time, the court date was bumped because the judge went on vacation and there wasn't a substitute.

When Jude turned eighteen, he got married, and at one point his wife had a health issue, so another court session was excused. Cindy even postponed the trial when her father, Larry, became ill and passed away. Each canceled session meant waiting weeks for a new court date. Month after month, Cindy fought frustration in her need for justice and resolution.

Because Jude had been fifteen at the time of the fire, it was considered a juvenile case, making it a closed courtroom—but the DA sent a subpoena to Cindy to appear, as he knew she wanted to be at every hearing if possible. Because she was subpoenaed, the court compensated her for her time and gas, which was a big help. Cindy's disability checks didn't go far in raising her two boys. Each day that she attended court was physically and mentally exhausting, and she felt like the trial was being dragged out for months on end—because it was.

The court heard many testimonies. The fire marshal testified that the fire was set with a flammable liquid, probably gasoline, and a match. A counselor, a psychiatrist, and Cindy also testified.

Although the counselor from the group home initially pleaded the Fifth Amendment to protect patient privacy, Judge Frances ordered her to disclose the confidential details from their sessions. As such, the counselor conveyed that Jude had been fixated on the fire and also on Cindy's and Jeremiah's recovery. She was able to reveal information that he had told her privately in session, and it was these details that were condemning.

There was also a court-appointed psychologist involved in the trial, whose analysis and prognosis of Jude's character was damning as well. The psychologist had asserted that Jude was a *sociopath*, a person with a personality disorder that manifested itself in extreme antisocial attitudes and behavior—and a lack of conscience.

At one point during the trial, Cindy called the psychologist at his office and pleaded for his help. She knew he couldn't talk about Jude with her, and she would deny this conversation had ever taken place, but she just had one question she was hoping he would answer: *Am I in danger?*

The doctor's response chilled her to the bone. "All I can say is this: I've been in practice for over thirty years, and this is the worst sociopath I have ever seen."

In the district attorney's summation, he painted a picture of what had happened that morning: After stealing a wallet from their neighbor, Sarah, taking the cash out, and dropping the wallet on Cindy's driveway, Jude let himself into Cindy's house and stole the $30 cash she had in her wallet, which was in her purse on the dining room table. *Thirty dollars.*

When he turned to leave, he heard creaking upstairs, heard Cindy cough, and realized she was home. Afraid that he would get caught and that he would be arrested for his third strike, he decided to cover his tracks and create a distraction.

On the first floor by the door was a gas can for the Skidoo snowmobile, and it was filled with gas. He picked it up, went up the stairs to the bottom of the third floor, and poured it on the only path for Cindy and Jeremiah to get out. He proceeded to fling it throughout the house as he retreated through the entryway to the outside stairs.

He then took a lighter from his pocket and lit the stairs, watching the petroleum rapidly catch fire and rush up the staircase. Jude then quickly raced home, shut the door behind him, and fingered the cash in his pocket.

He did not call 911.

Finally, five years after the fire and a long, drawn-out trial, the court reached a verdict: Jude was found *guilty*.

Although Jude had pleaded "not guilty" in court, there was enough circumstantial evidence against him, including his petty-theft history, his psychodrama reenactment, his lies that had been caught on the stand, and his psychological evaluation, which deemed him a sociopath.

After the sentencing, Judge Frances asked if Cindy wanted to address the court and address Jude. Cindy had some specific requests that she wanted made known. As she read her victim impact statement, she faced Jude and looked into his dark, resentful eyes. She acknowledged that he was a troubled young man and needed professional help. Then she made three requests of the judge:

1. She requested that Jude go to a facility where they had mandatory counseling so that he could rehabilitate. She had already looked it up and gave the judge a couple of example facilities that provided this.
2. She wanted to be kept informed where he was incarcerated and be able to check on his status periodically.
3. She wanted to know before he was released from prison.

Judge Frances granted Cindy her three requests. He also ordered Jude to pay Cindy $40,000 in restitution after he was released from prison.

Cindy watched as Jude was guided by the officers out of the courtroom in handcuffs, his head bent down, looking at his shackled ankles. She wondered what was going through his mind, whether it was anger, shock, or sadness. She doubted it was shame. She waited for the tension to ease in her chest, that tightness that had found a home inside her. She waited, but even with Jude locked in jail, it would be a long time before the anxiety would go away, before she felt safe and free of fear.

CHAPTER 79:
FACE TO FACE
May 1989

Jude was sentenced to only seven to nine years, since he had been a juvenile at the time the crime was committed. That meant he would be up for parole review after only two or three years.

After the two-year mark, in preparation for his review and possible release, Cindy was contacted to see if she wanted to present her viewpoint to the review board and to see if she was open to receiving a letter from Jude. She said yes to both.

Before Cindy addressed the review board, she wanted to talk to Jude face to face. She had to face him, face her fears, look into the eyes of the boy-man who had stolen so much of her life and see into his soul. She would not know how she felt about him until she did. In the courtroom, he had been cold as steel, like a sinister devil with no remorse. He continued to lie on the stand and deny what he had done, even when the judge called him out on it.

Cindy wrote Jude back and said that she would like to meet him in person to talk, and he wrote back and agreed.

Cindy flew down to Southern California, where Jude was being held in the youth detention center in Ontario. Her brother, Larry, joined her there for moral support.

So many people commended Cindy for being brave and for facing the evil that had burned her alive. But it wasn't a matter of being brave; it was a matter of need. Cindy had to do this for herself. She still had questions that had not been answered in the courtroom, and she wouldn't rest easy until she had the answers.

She was nervous—and she wasn't. She knew that if she didn't like what she saw or who he was, she could ask the board to keep him behind bars, and she felt confident that since this was the first time he was up for parole, they would listen to her.

After entering the jail, Cindy was led into a room and seated with her brother on one side of a table. Jude was then brought in with the center's social worker and an armed guard, who stood by the door. Everything was in order, and Cindy didn't feel afraid that he was going to hurt her, but she was afraid of how she was going to feel looking him in the eye. She didn't want that cold-steel look to be in his eyes like before. She didn't want to feel that fear she had felt every day in the courtroom.

Jude sat down across from her, and he looked at Cindy. Cindy looked straight at him, and he looked … normal. Cindy felt relieved.

She took a deep breath and spoke. "I just need to know why, Jude. I need to know why you did it."

At this point, Jude had not once admitted he did it. Not in court. Not to Cindy. But Cindy needed to hear him say it. She needed to know he was remorseful. She needed to know that he accepted responsibility for his actions. But she was not sure if he would admit it or would give her the internal validation she needed.

There was a heavy silence as Jude paused, searching for his response, and then he said, "I came in, and I stole thirty dollars out of your purse. And then I heard you upstairs, and I got scared. I panicked, and I didn't know what to do. I already had two strikes, and a third one would have sent me to jail. I was afraid of leaving my fingerprints, so I went down to the front door and saw the gasoline, and then I poured it all around downstairs, and I lit it on fire."

"Oh my God!" Cindy whispered. She had been waiting for years to hear his confession. Hearing him say it aloud was surreal.

"And I want you to know, I know you said in court that you felt like someone was watching you jump out the window, that someone was watching you in the fire," he continued, "but I want you to know that I didn't stay and watch. I wasn't watching you. I left."

Cindy nodded. "Well, that is a little bit of a relief to know that you didn't just stand and watch the fire happening."

"I got scared," he admitted. "And to tell you the truth, all I ever did was think about me and what would happen to me. Not what would happen to other people. What would happen to you? Or the big picture. I poured gasoline, and I set it on fire. I knew you guys were upstairs, and I just wanted to get away with it, and get gone, so that's what I did." Jude's eyes filled up with tears. "I am really sorry, Cindy. I ... that was horrible of me. I was wrong. I guess I didn't really think of the consequences. I was wrong."

Cindy looked at Jude, *really* looked at him. He was not offering excuses, but he did seem apologetic. He was crying in front of her, and his confession seemed heartfelt.

She wondered for a moment if she was being played. Sociopaths are known for being emotionally manipulative, and she didn't want to seem a fool. Yet try as she might to get through his façade, she couldn't do it. He seemed genuine. He seemed to have a softened heart.

"How did *you* get through it?" Jude inquired, the first time he could seek answers to his own questions.

Cindy's mind flashed back to hearing reports about how Jude had called his mom, Dee, each week from the boys' home asking for updates on Cindy's recovery in the hospital. And of course, Dee had always let everyone know about his concern. He had come across as a sympathetic neighbor then, but now, of course, she realized he was concerned about the damage he had caused and whether he was responsible for a murder—or two.

Cindy talked to Jude about how her faith in God had guided her through her recovery, how the love and support of her family had been everything, and how being present for her boys motivated her to recover. Jude admitted he had been attending church for the first time in his life. Cindy reached into her bag and pulled out a Bible—a Bible she had brought as a gift for him. She slid it across the table into his hands.

He opened it and read the inscription Cindy had written inside:

Jude—

The only way I got through this is with the Lord in my heart. While what you did was wrong, I don't want you to live with this for the rest of your life. I want you to know that God will guide you if you let Him. I want you to go on and live a positive life and do good in the world.

Cindy Ames

Jeremiah 29:11

Tears rolled down Jude's cheeks as he read the passage. This was forgiveness. Cindy was offering absolution.

"I am so grateful for this gift, Cindy," Jude said with heartfelt thanks. "You are the only one who has come to visit me in prison. My parents have never called me once and have just tried to forget about me, I guess. My wife divorced me after the conviction. You are the only one, and your being here, you especially, means a lot."

Cindy also gave Jude the two audiotapes of Pastor Brian's sermons—the sermons about leaning on God in time of need. These messages had helped Cindy overcome her dependency on drugs and alcohol, and she hoped they could help Jude.

After Cindy and Jude both seemed to get everything out, Cindy turned to Larry and asked if he and the counselor would mind stepping out of the room so that she could talk to Jude alone.

"Are you sure?" asked her brother.

"Yes, I'm sure," she assured him.

Both men left the room. Cindy looked at the guard just outside the door. Jude looked at Cindy curiously. Cindy stood up, and Jude followed her lead.

"I just want to pray with you, Jude. I really want to pray with you because I want your life to be something good. I don't want it to be horrible."

"I still can't believe you're forgiving me like this," Jude confessed. "I mean, after everything I did …"

"That's what we're supposed to do. Forgive. You were fifteen years old, and you did something stupid. I don't want this to hang over you for the rest of your life. I want you to live a life worthy of God. Come, let's pray together."

Cindy reached out and held his young hands with her scarred ones. She and Jude both bowed their heads as Cindy lifted him up to the Lord. Praying out loud, she asked God to forgive Jude for his sins and to open his heart to His glory. She asked that God guide him and help him live a good Christian life.

Afterward, Cindy looked at Jude. She could not see the "worst sociopath ever" anymore. Instead, she saw a young man who was remorseful, with tears in his eyes and a heart that was open.

CHAPTER 80:
PANDA BEAR

Jude wasn't ready for Cindy to leave. She was the only visitor he had ever had.

"Before you go, can I show you around the complex here?" he asked.

Cindy nodded her head in agreement.

Jude asked the guard if they could go on a walking tour.

"I just want you to see where I've been staying and what I've done and that I've really been trying," he said to Cindy. "I want you to know that. I hope to work with the prison system somehow and to make a difference."

"I've been working with the National Center for Victims of Violent Crime," Cindy replied. "It's a program that helps victims of crime rebuild their lives."

"That's what I want to do," Jude responded earnestly. "I want to do something that will help others that's positive. Something that will make a difference."

"Well, there's a lot of things that can be done. You should be able to find something when you leave, something that can make a positive impact."

Jude then took her across the yard where all the prisoners were, and Cindy looked around feeling uncomfortable—but knowing her brother and the guards were there gave her assurance. On the other side of the yard, Jude took them into his wing where he stayed. They went through the craft room where Jude showed them the clay and pottery area where he made figurines.

Then they went to his jail cell. Cindy looked around and noted it was a barren jail cell like she expected: one cot, a little table, and one shelf for his belongings—not too comfortable but just enough. Each prisoner was allowed a couple of personal items. One of Jude's items was a statue of a panda bear waterskiing with a boat, and on the boat were numbers: his birthday. Cindy was surprised at how intricate it was and that Jude had made it himself.

"Here, I want you to have this, Cindy," said Jude. "I don't have much to offer, but I'd like to give it to you as a token of my apology."

Cindy looked around the sparse room and knew this was something that meant a lot to him. Looking at the panda bear, for a moment Cindy glimpsed the young boy imprisoned in a jail cell.

"Thank you, Jude," Cindy said, appreciating the gesture.

Shortly after, Cindy and Larry left. On her flight home, Cindy reflected on their visit. She felt both vindicated by his confession and the serenity of offering him forgiveness. She would not carry the weight of any residual resentment or anger any longer. She would not let it taint her life. She knew in her heart that this was what Jesus wanted her to do, and she surrendered to Him, exhaling in peace.

CHAPTER 81:
JUDE'S LETTER

June 1, 1989

Dear Cindy & Family—

Speaking and meeting with you has done me more good than I think you could know. Ever since last Friday, you have been on my mind constantly. I can't tell you either just how much closer to the Lord your prayer and charitable heart have brought me. When I looked inside the flap of the Bible you brought, I cried for the beautiful words you wrote me. That you brought it was outrageously kind and unexpected, but such quality as well. I can't believe it still! Thank you ever so much!

Cindy, this may sound bad, and for this, I apologize. But I couldn't accept your forgiveness until I listened to the tapes. Brian has a way with the Gospel. Until I listened to them and you, I didn't forgive myself, and upon doing the exercise of imagining Jesus at my door, I found I was harboring resentments toward people I hadn't thought about in years! It is only through God's grace that you were able to come down here, but you left one very happy person behind. I love you for what you have shown me and will never forget the most Christian act I've ever experienced was from the lady I hurt the most! I did the unforgivable, and you were able to forgive me! I use you as my example of what kind of a person I want to be. I'll never forsake that! Thanks!

Love, Jude

CHAPTER 82:
CINDY'S LETTER

June 5, 1989

Jude—

I wanted to write and let you know I'm glad I had a chance to see you. I'm glad you were willing to talk with me. I'm sure it helped us both. I feel good about you and the steps you are taking in your life. I know you can make it with the help of the Lord. I will continue to pray for you like I've been doing for the past few years. I know the Lord's been listening!

I'm sorry you didn't get out to come up to Yuba City, but there is a reason for everything. Maybe you will have more time in the next three weeks to read the Bible, and the Lord will help strengthen you for your homecoming.

Jude, you seem like an intelligent young man who has a lot going for him. Put the past behind you and start fresh. You'll never forget, and neither will I, but we can go on with our lives in a new way. You are very talented in your art and appear to enjoy it. Pursue it if it seems right. If it means going to school in California, it's OK with me. I have no more fear of you. I only want what is best for you. Live where you want to live and do what is best for you, Jude, and what is going to help you lead a life without crime.

What you can do for me, Jude, is to be happy and content with yourself, and Praise the Lord for saving my life. I thank Him every day for my time on earth to enjoy the simple pleasures.

I look at life differently now than I did seven years ago. I see the sun brighter and the moon clearer. I get joy from my children that I used to take for granted. I am happy I can walk again and lead a mostly normal life.

I'm sure your life will be similar when you get out. It will be a new start for you. People will be the same when you go home, but you'll have changed. You'll see life in a whole new way. Take the Lord with you, Jude—He's a great friend to have. He'll love you, comfort you, and give you strength like no earthly person can.

Good luck and please keep in touch. I'm sending my address and phone number—call if you feel the need.

God bless you,

Cindy

CHAPTER 83:
A BRIGHTER FUTURE

After Cindy returned home to Truckee, she reflected on her visit with Jude for many days. She felt at peace with God and with Jude, and she knew this was important for her healing. It helped her move forward with her life. She knew that hate and anger could eat a person from the inside out, and she needed to heal. Even though it had already been seven years since the fire, she still struggled with physical ailments that would last her lifetime.

Jude, on the other hand, stepped out of jail in June of 1989, just two years into his term, and was free to move on with his life at the age of twenty-two, with sound health and an able body. Once a year or so, Cindy asked the sheriffs to check on his whereabouts, and they reported that he was in Florida. He wasn't in jail, and he wasn't dead, and Cindy was satisfied with that.

Every so often, Cindy found Jude on her mind, and she prayed for him. *God, I don't know what Jude is doing now or where he is, but I pray that he is in a good place and doing well.*

Cindy moved on. Despite the doctors having told her parents that Cindy might not live, she breathed. Despite being told by doctors that she would likely lose her sight, she marveled at the tall pine trees and Donner Lake's glistening water. She had been warned she might never walk again, but she went on regular hikes with her boys. She had been told she would probably never work as a nurse again, but she was back full-time at the Tahoe Forest Hospital in the perinatal program, working with expectant mothers and their babies.

Yes, her entire body was covered in burn scars, and she would endure many more surgeries in her life as a result of the trauma. There were physical limitations she learned to live with, and she would digest a cocktail of medications for the rest of her life.

But life was good. No—life was a gift, a precious gift that she would never take for granted. She would seek God in all things beautiful and seek joy in every day. She praised God for her children.

Jeremiah seemed to recover from the fire with only small burn scars on his arm and face. He was young enough when the fire happened that he was able to move on easily. Michael seemed to push the trauma deep down and kept it buried, never wanting to talk about it. Overall, they were joyful children, and while she and Ken were divorced, they raised their boys amicably, and the kids seemed well-adjusted.

Cindy used some of the insurance money to co-purchase a little gift shop in the historic strip in Truckee called the Merry-Go-Round with her friend Jeannie. The venture pushed Cindy back out into society, forcing her into the public eye. It was a fun adventure owning her own business. She and Jeannie remained best friends for the rest of their lives.

Even though the court imposed upon Jude a criminal fine of $40,000 to pay Cindy in restitution to help cover her medical bills, she never saw a cent. After Jude wrote her his letter, she never heard from him again.

Cindy never forgot Jesus' declaration that she had more to do on earth. She sought to find her purpose in life in various forms. When confronted with patients on their deathbed, she assured them there was an afterlife and that she had seen it. She also wanted to share her story in a book so that nurses and doctors would know what the experience was like for a burn patient on the other end of their care. She took in foster children and smothered them with love.

Cindy knew that God had a plan for her and that she had survived the fire for a reason. She remained curious to see what God had in store for the remainder of her life.

EPILOGUE: THE PARADISE FIRE

November 8, 2018

Cindy drove bumper to bumper on the road out of Paradise, California. Fire was burning on both sides of the road, and she could not see anything but a tunnel of charcoal smoke and bright orange flames. Occasionally, she spotted a flicker of a red taillight directly in front of her. Don, her husband of fifteen years, was in the truck and camper ahead of her, her beacon through the flames. George, her ninety-four-year-old neighbor, sat beside her while their dogs, Gizmo and Grizzly, sat in the back seat.

As the fire and heat closed in, Cindy began to feel trapped and started having a panic attack. Her post-traumatic stress disorder from the Truckee fire had her feeling nauseous, and she started hyperventilating. Her chest rose and fell as her breathing quickened.

She gripped the steering wheel, clinging to it for dear life, and her wild eyes started pouring tears. *Stop the car! You need to get out. You need to run*, she thought. Cindy stared at the wall of fire closing in on the road. *This can't be happening. I can't go through this again. I can't live through another fire like Truckee. I just can't. I can't do it.*

Cindy looked to her left at the wall of fire devouring the manzanita bushes and cedar trees only ten yards from the road. *I should just run into the fire,* she thought. *I should stop the car and run. I don't want to be burned alive in my car. I don't want to be burned and survive. I can't go through it all over again. I don't want to burn slowly; I want to die fast. Just end it, quickly. Just run into the fire. Just run …*

George squeezed her arm. She looked down at his hand, wrinkled and bespeckled with age spots, and then looked him in the eye. "Just keep moving forward," he said in a calm voice.

Cindy looked at the road with wide eyes. Her white knuckles gripped the steering wheel as she tried to slow down her panicked breaths.

"You're okay," he said.

"No, we need to get out of this," Cindy replied, crying. "We need to get away from this. We need to do something."

"You can do this," he assured her. "You can do this, sweetheart. You're a strong woman. You just follow your honey out of this."

Cindy glanced at George. *Oh God, of course*, she realized. *If I stop the car and run, he will have to get out, and he can't run. I can't leave him. The dogs would get loose and get hurt. The people behind me would have to stop and be trapped and would burn to death. What was I thinking? I have to keep going.*

Cindy looked back at the dogs, who were both alert and sitting upright together, sensing the disaster surrounding them. On the floor behind the passenger seat, Jeremiah's urn caught her eye. *My Miah.* She turned her head and looked to the road as warm tears rolled down her cheeks. The cars were moving slowly, five to seven miles an hour maybe, but they continued to move steadily forward.

Cindy tried taking deep breaths without taking her foot off the gas. Townhouses were on fire to the right, and she hoped nobody was in them. The thick, smoky air and eerie orange glow closed in. Somewhere in the dark wall of smoke, another transformer exploded.

Ash was flying through the air like frenzied snowflakes. She could hear the fiery wind swirl around them and feel the heat from the fire, making her scarred skin prickle. The smoke made it difficult to breathe.

"George, we're driving into this fire. We're driving *into* it ..." Cindy didn't want to finish with *and we'll burn to death*, but she let the sentence linger. "Oh my God, I can't believe this ..."

She kept her eyes looking forward, scanning for a glimpse of Don's taillights, willing an invisible tie between them. Memories flashed through her mind: letting go of Jeremiah's hands and dropping him to the ground, getting scrubbed during the Betadine baths, lying on the dreaded circle bed, years of painful physical therapy ... The drive was slow and endless as Cindy's flashbacks enveloped her, but they kept moving forward.

Then, for the first time, Cindy saw a small patch of blue in the sky break through the smoke, and it gave her hope. On the left, she could see some manzanita bushes as the smoke tunnel began to give way. She could hang on. They might be able to get through this.

There were more patches of blue sky, and Cindy's breathing started to regulate. She squeezed her eyes tightly in an attempt to stop the flow of tears while her hands still gripped the wheel.

Suddenly, as if with a snap of someone's fingers, they broke through the smoke and the sky was blue.

"Oh my God," Cindy said.

"You did it," assured George.

Cindy wanted to pull over. She felt lightheaded like she was going to pass out. But there was nowhere to go, and the cars kept moving forward. Suddenly, her cell phone rang, and it was Don.

"Where are you?" he asked, unsure where they were behind him. He sounded panicky.

"I'm right behind you," she assured him. The big camper and the smoke had hidden her from view.

"I need to pull over," she said, suddenly engulfed in full-body sobs. She felt the shock of the fire taking over her body, a response to the trauma.

"You can't pull over. Just follow me down the hill. Just stay behind me."

Cindy reluctantly agreed as they drove down the hill toward the highway. Don's voice had soothed her, and now she needed to let Michael know she had made it out safe, so she called her daughter-in-law Kim to let them know.

When Kim answered the phone on speaker, Cindy's four-year-old grandson, Bryce, yelled, "Grandma, hurry! Come down here! There is a fire, and you have to get out!"

"Grandpa and I are safe, honey. We're on our way to your house right now," assured Cindy.

The Skyway connecting Paradise with Highway 99 was only ten miles long, but it took over two hours for Cindy to reach it. Cars were lined up at the bottom with crowds of people looking up at the hill, hoping and praying their family members would break through the smoke. People had come out of their work buildings to watch.

When Cindy finally made it to the bottom, she rolled down her window where a small crowd had formed. A few looked at Cindy and then at George.

"We had to drive through the fire to get out of there," Cindy said, shaking her head. Her smeared mascara and tears on her cheeks spoke louder than her words. "It was horrible. Say a prayer."

Cindy glanced up at the Skyway, at the line of cars descending the inferno of Paradise, and she prayed they would keep coming.

She left her window down to breathe in the fresh air as she and Don, without stopping, got on the freeway heading to North Chico. Michael and Kim lived there with their three sons, and their home would serve as a safe haven. When Cindy got a chance to look at her phone, there were messages from Michael, Kim, Jeannie, and others, all left while she was in the dead zone, all concerned about her well-being.

As they pulled into Michael's driveway, Cindy felt a moment of déjà-vu. Mason, her eight-year-old grandson, had been in school all day, and none of the kids had any idea whether their relatives in Paradise were safe or not. Hurrying from the bus stop, Mason ran up to her just as she got out of the car with tears in his eyes, hugging her and crying with relief. She could feel the anxiety leaving his little body with each sob.

This is how Michael must have felt when our Truckee house caught on fire, she thought. *Wondering and not knowing if Jeremiah and I were safe. Unfortunately, that fire had a different outcome …*

Cindy was later thankful that she hadn't stopped en route, because she discovered that some people *had* stopped, and their tires melted, and they got trapped in the fire and died in their cars. Others couldn't outrun the fire. Some were trapped in their homes.

In the end, the Camp Fire, one of California's deadliest and most destructive wildfires—caused by an electrical transmission from a PG&E power line—killed eighty-five people. Nearly 19,000 homes and businesses were razed in the town of Paradise, which all but burned to the ground.

Cindy and Don's house was devoured by the flames. For the second time in Cindy's life, she lost her house and all her belongings to fire—but lived to tell her story.

PHOTO GALLERY

A rare photo of Cindy before the fire, age 24, with Jeremiah

*Edwards family photo, 1985: (top) Gail, Joy,
Cindy, Larry; (bottom) Reota, Larry*

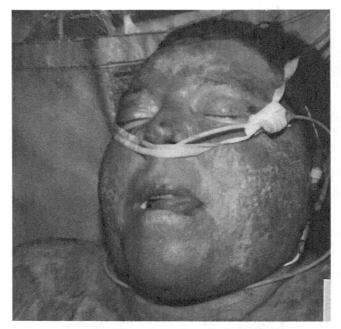

Fifteen days after the fire

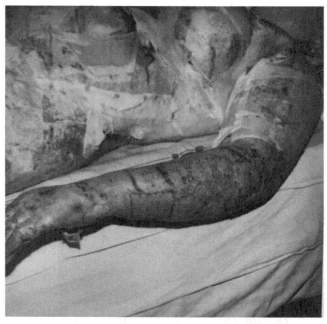

May 25, 1982

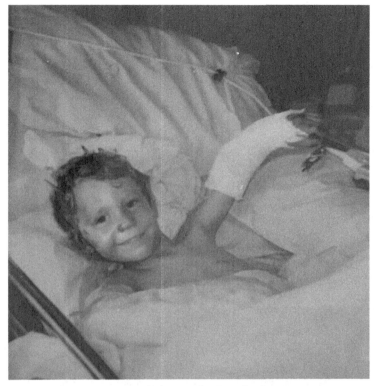

Jeremiah one week after the fire

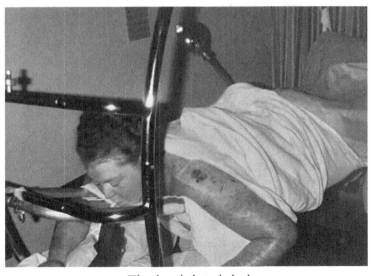

The dreaded circle bed

Walking for the first time to the corner of the room to kiss her mom

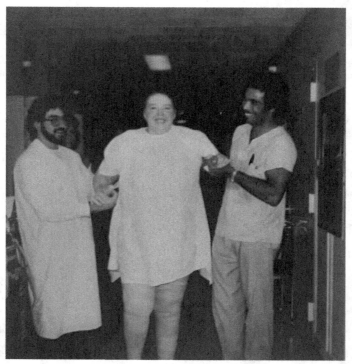

*Learning to walk again with Nurse Robbie
and her physical therapist*

Cindy's Freedom Dance with Dr. Hoefflin

Michael, Cindy, and Jeremiah in 1987

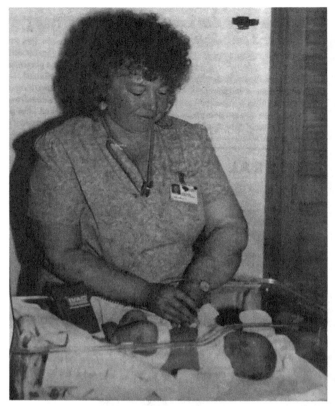

Back to work in the nursery

Don and Cindy Harding at their home in Paradise, California, before the fire

AFTERWORD: CINDY'S REFLECTIONS

Forty years after the fire, I think back on all I've been through—all I have *survived*. I've had more than my fair share of tragedy, and yet, it is due to my belief in God and knowledge that He has a purpose for my life that I have endured. While doing so, I have embraced joy in my life and never taken a day for granted.

When I was in the hospital, one of the nurses asked me, "Well, now that you lived through this, what are you going to do?"

I thought about it and said, "I am going to write a book." I realized I wanted to share what it is like being totally dependent on the medical community. I realized, as a nurse, that we don't always know what to say or how to relate to our patients. I want to share how a touch, a gentle whisper, a foot rub, or even a smile helps a patient feel safe. There were many details that I noticed that the staff did, both good and not so great. Hopefully, this book will help the medical world understand the critical patient better.

It is hard sometimes to move forward and let life take its course, but it is what we must do. God will help us get through whatever we face. One of my favorite poems is called "The Weaver" by Grant Colfax Tullar. It reminds us that we only see the top of the piece of art. Only God sees the underside and sees the results of our life and all that we do and go through. He sees the beauty of what we have done and what we have made of our challenges in life. Challenges can also be what makes our weaving beautiful. As we all go on our journeys in life, remember we have God to rely on and each other to cry on.

My Health

In the years after the fire, when friends or acquaintances asked me if I was back to normal, I usually said, "For the most part, yes," because people typically don't really want to hear about all the problems I am still dealing with. I have suffered more than most my entire life. It's important to know that most burn patients have ongoing health issues they're dealing with. Here are some of mine:

- For about five years after the fire, I was taken to surgery several times for large pustules of infection that kept emerging from my body. My surgeon, Dr. Boone, had to drain and cleanse them periodically.
- My immune system is compromised, so I'm on antibiotics frequently for infections.
- I was diagnosed with chronic fatigue syndrome. The chronic pain I still have is sometimes overwhelming, but I am able to find medications that help.
- I was hospitalized many times for my heart. Due to the stress put on it, I need medication to help stabilize it in a regular rhythm.
- I still can't bend the last two fingers on my right hand.
- My right hip and pelvis, which were fractured from the fall, fused together during the healing process in the hospital. While they healed enough that I could walk, it was still painful. In 2012, I finally received a hip replacement, and it has been a blessing.
- My scars are still tight and pull constantly. I went to physical therapy weekly for years with a personal routine of stretching. Even forty years later, I still have scar work done, but it's much less now.
- Due to my skin grafts, I do not perspire; therefore, I am more at risk for stroke when in high heat. I have to cool myself down with a spray bottle, a body of water, or lots of shade when I hike or walk. This is still true to this day. Living in California, a hot state, there are some days I cannot go outside.

There were many times when I told my friends, "If I die tomorrow, please tell my boys that it's okay because I'm not in pain anymore." That's how bad some days were. I wanted to live, but I got tired of the constant pain.

Most of my coworkers and friends did not know about my discomfort. I have tried to keep it to myself and to lead a "normal life." I have gone to counseling off and on over the years to help me cope with my life and the flashbacks of the fire and the hospitalization. I had to learn to accept this is a lifelong injury and to be thankful my injuries were not worse.

But even with these problems, I am very grateful every day to have lived and seen Michael and Jeremiah grow up. I asked God to let me just see them graduate from high school, and then He could take me home, and I did, and it was a blessing.

Medical care for burn patients has changed significantly since the 1980s. It is still incredibly painful, but there have been many advances. This book is based on my experiences in 1982; however, the approach that care is given to the patient is a constant.

Jeremiah

Jeremiah had a happy childhood. When he was twelve, Dr. Hoefflin did another dermabrasion on his cheek and the top of his arm to diminish the scar band. When he turned eighteen, he wanted to join the military but was not accepted, as they thought he had a heart anomaly. He then went to Denver to work with a friend in the tow truck business and enjoyed it.

One day after work, he witnessed an accident on the other side of the freeway. He was able to secure the scene until another truck from his company arrived. He secured the ladies on the side of the road safely. His truck lights were on with flares all around.

As he was walking back to his tow truck, he noticed a semi-truck swerving toward him. He tried to dive into his tow truck's front seat, but he didn't have enough time. The truck pulled him under and scraped him along the highway. When the firemen arrived, they tried to pull him out from under the truck, but they needed a jack.

There was a cardiologist who had stopped on the scene, and he was checking Jeremiah's pulse. He said they needed to get him out now, and Jeremiah yelled for them to "all just pull." He prayed and said, "Please let me live. I can't leave my mom without saying goodbye."

I got the call that evening that Jeremiah had been in an accident. He lost part of his fingers on his right hand, and he lost his left ear. I got on the first flight the next day. Michael flew there as well.

Jeremiah lived through the accident but was never the same again. He had a new ear made by a specialist at a hospital in LA, but the ear frequently got infected, the grafts would not take, and it was very painful. He had many surgeries on his hand and needed regular physical therapy.

After two years, he was admitted into a mental health facility in Colorado with severe PTSD. Jeremiah hadn't slept more than ten or fifteen minutes a day for the previous few months. His doctor wanted to start Jeremiah on a new medication to help him get some deep sleep.

After his assessment, he got a day pass to spend the rest of the day with me, as I had immediately flown there. We saw friends, and then he picked up some candy and sodas to bring back for movie night to share with the guys at the treatment center. Michael flew in that night, but it was late, so we scheduled a visit with all of us in the morning.

I got a call at six a.m. informing me that Jeremiah had died during the night. I was shocked. Michael and I rushed to the facility. It was heartbreaking to see my son lying there with no color on his face, a sight no parent should ever have to see. One thing I did witness, however, was a peaceful look on his face, something I hadn't seen in a couple of years.

His autopsy did show a heart anomaly; it was intramyocardial tunneling. However, that is not what caused his death. Per his doctor's orders, he had been given the new sleep medication, but instead of 40 mg as prescribed, he had been given 400 mg. Jeremiah died at the age of twenty-six.

As a mother, it is hard to have anger when your heart is so full of sorrow. I made sure the medical staff knew that I was aware of their mistake. I wanted to make sure it never happened again. I had Miah cremated, and while his ashes have been scattered in various special locations, like his favorite fishing spot on Donner Lake, his urn has stayed close to me ever since.

Michael

Michael loved it when we moved back to Truckee. He continued to pursue his skiing and his baseball, as he excelled in both. He was a responsible older brother and helped me a lot as a single mom.

He never talked much about the fire, but I remember once a teacher gave me a school assignment he wrote; it was all about the fire and what had happened. I was glad to see that he shared it with her.

Michael was asked to play baseball in Europe during his senior year in high school and was fortunate to play in a tournament over there. He went to college after that in Chico and went on to earn his bachelor's degree in business, and he has a successful career now with a power company. Michael and his three boys—Mason, Bryce, and Blake—all live near me in Chico. I am really blessed to have them in my life.

My Family

My father and mother were both able to see me get on my feet again and continued with their love and support when the boys and I moved back to Truckee. Daddy passed away in the winter of 1986. I moved back to West Covina to be near my mother in 2000 and was fortunate to spend the last ten years of her life near her and my family. Mother passed away in the summer of 2010.

Gail had her teaching credential and taught overseas until she retired in 2019. Joy continues to live in Southern California and enjoys her time with her children and grandchildren. My brother, Larry, did get his general contractor's Class A license and has had a successful career in construction.

He later struggled with his quick judgment regarding Ken and asked Ken for forgiveness.

Foster Care

I started doing foster care in 1991. It had always been a dream of mine. My first boy was Timmy, who was seven years old. I knew immediately that this was what I was supposed to be doing. Then I got David, who was four, and his older brother, who was twelve. These three became permanent members of my household. I adopted David and was granted guardianship of Timmy, and we are family. They have both gone on to get married and have wonderful wives and children. Altogether, I did foster care for twelve years.

My Husband Don

In 1998, God made it clear to me that my mother needed me to be closer to her. It took me two years to leave the job I loved and the support of the people in Truckee. I had only one foster child at home then, going through the adoption process with David, and he moved with me.

After I moved to L.A., I went on a dating app just to meet some friends and explore who was out there. A gentleman named Don Harding contacted me, and after some discussions, we made a date. As a single parent, he had a son at home who was the same age as David, and we all went to the beach on a Sunday for clam chowder and ice cream. We had our first real date on St. Patrick's Day. Something in me told me I was going to marry this guy. We just meshed.

I remember bringing him to my fiftieth birthday party at my mother's house. I always thought I was going to die young due to all my injuries, but meeting Don helped me realize that God planned for me to be here a while longer. I wasn't going to die young; I had a future and was going to live! Don and I got married in June 2003.

I thought back and remembered the day I sat on my deck at Donner Lake and asked God for a husband. We had a sermon that Sunday at church about being specific with God and telling Him exactly what our needs are, so I poured my heart out and asked for a husband who met all of my needs: someone who would love me, who could see past my scars, and who had medical insurance, which I couldn't get due to my burn history.

It amazes me that God provided for me in the way I prayed. Don has been a rock for me. He has a good heart, and I truly love him. I am really blessed that God put him in my life. Over twenty years later, we're still happily married. After we both retired, we moved from Southern California to Paradise until the fire destroyed our home. We currently live near Michael and his family in Chico.

Jeannie

After the fire, Jeannie O'Brien quickly became my new bestie in Truckee. She and I even purchased the Merry-Go-Round gift store together in historic downtown. She was also a single mom, and our families meshed well together. Her boys, Sean and Craig, were the same age as Michael and Jeremiah. She also had three older children: Dana, Rick, and Andrea.

Our families always had great times hiking, camping, and laughing together. Jeannie and I remained best friends for the next four decades until her recent passing. I miss her dearly.

Andrea

On the fortieth anniversary of the fire, I was flipping through an old scrapbook of newspaper articles and came across one in Truckee's newspaper, *The Sierra Sun*, titled "Cindy Ames to Write Book about Fire." Writing this book has been a lifelong goal of mine, and I've attempted to write it several times, even taking creative writing classes. But each time I sat down to relive it all again in writing, it became too much for me, too much pain to relive, too much heartache.

Jeannie's daughter Andrea Neptune was an English major in college, and I used to say, "Why don't you help me write my book?" Knowing she was growing her career and family, I figured it likely wouldn't happen.

Over the years, we have always stayed close; even her mom commented how much we Cancers were alike, and I fondly called her "my daughter from another mother."

Then one day, decades later, Andrea called me out of the blue and asked how the book was going and then volunteered to write it for me. It was a miracle. I knew God would bring me the right person when the time was right. She has worked so hard these last three years to capture my feelings and thoughts, to include all the meticulous details. She has cried with me, laughed with me, and helped me relive my worst nightmare.

Andrea has done an amazing job capturing my journey, and I am so grateful to her for making this dream happen. She is a real blessing in my life, not only because she has written this book for me but because of the special person she is. Thank you, Andrea!

Nancy

My friendship with Nancy Helton, whose nickname is Niki, is stronger than ever. She has been my cheerleader, my confidence booster, and my friend who would not let me give up on my passion to write my book. When I was discouraged, she encouraged me. When I was sad or depressed, she would remind me of all I had overcome. She knew I had a calling to get this story out, and she always believed in me, even when I was trying to write it myself.

When Andrea asked her to give some insight into what it was like seeing me in the hospital, she immediately offered to share her experience, and we all met for lunch. It was through tears that she was able to relive her experience. Thank you, Niki, for always being there and knowing just what to say.

Community Work

I am one of the blessed people who has been able to see good come out of tragedy. The following are some of the ways I was able to help the community:

- Soon after the fire, I did some volunteer work with the Alisa Ann Ruch Burn Foundation.
- I was asked by the California Youth Authority if I would be a speaker at the Nevada City facility to share my story with the men as part of their mandatory classes. They were teen boys and young men who had earned the right to be in a less-strict lockdown facility. I spent the next ten years volunteering at the California Youth Authority speaking to the prisoners about being a victim and sharing my journey. I received many letters from them with positive responses. I was honored with a Certificate of Appreciation from the state of California in April of 1997.
- I was one of the first in California to visit my perpetrator and to be involved in the Victim Awareness Program, and I was blessed to help it move forward.
- In June of 1997, I participated in a focus group called Victims, Judges, and Partnerships for Juvenile Court Reform Project in Sacramento, California, along with Gov. Grey Davis and Vice President Al Gore. We discussed the present victims' rights legislation and made suggestions on what needed to be changed.
- I was then invited to speak in September 1997 in Reno at the Janiculum Project, sponsored by the National Council of Juvenile and Family Court Judges. I was able to share my story on how I had to fight the court system every step of the way to get justice. Changes were made to the new juvenile court system later that year.

In Gratitude

I want to thank Elaine Rojas, RN, for reading through this book and helping Andrea and me with all the medical terminology. Your help and guidance have been invaluable. I am so glad to have made contact with you after all these years. You were a real blessing to me in the hospital with your uplifting yet firm care. You are the epitome of effective medical care. Thank you!

I want to thank the Truckee Fire Department, which helped with the fire and worked so hard to save the neighborhood.

Thank you to all the medical staff from the Tahoe Forest Hospital emergency room, my flight transfer, and my stay at Brotman Medical Center.

Thank you to the Truckee and West Covina communities. The support from friends and family was a real blessing.

I hope this book can help someone with their struggles to know that it can get better.

God bless you all.

TUNNEL OF FIRE

by Cindy Ames Harding

I look around at the embers falling.
The sky is dark grey all around
As I drive with my ninety-four-year-old neighbor,
We are both in awe of our town.

The cars are all bumper to bumper,
In a hurry to leave this hill.
Our homes are all behind us.
For us to come back will be God's will.

As we continue down the highway,
We see the flames jumping over the road.
We're now in a tunnel of wind and heat,
And we are hearing things explode.

Memories of my fire thirty-six years ago flood back,
My burns and my hospital stay.
I do not want that to happen again.
I burst into tears and I shake.

My neighbor, George, takes my hand
And tells me I am strong.
"Just follow your husband through the flames.
He is just ahead, move along."

In the car we feel the heat
And hear the burning trees snapping.
The power lines are hanging down.
I can't believe this is happening.

It seems like forever we drive through the flames
And wonder if we are driving to our death.
We don't know what's ahead of us.
We just know we can't turn back.

Up ahead we see some light
In the black smoky sky.
We made it through the tunnel of fire.
Maybe it's not our day to die.

We find out after two days
Our house and block are gone.
But I thank God we got out safe.
Now we must figure out how to move on.

ACKNOWLEDGMENTS: ANDREA NEPTUNE

I've known Cindy since I was twelve, when my mom, Jeannie, befriended her shortly after Cindy returned to Truckee following the fire. Cindy was always friendly and candid about her burns, and I quickly recognized she was a beautiful soul inside and out. I no longer see her scars. As a term of endearment, I've always called her my auntie Cindy. We've always had a special connection and understood each other. She is my family.

Cindy and my mom became best friends, and our families spent a lot of time together. I grew up hearing her incredible stories. Cindy became an important parental figure in my life during my teen years and remains so in adulthood. She has influenced my life in many ways, and it is partly because of Cindy that I have been a blood donor all my life.

One distinctive day as I was stoking a burn pile on our property, feeling the heat of the fire on my face, I started thinking about Cindy and all she had gone through. I started thinking about the book that she was always talking about, a book she had asked me to write as a college English major some thirty years earlier, and a book I knew she had struggled writing. I suddenly felt with absolute conviction that I needed to write the book for her—that she needed to have this book written before God decided her nine lives were up. And I was fairly sure she was on number eleven.

So I called her the next day and offered to write this book for her as a labor of love. With relief in her voice, she excitedly accepted my offer.

As an adult, after learning all the sordid details of her story and understanding all that she endured and continues to endure, it stuns me that everything that happened to her was all for thirty dollars. Yet Cindy's resilience, positive attitude, and joy for life are an inspiration. She is the first to laugh at life's minor setbacks, and she lets struggles slide off her scarred back like water. Those who know her are truly blessed to have her in their lives. She is a constant reminder to have gratitude for all of life's blessings, as no day can ever be taken for granted.

Some of these passages were challenging to write, whether they were intense, grotesque, or horrifying. Several years ago, I attended author Margaret Atwood's presentation in San Francisco, during which she said, "An artist never averts their eyes," and this became my mantra during this process. When challenged with a passage, I would ask Cindy or myself, "Did it happen?" and "Is it honest?" If both answers were yes, we included it.

In Gratitude

I first want to thank my husband, Gary Charles, who didn't bat an eye when I told him that fateful night that I wanted to write Cindy's book and was going to call her the next day. He had complete faith that I could do it and has been supportive during this journey more than three years later. He's even been a devoted editor, reading my initial drafts and giving me helpful feedback. He's my best friend, my person, my lobster, my Magstar ... thank you, my love!

A big thank you to my mother, Jeannie O'Brien, for bringing Cindy into our lives. Watching the two of them laugh until they cried was a powerful lesson in joy. My mom was always such a wonderful role model and my biggest supporter. I always knew I was loved. Unfortunately, she didn't get a chance to read the book in its entirety before she passed away. She is deeply missed.

I dedicate this book, in part, to my sons, Nolan Aguilar and Trevin Aguilar. Watching them grow into independent, intelligent, and grounded men has been the greatest source of pride in my life. You are both such a blessing!

I want to thank my sister Dana Cheney and my friends Katie

Braverman and Barbara Stone for enthusiastically reading the manuscript and giving me their honest feedback. You're the best!

I want to thank my friend and colleague Matt Jewett, a fire academy instructor and former firefighter, for providing accuracy and terminology for the fire's behavior. High five, Buddy!

Last, I want to thank all my friends and family who supported me during this process, checking in on my progress and offering encouragement. I'm so grateful you're in my life!

Andrea and Cindy (2019)

Printed in the United States
by Baker & Taylor Publisher Services